SYSTEMIC ACTION RESEARCH

A strategy for whole system change

Danny Burns

To Laura

First published in Great Britain in 2007 by

The Policy Press
University of Bristol
Fourth Floor
Beacon House
Queen's Road
Bristol BS8 1QU
UK

Tel +44 (0)117 331 4054
Fax +44 (0)117 331 4093
e-mail tpp-info@bristol.ac.uk
www.policypress.org.uk

© Danny Burns 2007

British Library Cataloguing in Publication Data
A catalogue record for this book is available from the British Library.

Library of Congress Cataloging-in-Publication Data
A catalog record for this book has been requested.

ISBN 978 1 86134 737 4 paperback
ISBN 978 1 86134 738 1 hardcover

The right of Danny Burns to be identified as author of this work has been asserted by him in accordance with the 1988 Copyright, Designs and Patents Act.

Cover design by Qube Design Associates, Bristol.
Front cover image kindly supplied by Zeth Lorenzo.
Printed and bound in Great Britain by MPG Books, Bodmin.

Contents

Acknowledgements   iv

About the author   v

List of abbreviations   vi

Introduction   1

one   Action research   11

two   A systemic perspective   21

three   Working across systems   41

four   Some systemic action research projects explored   55

five   Some design principles for systemic action research   85

six   Practices of systemic action inquiry   103

seven   Issues for action research facilitators   137

eight   Quality and ethics in systemic action research   155

nine   Systemic action research in policy and politics   173

A final reflection   179

References   181

Index   189

Acknowledgements

This book owes its greatest debt to Susan Weil who, through the creation of SOLAR (Social and Organisational Learning as Action Research), and subsequently through our joint work, and our many conversations, opened the door to the thinking that underpinned it. It is equally important, for me to acknowledge my other colleagues at SOLAR: Barry Percy-Smith, Dianne Walsh, Matthieu Daum and David Evans. Over the years both SOLAR and I have been supported by many administrators, and I would like to thank them all – in particular, Madeleine Munro, who did an immense job in setting up SOLAR at the University of the West of England (UWE).

I would like to give special thanks to Margaret Boushel, Ann Goymer and Lil Bowers, who backed a highly experimental large system inquiry in Bristol, and endured the many ragged edges associated with learning as we went. Without the learning from this project, I would not have been able to conceptualise even half of what is contained in this book. I would also like to thank a number of other clients: Anne Stevenson, Helen Bushell and Alan Burge (Welsh Assembly Government [WAG]), Nick Starkey and Margaret Lally (British Red Cross) and Stuart Worsley (SNV Kenya and Southern Sudan), who, from an early stage, saw the potential of large system action research in international development contexts.

I would like to acknowledge the work of Alison Gilchrist, Linda Gordon and Marina Prieto-Carron – three PhD students whose action research studies helped to crystallise for me many of the issues and dilemmas that needed to be addressed. I have also learned a huge amount from the third cohort of SOLAR PhD students – Anne Archer, Susan Ballard, Liz Hayes, Clare Hopkinston, Alan Taylor and Bjorn Uldall – who modelled different forms of systemic inquiry.

Reaching a little further back into the past I would like to acknowledge some of my colleagues on the MSc in Management Development and Social Responsibility who helped to take my thinking in a different direction. In particular, Tom Davies, Margaret Page and Gill Coleman, and, as ever, Paul Hoggett, who in this endeavour, as with many others, has been profoundly influential.

Turning specifically to this book, I am immensely grateful to Matthieu Daum, Gerald Midgley, Yoland Wadsworth, Susan Weil and Stuart Worsley for their detailed reviews of the penultimate draft of this book. I would also like to thank The Policy Press. In particular, Julia Mortimer, who was a constant source of sensible advice; Dawn Rushen, who both mapped the book out with me at the commissioning stage and copy edited it; Dave Worth, who helped to achieve a complex design; Emily Watt and Philip de Bary, who supported me in the editing process; and Ali Shaw, for establishing and running such a great publishing house.

About the author

Danny Burns is Professor of Social and Organisational Learning at the University of the West of England and Director of SOLAR (Social and Organisational Learning as Action Research).

His previous publications include:

Poll tax rebellion (AK Press, 1992)

The politics of decentralisation: Revitalizing local democracy (Macmillan, 1994) with Paul Hoggett and Robin Hambleton

Mutual aid and self help (The Policy Press, 1997) with Marilyn Taylor

Community self-help (Palgrave Macmillan, 2004) with Colin. C. Williams and Jan Windebank

Making participation meaningful (The Policy Press, 2004) and *What works in assessing community participation?* (The Policy Press/Joseph Rowntree Foundation, 2004) with Frances Heywood, Marilyn Taylor, Mandy Wilson and Pete Wilde

SOLAR is a research and development team that specialises in systemic action research. It has facilitated action research projects for clients including the Welsh Assembly Government (WAG), the British Red Cross and the National Health Service (NHS). It also runs a cohort-based PhD programme and regular inquiry forums. These have been led by, among others, Donald Schon, Patricia Shaw, Ralph Stacey, Gareth Morgan, Stephen Kemmis, Peter Reason, Judi Marshall, Etienne Wenger, Arie de Geus, Suzi Goff and Danny Wildermerch. SOLAR was set up in 1996 by Susan Weil at University College Northampton. It has been based at UWE since 2001 under the co-directorship of Danny Burns and Susan Weil.

List of abbreviations

Organisations

ALARPM	Action Learning, Action Research and Process Management international association
CARPP	Centre for Action Research in Professional Practice (University of Bath)
HHW	Hartcliffe, Highridge and Withywood Sure Start (a neighbourhood in Bristol)
NHS	National Health Service
SNV	Netherlands development organisation
SOLAR	Social and Organisational Learning as Action Research
SOLAR 3	The third cohort of SOLAR PhD students supervised by Danny Burns and Susan Weil at UWE
UWE	University of the West of England
WAG	Welsh Assembly Government

Projects

BCI	Bristol Children's Initiatives action inquiry project
U&I	Melbourne Understanding and Involvement project

Other

CFSN	Communities First Support Network
IMD	Index of Multiple Deprivation
FGM	Female genital mutilation
MDSR	[Masters in] Management Development and Social Responsibility
MRPCMA	Moiben River Catchments Protection, Conservation and Management Association
NCSL	National College for School Leadership
NGO	Non-governmental organisation
RDA	Regional Development Agency
Susan	Susan Weil
Matthieu	Matthieu Daum
Gerald	Gerald Midgley
Yoland	Yoland Wadsworth

Introduction

What this book is about

This book is about achieving holistic change in complex social and organisational settings. This is sometimes called 'whole system change'. A holistic approach to intervention is crucial because complex issues cannot be adequately comprehended in isolation from the wider system of which they are a part. Things that happen within one arena affect, and are affected by, things that happen in other arenas, in ways which are often not easy to see. It is not enough just to *see* things holistically. Effective whole system change has to be underpinned by processes of in-depth inquiry, multi-stakeholder analysis, experimental action and experiential learning, enacted across a wide terrain. *Systemic action research* offers a learning architecture for this sort of change process.

Systemic action research[1] is a process through which communities and organisations can adapt and respond purposefully to their constantly changing environments. It supports participative solutions to entrenched problems, and enables us to work with uncertainty:

> It is through systemic thinking that we know of the unknowable. It is with action research that we learn and may act meaningfully within the unknowable. (Flood, 2001, p 142)

> As we face more and more that is unknown and not capable of being understood or controlled, we must approach learning and change as relational and improvisational processes. This inevitably means building cultures that support new forms of collaborative inquiry and action research. (Weil, 1997)

Systemic action research opens up the possibility of strategy development that can meaningfully engage with the complexities of the real world. In this respect it is a challenge to the rolling out of 'best practice', to 'strategic planning', and to the models of linear causation that dominate our organisational and political landscape. These consistently fail because they are based on an assumption that intervention outcomes are relatively straightforward to predict, if only we could get enough of the right sort of evidence:

> ... once we can predict, we can engineer the world and make it work in the way that we want it to.... The trouble is that much, and probably

> most, of the world doesn't work in this way. Most systems do not work
> in a simple linear fashion.... (Byrne, 1998, p 19)

How many urban planners predicted that those wonderful 1960s tower blocks would become the sink estates of the 1990s, or computer technicians that the internet would completely transform the way in which we shop? We could have predicted that the Iraq war would impact on race relations within the UK, but to predict the many ways in which this would happen would have been impossible. Would it have been different if the Pope hadn't died when he did? Or the 9/11 bombs hadn't hit their targets? Or if a Brazilian citizen hadn't been shot at a London Tube station? Would the issue of wearing the veil have emerged as a significant issue for our schoolteachers in 2006? Could we have predicted how that would impact on other aspects of school life? Everything is contextually situated, everything is interconnected and everything changes everything else. So instead of trying to understand linear relationships we need to understand the complex *dynamics* of social systems (Byrne, 1998). For

> ... if we can see what makes the difference, we can make the difference.
> (Byrne, 1998, p 42)

We can never fully understand, explain or predict reality, and we can only ever see a bit of it, but we can try to make enough sense of it to be able to act effectively within it. This sense making is not only an analytical process that takes place after the event; it is a relational and experiential process that takes place as things are happening.

Sense making is often about creating a whole out of fragments. But it is about more than juxtaposing and arbitrarily linking them. It is about finding the patterns that connect them, and constructing a meaningful narrative to hold them. Meaning is not only constructed intellectually and analytically; it also derives from our emotions and our senses. To make sense requires us to draw on our senses. Our smell, sound, touch, taste and sight are crucial to how we come to know and understand the world we live in. A picture drawn by a child can suddenly explain a history of violence. A piece of music or the smell of a flower can evoke a powerful memory that would otherwise never have emerged. You can walk into a room in which you can 'cut the atmosphere with a knife' and learn more about a situation than if you interviewed all of the staff. You can sense danger. A person's life can be embodied in their gait, their expressions, the lines on their faces and the clothes that they wear. Fragments of unexplained behaviour can be explained in the instant that you see your partner's eyes meet the eyes of your friend, and you realise that they have been having an affair. Positivist science would seek hard evidence of the affair, but the look may be all that is needed to act meaningfully in the situation.

Meaning is derived in action itself. It is the exhilaration that we feel when we are playing a fast sport that gives meaning to the experience, not our analysis of that exhilaration. It is the feeling of hunger that gives meaning to poverty, not our analysis of hunger. It is the experience of 'being with' and 'doing with' our families that gives meaning to our 'family' ('fear', 'home', 'a sense of place', 'security'), not an analysis of family. In an action learning set that I ran with Directors of Social Services in 1998 the key issue to emerge across the group was that judgement was being replaced by knowledge. Social workers were losing the skills to 'read' a situation because their analysis was based on checklists *about* situations.

> When we have knowledge, don't we lose everything but knowledge.... If I know about the flower, don't I lose the flower and only have the knowledge; aren't we exchanging the substance for the shadow, aren't we forfeiting this dead quality of knowledge; and what does it meant to me after all; What does all of this knowing mean to me? It means nothing. (D.H. Lawrence, *Women in love*, 1920)

And knowledge without an embedded understanding can mean very little indeed.

Action research has been articulated as a process of coming to know. There are of course different ways of knowing:

> ... *experiential knowing* is through direct face-to-face encounter with a person, place or thing; it is knowing through empathy and resonance, that kind of in-depth knowing which is almost impossible to put into words; *presentational knowing* grows out of experiential knowing, and provides the first form of expression through story, drawing, sculpture, movement, dance, drawing on aesthetic imagery; *propositional knowing* draws on concepts and ideas; and *practical knowing* consummates the other forms of knowing in action in the world. (Heron, 1996; Heron and Reason, 2001)

It is crucial that these are all engaged with in the action research process because:

> ... processes that work merely at the level of the discursive or analytic ... shield us from an appreciation of the complex interplay of paradoxes, contradictions, multiple realities and various processes of meaning making that are at play in any learning or change process. (Weil, 1997, p 375)

Sense making is thus highly personalised although not necessarily individualised (we can collectively make sense of things by seeking resonances across our life worlds), and it is highly contextualised. The lenses that each of us see through are framed by strong social and cultural norms. Personal experiences may re-enforce or override those norms. Nevertheless, things make sense in particular cultural contexts and if the culture changes they may no longer make sense. Smoking made sense to lots of people when I was a child, but it appears quite absurd to most of my children's generation. Wearing a veil may make sense to Muslim women but not to most western women. These represent multiple realities and there is no single truth to be found. So, in the words of Peter Reason, as we move from a positivist world view:

> ... human inquiry, as it ceases to be an attempt to correspond with an intrinsic nature of reality, becomes an exercise in human problem solving. (Reason, 2003)

Through human inquiry shared understandings can be built; ways of living alongside each other and doing things together can be found; problems can be solved; conflicts can be resolved; power imbalances can be challenged. This can and should mean that transforming the world so that it is a place of less conflict, hunger, suffering and inequality remains possible. But if we have learned anything, we have surely learned that central planning is not the answer.

Systemic action research takes a different approach. It is an embedded learning process through which policy and practice can be constructed on the ground. It is a means for getting things done, which is owned by the many stakeholders who are affected by problems, and have a part to play in their resolution. As such it is a process that can be built into the 'everyday' practice of community activists, professionals, policy makers and change agents (as well as students and researchers) rather than a specialist process for an expert researcher. The premise on which this book is built is that *we can all do it*.

My journey travelled

So that is what I am writing about. But let me briefly digress and say something about what brought me to these issues and what drew me to this approach. Most of my early work involved qualitative research, consultancy and policy advice on decentralisation and public participation. By the late 1990s, while still committed to these causes, I was challenged in two significant ways. Firstly, I was troubled by the paradox that while my work focused on participation, it was not participative. Like most traditional researchers I was 'the expert' who observed the practice of others and made judgements about it. I needed to find some congruence between the content of my work, and the methods that I used to pursue it. Secondly, I had observed over a decade how the participatory decision-making processes that I had supported consistently failed to develop in the ways that I and others had anticipated. There were always unseen power flows that blocked or derailed initiatives, unintended consequences of actions that undermined them, and so on. A different outlook on both the issues and how I engaged with them was needed.

In 1997 I took on the directorship of the Masters in Management Development and Social Responsibility (MDSR) at the University of Bristol. The programme worked with middle and senior managers who were grappling with how to bring their values into the management and leadership process. It was grounded in 'new paradigm' thinking (Heron and Reason, 1997) and for many years it had taught students action research and inquiry methods to support their sense-making endeavours. It was through this programme that I first saw the potential of action research as a response to my doubts about the work on participation that I was carrying out.

At the same time, I was supervising three PhD students whose work had an important influence on my thinking. Alison Gilchrist's work (Gilchrist, 2001) explored the relationship between community development and networking. Linda Gordon's research (Savoury-Gordon, 2003) looked at the ways in which the changes in outlook and behaviour which resulted from the worker buy-out of a major steel plant spilled over from the plant into the realm of family and community. Marina Prieto-Carron (Prieto-Carron, 2006) was looking at whether corporate social responsibility codes of conduct had any impact on female workers in Central and South America. All of the PhD students used an action research methodology, and were trying to work across a wider terrain than is normally possible through cooperative inquiry (for example, global supply chains). Their research design was highly emergent and necessarily highly improvised. As they grappled with different ways to engage with this complex terrain, I began to see the shape of what we now call 'networked systemic inquiry'. This is described in more detail in Chapter Four, but for now the important point is that all of these pieces of work were communicating the same message – that transformational research work of this sort needed not only to be participative but also systemic.

Meanwhile, the MDSR programme was looking for a new external examiner, and my colleague Tom Davis recommended Susan Weil. It was through my engagement with Susan's work that my emerging interest in systemic approaches to action research was accelerated. Susan was based at University College Northampton where some years earlier she had set up SOLAR (Social and Organisational Learning as Action Research) with the encouragement of Donald Schon. She had become disillusioned by the dominance of what she saw as an 'expert' and 'control-oriented model' of consultant intervention. SOLAR was set up as a space where the many different ways of 'knowing' and 'sense making' could find expression. She was also concerned with 'post-disciplinary' interventions that were rooted in the mess of real lives and the complexities of real social and organisational processes, rather than the intellectual and professional disciplines of academics and practitioners. Susan was developing ideas and research practices with others in SOLAR that signalled to me how action research might engage with larger systemic processes.

By now I was convinced of the potential of action research to transform locally situated understandings and practice, but I still had significant concerns about their wider application. It appeared to be transformational to the individuals involved, and sometimes, by extension, to their teams and organisations, but it still seemed difficult to harness such a process to the end of wider social change. How could it be developed to work across organisational boundaries; to support national and international policy making; to engage with issues that spanned entire international product chains; to enable the development and sustainability of major programmes?

Intrigued by Susan's work, I joined her at SOLAR on a year's secondment. Within a year we had decided to move SOLAR to the University of the West of England (UWE) where we have developed a range of systemic action research projects. We set up a third PhD cohort who are themselves pushing the boundaries of systemic action research. The span of our parallel and collective work has supported our inevitably different (but for the most part mutually supportive) interpretations of large system action research, and I have drawn extensively on it to illustrate concepts in this book.

Nature of the book

This book is written within a participatory paradigm (Reason and Rowan, 1981). It is not a positivist text whose aim is to *prove* the effectiveness of systemic action research. This means that the focus of this work is on narrating and explaining (and hopefully inspiring), not on justifying. So while I have sought to ground this book in the thinking and practice of those many pioneering participatory researchers and systems thinkers, I do not accord these academic writings any special privilege. I offer them as supportive data with the same status as any other data. If anything, this book privileges the stories and metaphors that make the concepts come to life and enable them to resonate with the reader's experience.

I have tried in a limited way to widen the boundaries of the narrative by including 'reflection boxes' at the side of the text. These contain helpful reflections or elaborations from those who reviewed the drafts of this book in detail: Matthieu Daum, Gerald Midgley, Yoland Wadsworth and Susan Weil.

Some key definitions

There are a few clarifications that I need to make at this early stage in the book. They are explained in more detail later, but in order to avoid confusion it is necessary to pre-empt that discussion.

Systemic thinking

This book is about *systemic thinking and practice*. It does not see 'systems' as real things that can be engineered. Systems in this context are constructions that enable us to see the different factors that are important, the connections between them and the boundaries around them. In that sense this book reflects the radical shift in systems theory that has taken place over the past 50 years or so. Midgley identifies three waves of systems theory (Midgley, 2000, 2006). The first is represented by hard systems where systems are seen as real sets of relationships that are constantly seeking equilibrium. As Flood (1999) put it, these theorists saw systems as 'physical entities just like organisms', which encouraged them to 'seek out and identify systems in the world'. They thought that by modelling 'real world' interrelationships and interconnections, it would be possible to develop effective interventions. Second-wave systems theory challenged this approach by articulating systems as social constructs:

> ... writers such as C. West Churchman and Peter Checkland argue that human systems are better understood in terms of systems of meaning (ideas, concepts, values, etc) people ascribe to the world ... to appreciate human systems therefore requires learning and understanding about systems of meaning and conflict that arises between them. (Flood 1999)

This saw the emergence of 'soft systems' (Checkland and Scholes, 2004). Here systems are presented metaphorically to aid the process of insight generation. Emphasis is given not only to the interrelationships between things, but also to the multiple voices that have a stake in those things. So 'it is less important to "model" behaviour and more important to understand the different meanings that people create within a situation, taking account of multiple perspectives' (Williams, 2007). Third-wave systems theory brought issues of power much more firmly into the frame and showed how the way in which we construct boundaries around issues fundamentally affects what happens (Ulrich, 1983; Midgley, 2000). So as the theory has developed it has become clearer that the systems are not reality; they are ways of thinking that help us to understand the multiple realities that different stakeholders experience.

Action research and action inquiry

This book is inevitably filled with references to 'action research' and 'action inquiry'. I use these in a very specific way.

   Systemic action research is a form of action research that locates local action inquiry within a wider system taking into account both the effects that the system has on local issues, and vice versa. I describe two approaches: *large system action research* and *networked systemic inquiry*. These have been developed within SOLAR to enable effective engagement across large and complex systems.

When I refer to action inquiry I refer to the inquiry practices (see chapter six) that underpin systemic action research. These are enacted within inquiry streams. An *inquiry stream* is a series of linked meetings which explore issues and constructs action over a period of time. These take the form of conversations which are supported by a wide range of insight-generating processes. The conversations may take the form of informal 'dialogue' or a series of 'group discussions', but within an action inquiry process they are deliberately connected to each other, and then guided toward action. Conversation, like the issues that we are concerned with, is messy and fragmented, partial and like everything else, subject to power, so I think it is crucial not to get too focused on 'ideal' dialogic processes. I would, however, distinguish conversation from much of the 'talk' that takes place in meetings structured by agendas. This tends to be characterised by 'defending positions' and 'making decisions'. A conversation implies interrelationship and the possibility that something new emerges (Shaw, 2002), and action inquiry supports action in those emergent spaces.

Figure 1: Systemic Action Research

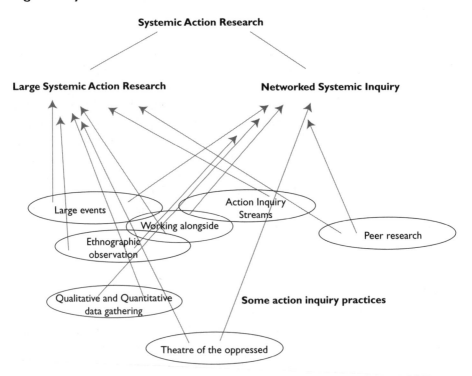

Interventions

At times in this book I refer to 'intervention' as a form of action. Intervention is a controversial word because it can be associated with 'external meddling', 'social engineering' or 'top-down development'. I see interventions as interruptions to disabling or disempowering systemic patterns. Interventions of this sort can be generated internally or with the aid of external perspectives, facilitation or resources. If, for example, victims and others take action in response to a local culture that is perceived as supporting domestic violence, then they are making an intervention in relation to local social norms.

Structure of the book

Chapter One looks at the nature of action research and explores how it needs to be developed to realise its potential as a catalyst for social transformation. Chapter Two introduces the reader to systemic thinking. It offers a way of engaging with complexity that can work effectively with paradox, uncertainty and non-linear causality. The chapter illustrates through stories and intervention scenarios some of the limitations of analytical frameworks and strategies that do not engage with complex systemic interrelationships. Chapter Three explores some key implications of systems thinking and complexity theory for action research. It highlights the importance of three interrelated concepts: improvisation, parallel development and resonance. Chapter Four draws on four systemic action research projects to explore the evolution of large system action research design. Chapter Five uses these examples to draw out a number of design principles that need to be considered both at the initial design stage of the research and as it emerges. Chapter Six explores in more detail some of the methods that are used in action research, such as the construction of inquiry streams, the use of large events and visual approaches. The idea of systemic action research as a hub within which multiple methods can be located, through which multiple interpretations can be collectively processed, and from which action can be constructed is developed. Chapter Seven is about the role of external facilitators in the action research process. It explores the skills that they need, their relationship to the groups that they work with and many of the dilemmas that they face. Chapter Eight develops some arguments about quality and ethics in systemic action research. These build on an emerging literature within the field of action research about what good research is within a participative paradigm. Chapter Nine explores the implications of this discussion for the policy-making community. It argues that systemic action research is a process that could be embedded throughout the public sphere offering solutions to endemic social and organisational problems. The book concludes with 'A final reflection' on the many issues that have been explored.

Note

[1] The term 'systemic action research' is not new. It has been used in a variety of contexts over the past 15 years or so. Early references (Bawden and Packham, 1991, Packham and Sriskandarajah, 2005) had a strong agricultural focus . More recently it has been used in the context of organisational change (Cochlan, 2002) and more widely to engage with complex social and organisational environments (Ison and Russel, 2000; Burns, 2003 and 2006a, Burns and Weil, 2006; Weil et al, 2005). The focus of these authors is diverse but they share a concern to take into account the wider context within which issues are situated.

ONE

Action research

By integrating 'learning by doing' with deep reflection, action research has always held the promise of an embedded learning process that can simultaneously inform and create change. The approach has been developed and refined over decades so that it is now able to comprehensively answer challenges about its robustness, rigour and quality[1] (see Chapter Eight), but I will argue it has also been limited by scale, by a linear model of change and by an over-reliance on consensual and dialogic processes which, although important, have neglected the impact of power. This book offers a vision of action research that I hope is able to meet those challenges.

I do not propose to trace the history of action research in this chapter as this has been done in numerous texts (see, for example, Greenwood and Levin; 1998; Reason and Bradbury, 2001). Rather, I intend to explain what I mean by action research, to map some of the arguments for shifting beyond either an 'individual' or 'small group' focus, and to signal how I and colleagues in SOLAR have been developing it as a process for supporting large-scale social and organisational change.

What is action research?

> Action research must not be seen as simply another methodology in the toolkit of disinterested social science: action research is an orientation to inquiry rather than a methodology. It has different purposes, it is based in different relationships, and it has different ways of conceiving knowledge and its relation to practice. (Reason, 2003, p 106)

Action research is not a methodology. It is an approach to inquiry that supports many methods in the service of sense making through experimental action. It combines inquiry with action as a means of stimulating and supporting change and as a way of assessing the impact of that change. By inquiry I refer to a process of insight generation about issues of importance. This process combines intellectual analysis with experiential knowing, and works with many forms of evidence. The evidence can range from stories, to statistical data, to qualitative questionnaires, images and so on. These are made sense of within an action research hub. The process provides a picture of what is really happening by unravelling the consequences of action, which in turn provides a foundation for new action. As Levin put it: 'the best way to understand something is to try to change it'

(Greenwood and Levin, 1998, p 19). So action research is centrally concerned with learning through reflection and doing, and being 'in it'. It differs from action learning in its deliberate intention and recording, but is built around the same cyclical concepts. There are many representations of this cyclical process, but put simply action research practice is most commonly rooted in the sequence *plan, act, observe, reflect* loosely derived from the 'Kolb cycle' (Kolb, 1984). This is repeated as participants move into ever new cycles of action planning for as long as the process remains useful.

There are many interpretations of these terms. The meaning that I give to them in this context is as follows. By planning, I mean a process of thinking through and developing our intention to act. By acting, I mean intervening in complex social processes. By

Figure 2: A simple action research cycle

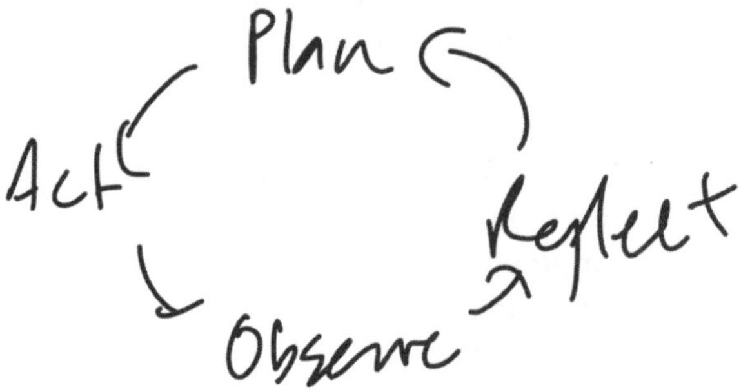

observing, I mean seeing or finding out what happened as a result of our actions. By reflecting, I mean cognitive, sensual and emotional sense making. Greenwood and Levin describe this as:

> ... a cogeneration process through which professional researchers and interested members of a local organization, community or specially created organization collaborate to research, understand and resolve problems of mutual interest. AR [action research] is a social process in which professional knowledge, local knowledge, process skills, and democratic values are the basis for co-created knowledge and social change. (Greenwood and Levin, 1998, p 93)

They see action research as having the following core characteristics:

- it is context bound and addresses real-life problems;
- it is inquiry where participants and researchers contribute to knowledge through collaborative communication processes in which all participants' contributions are taken seriously;
- it treats the diversity of experience and capacities within the local group as an opportunity for the enrichment of the research–action process;
- the meanings in the inquiry process lead to social action or these reflections on action lead to the construction of new meanings;
- the credibility of action research knowledge is measured according to whether actions that arise from it solve problems (workability) and increase participants' control over their own situation.

Put together with Lewin's (1952) key principles summarised by Barcal (2006, p 368), we begin to get a picture of the underlying ethos of action research:

- it combines a systematic study, sometimes experimental, of a social problem as well as endeavouring to solve it;
- it includes a spiral process of data collation to determine goals and assessment of the results of intervention;
- it demands feedback of the results of intervention to all parties involved in the research;
- it implies continuous cooperation between researchers and practitioners;
- it relies on the principles of group dynamics and is anchored in its change phases. The phases are unfreezing, moving and refreezing. Decision making is mutual and is carried out in a public way;
- it takes into account issues of values, objectives and the power needs of the parties involved;
- it serves to create knowledge, to formulate principles of intervention and also to develop instruments for selection, intervention and training;
- within the framework of action research there is much emphasis on recruitment, training and support of the change agents.

There are many other formulations, and I am not going to try to synthesise these into core principles. These two examples from Greenwood and Levin and Lewin give us a feel for what action research is, and how it differs from traditional research. Its construction as 'a dynamic and continuous enquiry process' (Weil, 1998, p 59) enables feedback in real time, in contrast with traditional research and evaluation reports that present findings after the event. Its focus on action enables learning from experience. Its focus on participation ensures that stakeholders have ownership of the process that in turn harnesses their passion:

> And when the people acted upon are themselves made the true partners in the actions, and co-discoverers of the corrections of error, then through and through, and in spite of blunders or even by virtue of them, the vital energies are increased, confidence increases, power increases, experience builds towards wisdom, and the most potent of all principles and ideals, deep democracy slowly wins the field. (Collier, quoted in Neilson, 2006)

Extensive and diverse participation also ensures that there are multiple lenses on what is emerging, enabling better issue identification and consequently better problem solving. It is not a challenge to the idea of evidence-based practice per se, but strongly challenges the dominant discourse about what is and what is not evidence. Its holistic focus contextualises the research and consequently enables it to engage with more complex problems.

> AR [action research] generally takes on much more complex problems than the conventional social sciences.... Academic social researchers seem content to chop up reality to make it simpler to handle, more suited to theoretical manipulation, and to make the social scientists' life easier to manage. AR does not accept these compromises. (Greenwood and Levin, 1998, p 75)

Why action research?

So what is the purpose of action research? I would strongly subscribe to Reason and Bradbury's assertion that:

> A primary purpose of action research is to produce practical knowledge that is useful to people in the everyday conduct of their lives. A wider purpose of action research is to contribute through this practical knowledge to the increased well-being – economic, political, psychological, spiritual – of human persons and communities, and to a more equitable and sustainable relationship with the wider energy of the planet of which we are an intrinsic part. (Reason and Bradbury, 2001, p 2)

The broader sentiment goes right back to the roots of action research. While many have identified the originator of action research as Kurt Lewin, he was significantly influenced by Jacob Moreno. Lewin's more 'analytic focus' was preceded by a more embodied 'activist focus':

> When Lewin went to the US, he had been much influenced by Moreno, the inventor of group dynamics and sociodrama and psychodrama. Moreno had already developed a view of action research in which the "action" was about activism, not just about changing practice or behaviour understood in narrowly individualistic terms. Moreno was interested in research as a part of social movement. (Kemmis, 1993)

Neilson makes a similar observation, comparing Lewin's thinking with that of Collier:

> Collier wanted to promote the further use of action research as a technique for solving important social problems, while Lewin, still sympathetic to Collier's aim, wanted to promote action research itself as a legitimate dimension of scientific study.... Collier wanted to use action research to ameliorate the conditions of oppressed people. Lewin wanted to advance the science of doing this. (Neilson, 2006, p 397)

Many contemporary action research facilitators, particularly those associated with the participatory action research tradition, have echoed this political sentiment. Kemmis (1993) and Greenwood and Levin (1998), for example, advocate a direct link between action research and social change:

> Some versions of action research - the one I favour (see Carr and Kemmis, 1986), and also associated with the work of people like Richard Winter (1987, 1989) in England, and Orlando Fals Borda (1990, 1991) in Colombia, and Cesar Cascante (1991) in Asturias, Spain - aim to make strong and explicit connections between action research and social movement. (Kemmis, 1993)

> ... action research is a form of research that generates knowledge for the express purpose of taking action to promote social change and social analysis. But the social change we refer to is not just any kind of change. Action research aims to increase the ability of the involved community or organisation members to control their own destinies more effectively and to keep improving their capacity to do so. (Greenwood and Levin, 1998, p 6)

> AR [action research] explicitly seems to disrupt existing power relations for the purpose of democratising society. (Greenwood and Levin, 1998, p 88)

The lineage is significant because it illustrates how concern with political action, the importance of working on a larger scale and an understanding of the power of embodied and 'enacted' knowing have been present in action research thinking right from the start. What follows from this, however, is that if action research is to be an effective political tool then it has to move beyond the single local group, team or organisation to work across organisations, networks and partnerships, on multiple sites and at multiple levels. It also has to be able to engage with wider social norms.

Until recently, with exceptions in the 'global south', most action research practice has focused on action research as a form of individual reflective practice (Marshall, 1999, 2004) or on group-based processes such as cooperative inquiry (Heron, 1996; Reason, 1994; Heron and Reason, 2001) and appreciative inquiry (Ludema et al, 2000). In this book we explore how to scale this work up to engage with the wider systems within which they are situated.

Various writers have articulated the different scales at which inquiry might operate. Reason and Bradbury (2001) talk about first, second and third-person action research:

> First-person action research/practice skills and methods address the ability of the researcher to foster an inquiring approach to his or her own life.
>
> Second-person action research/practice addresses our ability to inquire face-to-face with others into issues of mutual concern.
>
> Third-person strategies aim to create a wider community of inquiry … the most compelling and enduring kind of action research will engage all three strategies. (Reason and Bradbury, 2001, p xxvi)

Torbert speaks of the 'personal, relational and organizational scales' (Torbert, 2001, p 257). I tend to think of inquiry operating at individual, group and systemic levels. While each of these formulations convey the notion of 'scaling up', they are not entirely synonymous with each other. The relational, for example, cannot be conflated with the level of the group. Much of SOLAR's work has been about developing new forms of relational practice at a system level and bringing different parts of the 'system' into relationship with each other. Nevertheless, Torbert's point that there is a relationship between these levels is well made:

> Second-person research/practice presupposes and works to co-generate first-person research/practice. Similarly one of the key characteristics of successful third-person research/practice is that it is an action inquiry leadership practice that presupposes first and second person research-practice capacity in the part of leadership. (Torbert, 2001, p 257)

Good systemic work is dependent on a strong network of group-based inquiries that are in turn dependent on strong reflective practice at the individual level.

While there has been scant practice and even less theorisation, a few contemporary writers have recently begun to make the case for action research to extend beyond the realms of the single group or the single case. Kemmis, for example, articulates the need for action research to bridge the gap between practice learning and policy learning:[2]

> Some hold that action research is the key to making research relevant to the concerns and needs of teachers and the education profession; some hold that large-scale policy research which connects more directly with professional concerns is what is needed – not necessarily action research. This way of putting the problem involves a troublesome distinction between the "micro" and the "macro" in educational research. (Kemmis, 1993)

Others have talked about extending the reach of action research. Gustavsen argues that it is:

> ... important to create many events of low intensity and diffuse boundaries than fewer events that correspond to the classical notion of a "case". Instead of using much resources in a single spot to pursue things into a continuously higher degree of detail in this spot, resources are spread over a much larger terrain to intervene in as many places in the overall movement as possible. (Gustavsen, 2003, pp 96-7)

A number of authors have advanced arguments for large scale systemic work. Weil (1998, p 58) speaks of the need to learn from disabling systemic patterns and contradictions, and to challenge underlying assumptions and world views across a system. Wadsworth (2005) talks about the importance of 'scaling up' invoking an image of locally based inquiry that builds upward and outward. Burns (2003 and 2006a) highlights the need for systemic action research which can meaningfully engage with complex governance environments. Ison and Armson (2006) argue for the development of 'systemic inquiry' as a way of facilitating social learning (defined as 'concerted action by multiple stakeholders in situations of complexity and uncertainty'). Foth highlights the importance of networks, inviting us to consider 'the network qualities of community and the implications it has for action research' (Foth, 2006, p 206):

> Networking taps into the "capillary communicative structure" of communities and enables action researchers to ensure that the open learning and inquiry processes that community leaders and volunteers are encouraged to engage in will spread through the community at large. (Foth, 2006, p 210)

> ... network action research moves away from a pure homogeneous model of community and acknowledges the fluid, dynamic, swarming, chaotic qualities of social networks that are present in communities. The primary objective of network action research is to map the existing (formal and informal) networks that operate within the community and initiate small participatory action research projects within each of them. The task of the action researcher is then to link and harness each of their sub-networks of inquiry to form a larger networked community of practice. (Foth, 2006, p 212)

What is implicit in all of these commentaries on action research is that if action research is to have a major impact on society more generally, and whole organisations and communities specifically, then it needs to extend beyond an individual and group focus. If action research is to get to grips with the complex dynamics of 'messy' reality then it needs to build systemic pictures of what is going on, and systemic intervention strategies:

> such an initiative would require facilitators accustomed to working with large scale dialogic and co-inquiry processes. It would necessitate politicians and others "holding open the programme action inquiry space" in ways that support the emergence (and further funding) of multi stranded developments that unfreeze existing thinking and practice. Different seed dialogues, within and across ... could slowly build, participation, momentum and insight.... Further strengthened by research that was legitimated in pursuing potential strands of inquiry that track and "played back" emerging insights into the connective inquiry process. (Weil et al, 2005, p 236)

In this book, building on a varied portfolio of SOLAR projects, I explore some different approaches to these visions. I articulate two distinct but connected forms of systemic action research: *large system action research* and *networked systemic inquiry*.

Large system action research refers to action research projects that comprise large numbers of parallel or interacting inquiry processes. Here, the action research process is not externalised as a project or discreet piece of research; it is embedded into the way that a whole organisation or organisational system works. A boundary will be held around the core concerns of a funder, but this may be held extremely lightly and the territory may be very large. As we will see later, this framing includes the work of Yoland Wadsworth that we discuss in more detail in Chapter Four. SOLAR's approach to design, departs from that described in Wadsworth (2001) in one important respect. Where Wadsworth describes a process that builds outward from a single starting point to develop multiple inquiries, our work has tended to build from multiple starting points. We have found that this has enabled a nuanced systemic picture to be built from different locations within the system (Burns, 2006a). We have been concerned that if an 'inquiry path' is constructed from the view of a single stakeholder – albeit the most important one (the psychiatric patients in the work on which Wadsworth reports) – then it can only go to places that it sees. Other places may be crucial to unlocking the problems that that stakeholder seeks to resolve. By seeding inquiries across the terrain we may be able to build a clearer picture of the boundaries within which new inquiries might be developed. Undoubtedly the richness and depth that some of our SOLAR projects have achieved was also reached in the Melbourne project (see Chapter Four), but this may not have been possible in a shorter piece of work.

Networked systemic inquiry refers to a more organic form of action inquiry that Susan and I have been able to articulate through our work with PhD students. Because they are not 'commissioned', the action research has greater freedom to go wherever the inquiry leads. Furthermore, new inquiries are not necessarily derived from existing ones. The form is less linear and connections are often made through the juxtaposition of patches of patchwork. These diverse inquiries can be held in relationship to each other by action research facilitators themselves, which not only places them firmly 'in' the research but makes them the heartbeat of the research.

In both of these formulations the action research process is characterised by establishing multiple action inquiry streams across an issue terrain, enabling multiple perspectives to be surfaced. The large system inquiry process connects with different action inquiry streams and opens up a coherent learning process to track the effect of different strategies. Bringing such diversity to the analysis of large systems is important. By engaging with groups across the breadth of a system we can stimulate ongoing cycles of evidence gathering and insight generation, action planning, action and reflection on action. This allows change strategies to emerge iteratively and to change direction swiftly and flexibly where we discover that one intervention is not working. The process enables us to develop an understanding of the effects of actions elsewhere in the system, and the impact of other people's actions on our central arena for action. It also provides an arena within which distributed leadership can emerge, thereby creating a resource to both generate and sustain local change. Both of these framings of systemic action research are developed in more detail in Chapter Four.

Notes

[1] I won't attempt to cite all of the authors that have contributed to this process as the names would stretch over many pages. A good overview from many of the key contributors is contained in Reason and Bradbury (2001).

[2] Some of my SOLAR colleagues have been working in this area for some time. See, for example, Percy-Smith (2004), Percy-Smith and Walsh (2006) and Percy-Smith and Weil (2003).

TWO

A systemic perspective

> Complexity is of course inherently systemic. What is crucially important about it is that it is systemic without being conservative. On the contrary, the dynamics of complex systems are inherently dynamic and transformational. (Byrne, 1998, p 51)

In Chapter One I said that the shift from individual and group-based action research was being triggered by calls for systemic learning processes to address large-scale political and policy change. It is also a response to the challenges posed by complexity and non-linearity. It is to these issues that we now turn. Once we have established why systemic thinking is so important, we can draw out its implications for the action research process. My approach is not to conduct a comprehensive analysis of all of the different variants of systems theory, and then apply my favoured approach to action research, but rather to use stories to illustrate how systems ideas help us to conceptualise and work with complex issues. From a theoretical perspective I take a similar position to Flood (1999), who argues that systems theorists such as von Bertalanffy, Beer, Ackoff, Checkland and Churchman offer a range of different insights into systemic thinking that are all useful.

Systemic thinking

> Systemic thinking is not an approach to action research, but a grounding for action research that may broaden action and deepen research. (Flood, 2001, p 143)

Systemic thinking means 'taking into account the whole', and seeks meaning in the complex patterning of interrelationships between people and groups of people. Put another way, 'systemic thinking requires people to look at sets of interacting activities' (Packham and Sriskandarajah, 2005). This highlights dynamics that are not always visible through the scrutiny of individual interactions. This is crucial because outcomes (positive or negative) will often have more to do with the interrelationship between interacting interventions than the effect of any individual action. Action rarely impacts in a linear way (Burns, 2006a).

Looking at things systemically is useful because it helps us to make connections that we would not otherwise make. Having said this, it is always important to remember that we can only ever see a part of the whole (Churchman, 1970; Ulrich, 1983; Midgley, 2000). This is the paradox of whole systems thinking

(Ulrich 1990; Pratt et al 1999; Atwood et al 2003). On the one hand we are drawn by the deficiencies of linear models of causality to engage with the wider system in order to understand it. On the other hand we have to acknowledge that this will always be an aspiration we can get closer to but which we can never entirely achieve:

> Systems theory and many of the developments of post-modern and poststructuralist theory rightly persuade us that this notion of a social whole is illusory. There are no "whole" societies, or "whole" systems, or "whole" states which are the addressees of social theory or practice. There are just interwoven, interlocking, overlapping networks of social relations which galvanize power and discourses in different directions and in different ways in relation to the personal and social and cultural realms. (Kemmis, 2001, p 99)

> Complexity theory is useful here for understanding the conditions that constitute action research practise. The theory conceptualizes social conditions as representing a complex set of interrelationships with multiple feedback loops and the capacity for spontaneous self-organisation (Flood, 1999). This theory argues that, at best, participants will attain only temporary and partial interpretations of events. (Boser, 2006, p 13)

So the concept of 'whole systems' is useful only as long as we interpret it as an attempt to see more of the whole, rather than as an attempt to see *the* whole. When 'organisational change' facilitators organise large events that are designed to 'bring the whole system into the room', they should not take their rhetoric too seriously. The acceptance of partiality leads us to very pragmatic conclusions. We have to be able to see 'enough' and understand 'enough' to make sense of our world such that we can act meaningfully and purposefully within it. We also have to have mechanisms that tell us something of the significance of what we see. Later I talk about testing resonance as a way of doing this (**see page 53**).

I refer to *systemic thinking* rather than systems because the systems that we conceptualise cannot be regarded as representations of reality but as constructions to enable learning. They are like 'a pair of spectacles through which we can look and interpret reality' (Flood, 2001, p 138). Flood (1996) invites us to 'study organisational forms *as if* they were systemic'. This is not to say that the interrelationships are not real, only that they are open to multiple interpretations. Weil (1998) echoes this view in describing what she calls critically reflexive action research:

> CRAR [critically reflexive action research] does not aim to create one representation of reality but, rather, the unravelling (and

documentation) of multiple realities and rhetorics that are in mutual and simultaneous interaction. (Weil, 1998, p 58)

Bateson makes a similar point below, which is crucial for action research facilitators to grasp:

> Solutions to problems often depend on how they are defined. If you look at unfolding lives, you immediately become aware of the processes of redefinition: shelters may come to be seen as constraining walls, interruptions are recognised as moments of fertilisation, outrage becomes empowering and freeing. It is possible to look for pattern in seeming disorder and propose a search for potential benefit in every problem. (Bateson, 1990, p 239)

We often limit the possibilities for transformative action because of the way in which we frame the issues and problems with which we are concerned. The notion of boundary critique is important here (Churchman, 1970; Ulrich, 1983; Midgley, 2000). Midgley (2000) argues that how we construct the boundaries of our inquiry has a profound impact on what we can learn. Because actions and interventions in one sphere can have major implications for other spheres, then the way in which we draw the boundaries (to define our focus of attention) fundamentally affects what we see and how we assess its effectiveness. The following example from a social care setting is instructive.

The systemic impact of catheterisation on a hospital ward

I was working with the senior management teams of a city council and the local primary care trust. They got to talking about care pathways for older people, and were musing on a puzzle that they had observed. This was that there seemed to be a one directional path from caring for yourself in the home, to homecare, to residential care, to nursing care and ultimately into acute hospital beds. If someone had a short-term medical problem and ended having to go to hospital they almost invariably ended up staying there longer than anticipated, and from there, instead of going back home or back to residential care they ended up in nursing care. Some of them started to talk about the experiences of their own parents. One talked of the way in which older people who came onto the wards were routinely catheterised (a catheter is a flexible tube introduced into the urethra for emptying the urinary bladder). This was because it took 15 minutes to take each patient to the toilet and 15 minutes to take them back again. There simply was not enough nurse time to do this. The effect of this was that virtually all of the older people who came onto the wards as independent individuals came out dependent. So they could no longer go back into their homes or into residential care. This meant that much greater pressure was put on available nursing care. Put this in the context of the national 'bed-blocking' crisis as depicted in the quote below:

A report on hospital bed management showed that two million bed days had been lost each year because of delays in discharging people who were fit to leave hospital. Two thirds of beds were occupied by people over the age of 65 and a key factor in their delayed discharge was the difficulty in finding them places in community facilities. (*The Guardian*, 17 April 2002)

and we can begin to see that the hospital service might begin to find the answers to its bed-blocking crisis within its own ward practices, but it could not see this. It needed a systemic inquiry initiated from outside its own boundaries (within the social care sector) to see this.

Source: Burns (2006a)

This story illustrates firstly how difficult it is to see the systemic patterning from within a local problem context. This is one reason why it is essential to open up multi-sited inquiries across a whole system. Secondly, the story shows how micro changes have macro impacts. It was not obvious to those on the hospital wards that investing in taking people to the toilet might contribute to unlocking a multi-million pound bed-blocking problem. Thirdly, the story illustrates how theory can be generated from within a local inquiry and tested for resonance within a wider system.

Whereas this example shows the need for systemic thinking in *large-scale* organisational settings, the following story from a study of acute psychiatric services in Melbourne shows the impact of boundary construction on a *small scale*. Here bureaucratic boundaries have been drawn that make a complete nonsense of the reality experienced by two patients who are processed within an organisational system as if they were not connected.

I would like to say that they have bent the rules here for my wife and I during the day but not at night. We would like to spend the night together but we are not allowed. It is against the rules here to be in the same room, the same ward, the same bed. This is contributing to my wife's illness. People with mental illness often marry other people with mental illness and then they cannot spend time together when they have to go to hospital. What I would like to see is another section where married people can sleep in the same room and spend time together. We miss out on the groups, because we can't go to one another's ward outings and we don't want to go alone....

Married couples should be discharged at the same time. Not one going out alone. We would be better off together. We would learn and we would be in peace. (quoted in McGuiness and Wadsworth, 1991, p 21)

The boundary is placed around the individual and the system does not know how (or does not want) to consider them in relation to each other. Now consider the following case outlined by Caroline Toroitich, who works with SNV Kenya:

Female genital mutilation in Kenya

Organisations have been focusing on eradicating female genital mutilation (FGM) for a long period. Female genital mutilation is still being practised on 32% of females in Kenya. Even in regions where the practice has gone down, there has been some resurgence among women aged 40 and above (who are increasingly subjected to it). As the practice is contrary to human rights several NGOs [non-governmental organisations] "rescue" girls from FGM. These girls are taken to refuge centres but there seems to be no recognition of what would happen if the NGO money runs out. The conflict between NGOs and local traditional communities can spill over into relationships with all NGOs and put other important work in jeopardy.

Female genital mutilation is about cultural and gender identity; if women haven't been circumcised they cannot marry within their communities because they are not regarded as adults. Organisations like SNV have explored the possibilities of alternative initiation ceremonies, and it is beginning to bear fruit in some communities although in others they still perform FGM on the girls after going through the alternative rite. Following the life trajectories of these young girls who run away from FGM leads us to discover that many end up dropping out of school and leading a miserable life because of the rejection by their communities and their families. Is this a better fate than the one that they were being protected from?

Meanwhile a parallel narrative is evolving. Some hospitals have decided to carry out the procedure themselves. Their motivation is to ensure that the procedure is carried out safely and that danger to the woman is minimised. This is having the effect of medicalising the process – making it much harder to challenge using medical arguments.

A more positive narrative is emerging – that is a positive articulation of female sexuality. Is this debate made more or less difficult by the HIV/AIDS epidemic?

Sexuality can bring misery through sexual violence, HIV/AIDS, maternal mortality, FGM, marginalisation of those who break the norm such as single women, sex workers, same-sex sexualities and transgender people. It can also bring joy, affirmation, intimacy and well being. How can we bring joy and less misery?

Caroline's question is a good starting point for an action inquiry. But thinking through how to go about it is not straightforward. We might open up a dialogue with tribal leaders about the nature of this practice and whether there are any alternatives, but this would be difficult if we were not also having a dialogue with the hospitals who were influencing the debate in ways in which they might not have intended. We also need to look at the time boundaries that are drawn. The non-governmental organisations (NGOs) may be considering the ethical issues with regard to the difficulties facing the child now, not the difficulties that she will face in the whole of her life. Because everything is interconnected we need to build a systemic picture of the dynamics of the situation. A positive assertion of female sexuality cannot be advanced without grounding it in the complex realities of HIV/AIDS. The way in which tribes are adapting or not adapting to HIV is not unconnected to how they are adapting to other issues. Action research in this context will necessarily be a multi-stranded inquiry process that involves work with, for example, the girls, their families, the NGOs, the hospitals and communities. These will probably need to start as separate strands, interacting and converging with other strands as opportunities emerge.

The example above illustrates how problematic it is to intervene in situations without taking into consideration interdependencies within the wider system of which they are part. The same applies to strategic policy and the implementation of strategic plans. Take the following example of water provision and management in Kenya.

The Moiben Dam

In the late 1990s in the North Rift region of Western Kenya, the Moiben River was dammed to provide water to the growing city of Eldoret. The dam was built and subsequently managed and controlled by the Eldoret Municipal Council. However, the dam itself was located in the neighbouring county of Marakwet. A memorandum of understanding was signed between Eldoret and Marakwet that should have ensured that drinking water would also be provided to people in Marakwet. The deal was reneged on. It is not entirely clear why. Meanwhile the lake behind the dam is becoming a breeding ground for mosquitoes and malaria has spread. People have drowned in the lake. The people of Marakwet have become angry and some have become organised. Calls have gone out to break the dam. With the new water reform programme in Kenya, the dam was transferred in 2004 to a private water supply company called ELDOWAS. The company move in response to this agitation was to set up the Moiben River Catchments Protection, Conservation and Management Association (MRPCMA). The local MP (Member of Parliament) is on the group. Was this an attempt to buy off the opposition?

As the years go by the external forces grow on Eldoret to maintain tight control over the water. The population is getting bigger and the town is in even more need of the water. Yet even if the 'militancy' of the people of Marakwet can be controlled there is a longer-term systemic problem. The water catchment area for the dam runs through Marakwet. A sustainable supply of good water is dependent on protection of the natural environment. ELDOWAS offers cheap seedlings through the MRPCMA, but what incentive is there for people to plant them? And why should they pay anything for them when they are not getting the water they were promised?

National water reform is under way. Water resource user groups are being set up to facilitate local representation. Water resource management boards and water resource user associations will make strategic decisions for the province. But these new bodies do not enter into a virgin political landscape.

What is clear from this story is that the success of the dam will not be determined by the quality of its technical implementation. Flood stresses the point that 'no problem exists that is purely technical. People are always involved' (Flood, 1999, p 71). In this case the success of this dam will rest on the creation of a social, economic and environmental equilibrium that supports it. Because there has been little or no attention to these complex interrelationships, the whole project could be undermined. The Moiben dam is a good example of the interdependent relationship between environmental systems (for example, malaria, public health and nutrition, water catchment management, urban growth) and social systems.

So far I have only illustrated the negative effects of how system boundaries are drawn. To conclude this section I want to offer a positive example of the way in which drawing a different boundary can suddenly open up possibilities. This did not have a successful outcome, but it did enable me to see the problem in an entirely new way. For many years I (with others) was trying to get a community centre built in my neighbourhood. We spent years building a consensus among community groups. We acquired the land. We had detailed architects' drawings made up and planning permission was granted. We had outline approval from the European regeneration funding stream Objective 2. To qualify for Objective 2 funding we had to have at least 50% matched funding. We went to five other major funders who all said it was a great project but they could not consider funding it unless we already had full matched funding. I am sure many readers will recognise this Catch-22.

Some months later I happened to be at a meeting at the local council where I met someone from a community organisation in another part of the city. He said that he had managed to get funding for his project when he started to view the whole matched funding issue through a different lens. Instead of drawing the boundary around his project he drew the boundary wider and started to look at what was happening in the whole of that neighbourhood. He discovered that the bus company was about to invest in new transport links and that other public agencies were investing in other things. He talked to them and asked them if they would enter a formal partnership with him. They agreed. This allowed him to construct a much larger project, 50% of which was 100% of his original project. So he now had a 50% match in the form of partners' investments in the area (which were already planned). In my area there were plans for a new Bristol arena to be built. I wondered if the Regional Development Agency (RDA) and the developers would be happy to be part of a Totterdown Area Regeneration Programme, half of which comprised our community centre. That would allow us to bid for 100% of the community centre cost. In the end we did secure agreement, but by the time we had done so there was not enough money left in the South West Objective 2 pot. We still do not have a community centre, but I learned something profound about how widening the boundary opens up possibilities that were previously obscured.

Systemic effects

In large system work we are concerned to understand patterns that emerge at the level of the system and the dynamics of change that bring them about. These are often the result of unintended consequences arising from the fact that a single action can have multiple impacts on different places; that interventions often do not have a linear effect; and that cumulative impacts might produce the opposite outcome to individual impacts. As Byrne puts it:

> Outcomes are determined not by single causes, but by multiple causes, and these causes may, and usually do interact in a non-additive fashion. In other words the combined effect is not necessarily the sum of the separate effects. (Byrne, 1998, p 20)

In practical terms some of the most common effects that I have observed in social situations are as follows:

- unpredictable outcomes
- consequential outcomes
- cumulative impacts
- collective impacts
- paradoxical effects

Unpredictable outcomes

Unpredictable outcomes frequently emerge where change is 'constructed' as a linear process that assumes that certain sorts of interventions lead to certain sorts of outcomes (if you do *x* then it is likely that *y* will happen). This approach is rooted in 19th-century physics and is characterised by 'reductionism'.

> Reductionism breaks things into parts and studies forces acting on them, seeking to establish laws and principles of behaviour. It does this by treating parts as closed systems, that is, separate units of analysis. (Flood, 1999, p 29)

It is typical of top-down policy-making and 'best practice' models of policy implementation, where evidence is gathered, a 'solution' to a problem is developed, and it is then 'rolled out'. Unfortunately, when it interacts with the complexity of local circumstances it does not behave in the way that was predicted. In 'complex governance environments', where many things are happening at the same time, interacting with each other, and simultaneously impacting on each other, simple explanations are very difficult to find. Given this it is extraordinary how often policy makers request researchers to find the link between intervention A and outcome B. Where 'positivist' researchers are concerned to isolate the influence of multiple variables so that the causal relationship between A and B can be verified, a systemic perspective tries to understand the relationship between the different elements. Rather than trying to 'isolate variables', we need to understand what happens when they combine. If I am eating a delicious fruitcake, it is of limited value for me to know how eggs and Brazil nuts taste together, or sugar and cherries. It is the interaction between all of the ingredients that counts. Furthermore, when I eat that fruitcake my enjoyment of it may depend on whether I like cake (my personal taste), what happened the last time I ate cake, who I believe made the cake, and so on. So a complex mix of interrelating elements interacts with another complex mix to produce an outcome.

Consequential outcomes

The section above illustrates the problem of negative unintended consequences impacting on the arena within which an intervention is made. Another common scenario is where an action, which has a very positive impact on the problem that it is specifically addressing, has unintended effects elsewhere in the system. In other words the consequences of a positive impact *here* could be a negative impact *there*. These may occur across system boundaries. The story of catheterisation that I recounted on pages 23-4 is a good example of this.

Another issue that we need to be aware of is the way in which positive interventions in parts of systems affect the ability of the system as a whole to coordinate its activities, thereby disabling the system at another level. The UK government currently argues that two of the most important elements of good public service management are (1) the setting of and adherence to performance targets, and (2) partnership. Yet time and time again we see how even small changes to organisational and departmental service targets completely undermine local partnerships. Partnership at its best is a negotiated process in which integrated solutions are built to support the needs of organisations and their clients. If new targets are imposed on one or more of the organisations so that they have to put their resources elsewhere, then the basis for the partnership has collapsed. The partnership problem is an important one, not least because these effects mean that what is called partnership very rarely involves integration of any sort.

Cumulative impacts

Sometimes one instance of an action can have an extremely positive effect but its cumulative effect can become negative. When people give presents to my son they are building a relationship with him. The value that he places on the gift strengthens the relationship. But when he is showered by presents by all of my relatives, he begins to take the gifts for granted and they no longer have the same value. As an episode the exchange is unproblematic; as a part of systemic pattern it can be seriously problematic. This can happen in social and organisational contexts. A very simple but obvious example of this is email, which has made life so much easier for so many of us, but has also made life so much harder. The fact that I often have 200 emails in a day actually makes the day very hard to manage. The cumulative effect on the whole system can be disabling.

Collective impacts

Taking this up a level we can observe a myriad of positive impacts for individuals that are negative when aggregated to the level of community and society. Individual car drivers and air travellers benefit from increased mobility, but the resultant carbon emissions are leading to global warming and are destabilising the ecosystem. Large out-of-town shopping centres can make shopping more convenient and cheaper (for some), but they are breaking up the social fabric of society leading to greater isolation of older people, more local crime and major traffic congestion. The advance of an individual rights perspective within public sector discourse has led to an increase in complaints and demands for redress, and consequently to an increase in litigation. While those 'wronged' benefit from a 'system' that is more likely to give redress to individuals for negligence, society (and consequently the individuals within it) suffers as a result of a much more defensive pattern of service delivery that is rooted in risk averse management rather than innovating to produce the best services.

Paradoxical effects

Another set of patterns that we must be alert to are the playing out of paradoxes within a system. The classic example of this in the public sector at the moment is the way in which very high levels of regulation have resulted in middle and senior managers fabricating accounts to give their own managers the information they think that they want to hear. This leaves managers with less information than they had in the first place. Attempts to control lead to an undermining of control.

These systemic patterns are common, but there are many others that can be explored, some of which I pick up elsewhere in the book. Both the stories and concepts that I have outlined in this chapter underline how crucial it is for interventions around contemporary social and organisational issues to get to grips with complexity, and to meaningfully engage with non–linear dynamics. This begs the crucial question asked by Susan Weil of how we can 'begin to transform the perspectives of people caught up in the linear archetype of cause and effect' (Weil, 1997).

Systemic change

> It is not realistic to believe that we can learn about all the things that might affect us, or what is going to happen as things unfold. We will always be faced with uncertainty. (Flood, 1999, p 2)

With its focus on interrelationships; emergence and spontaneous self-organisation, complexity theory offers us an explanation of why these patterns emerge, and how we might make effective interventions in such a complex unpredictable terrain.

Ralph Stacey (Stacey, 2001 and 2003) and Patricia Shaw (Shaw, 2002) in particular offer an account of the change process that is strongly resonant with my own experience. Stacey's 2003 article 'Organizations as complex responsive processes of relating' lucidly articulates how chaos theory and then complexity theory challenge some of the fundamental tenets of organisational change theory. Firstly, chaos theory challenges the idea of linear causality:

> In trying to understand what chaos theory was all about, I was struck by the theory's implication that unpredictability is a property of nonlinear interaction. If this has anything to do with human interaction, then organizations could well be characterized by intrinsic unpredictability. And if that is the case, then it is perfectly understandable that our plans are not materialized. If our intentional interacting with each other produces intrinsically unpredictable outcomes in the long term, then our planning efforts cannot be expected to lead to the outcomes we intended; something else will happen. (Stacey, 2003, p 27)

But chaos theory is still problematic because it is highly deterministic. Complexity theory describes a process where local rules guide complex interactions:

> … the key concepts are self-organization and emergence, which means that interaction is patterning itself. (Stacey, 2003, p 27)

The patterning of self-organisation and emergence is quite different from that which emerges from computer simulations of agents following multiple rules. It contains far greater unpredictability because humans, although guided by norms, also have, the ability to resist them as a result of their capacity to reflect, their emotional responses, their loyalty and so on, and because, as we have established, the interactions of multiple elements do not behave in linear or predicable ways.

As a result theorists such as Eve Mittleton-Kelly and Ralph Stacey have begun to re-think the idea of complex adaptive systems that emerged in the 1990s. Mittleton-Kelly talks about complex evolving systems:

> A complex evolving system is one of intricate and multiple intertwined interactions and relationships, and of multi-directional influences and links, both direct and many-removed. Connectivity and interdependence propagates the effects of actions, decisions and behaviours through the ecosystem, but that propagation or influence is not uniform as it depends on degrees of connectivity. (Mittleton-Kelly, 2003)

Stacey speaks of complex responsive processes of relating:

> I have said that complex adaptive systems provide analogies for human action. However, part of the complexity of human relating is that people don't always adapt to each other – they often intentionally refuse to adapt to each other. But in doing so, they are still responding. So there is this complex dynamic going on of adapting and not adapting, of responding, of relating. And all of that taken together is what we mean by complex responsive processes of relating. (Stacey, 2003, p 35)

> From a complex responsive process perspective, one influences others in that everything one does is playing a part in what emerges. (Stacey, 2003, p 37)

This means that each situation is unique and its transformative potential lies in the relationships between interconnected people and organisations. Stacey no longer sees these processes as congruent with systemic thinking. But I think it is entirely compatible. Indeed I have already indicated that I agree with various soft systems thinkers that systems should be seen as a way of thinking about human relations rather than as a map of reality. This seems to accord closely with Stacey's own view of complexity theory and also those of other theorists who are working with complexity thinking in social and organisational contexts.

> It has become increasingly clear to me that one can't take chaos theory, or the theory of complex adaptive systems, and simply apply it to organizations, as many writers are attempting to do. Rather, the value of the complexity sciences is that they provoke us to explore the way we're thinking. (Stacey, 2003, p 27)

The theories of complexity provide a conceptual framework, a way of thinking and a way of seeing the world. (Mittleton Kelly, 1998, p 7)

If systems are seen as the complex web of interdependencies that are constellated within the boundaries that *we* construct around issues (both individually and collectively), then I think we are essentially talking about complex responsive processes taking place within socially constructed boundaries. Stacey might still see the systemic metaphor as problematic because:

> What one can't do is to get outside the interaction and directly influence it. Systems thinking is based on the idea that one can be outside the system and design it or move it. (Stacey, 2003, p 27)

But systemic action researchers would strongly challenge this perspective. Our starting point is to construct a 'working picture' of the multiple systems that we inhabit, from both within and outside them, and then to identify opportunities to act within them. We can be *in* the interaction and influence it. We can be *in* the system and change it.

If change in human society is characterised by emergence, then our strategies for catalysing change must take into account its non-linear nature. Guidance as to how we might develop this at SOLAR came from the work of Stacey's colleague Pat Shaw. Her work also embeds change explicitly in relationships. Change occurs through the act of conversation rather than as a result of conversation. Any action taken is simultaneously acting on and being acted on. In other words, if I engage in a dialogue with you I am simultaneously changing you and being changed by you. Shaw describes:

> ... the living craft of participating as an intentional fellow sense-maker in conversation after conversation (both public and imagined), encounter after encounter, activity after activity. I want to help us appreciate ourselves as fellow improvisers in ensemble work, constantly constructing the future and our part in it as daily activity as we convene or join or unexpectedly find ourselves in conversations. (Shaw, 2002, p 172)

With each conversation, encounter and activity the whole field of possibilities changes, and this happens in the moment rather than following from the dialogue. As I understand it, action here means not only acting on a 'field', but also changing the field within which actors are acting on. This means that self-organising processes will flow like water into the new spaces. Emergent understandings will fashion new pathways for action in the 'real time' of their creation. In my introduction to this book I outlined a scenario in which 'you see your partner meet the eyes of your friend and you realise that they are having an affair'. This also illustrates the simultaneity of revelation and change. Change does not follow from the revelation. With the revelation everything has changed. The relationship between the man and his partner are entirely different. The possible actions that might follow are entirely different to what they were before that moment. Consequential action may follow but the environment has already changed. And so it is with conversation.

Here we need to distinguish between the generation of insight as a reflection on both the dynamics and outcomes of action, and the generation of insight in action.

> Our Potter is in the studio, rolling the clay to make a wafer-like structure. The clay sticks to the rolling pin, and a round form appears. Why not make a cylindrical vase. One idea leads to another, until a new pattern forms. Action has driven thinking; a strategy has emerged. (Mintzberg, 1989)

In organisations action is typically articulated as the result of planning. Thinking, it is believed, should drive action, but in reality action often results from action, as one thing leads to another. Implicit in the ideas of Stacey and Shaw is the simultaneity of action and decision making. This observation represents a profound challenge to dominant theories of organisational decision making that see planning and formal decision making as pre-requisites of effective action.

Interestingly both Yoland Wadsworth and Gerald Midgley responded to this point when reviewing the draft of this book.

> **Yoland writes:'I** think that this is both true for some and not so accurate for others…. Sometimes it is an immediate and complete intuitive field of response as you describe, sometimes it takes "getting around the AR [action research] cycle" even if in one's own head. I think this may be even more so for people who are not naturally "big picture" field thinkers or highly intuitive, but instead await a larger body of evidence before being able to "jump" to conclusions. But whatever people's preferences are, it still seems to me to be eventually conversational and relational – that's the important thing. It perhaps only has the appearance of conclusions being separate from the experience in which they arose'.
>
> **Gerald writes: 'I** agree with Shaw and others that conversation can reshape the possibilities for action in that very moment, and the metaphor of action flowing like liquid into spaces created by conversation is apt. Nevertheless, this doesn't explain the experience that most policy makers, managers and researchers will have had of planning meetings generating

> significant insights (ah ha moments) that are then never translated into action because of systemic pressures or unforeseen events. It seems to me that the smooth flow of action following a change in understanding relies on (1) the new understanding being sufficiently context sensitive and (2) the context remaining relatively stable over time'.

Taking the reflections of Midgley and Wadsworth into account, I would conclude that we must be aware of the opportunities that lie in both the simultaneous and sequential processes.

Systemic patterns, social norms and power

Systemic patterns are embedded and sustained by systemic assumptions that are manifest in repeated habitual behaviour. Organisational culture is another way of talking about systemic patterning. Stacey (2003) suggests that 'an organization's culture is the emergence of pattern in the form of habits'. Susan Weil also highlights the importance of repeated patterns (see below).

> **'I see social** and organisational learning as inquiry into systemic resonances and tensions; an exploration of where and how they emerge; and the intended and unintended effects they have. To draw a parallel, in every family, often no matter how many years have passed, certain behaviours or dynamics "between" certain family members under certain circumstances will trigger familiar reactive patterns. These will both galvanise and de-energise different members of the family system with disabling and enabling impacts. These behaviours can recur in a flash, no matter how much learning and insight into such patterns each individual might have gained into these since their last reunion.' (Susan Weil)

The same applies to social or community cultures, and sometimes we call these social norms. By local social norms I mean attitudes and behaviours that people regard as normal for their peer group. These often become reified into rules, beliefs, principles and moral attitudes, but they are rooted in repeated behavioural practice.

> Social norms are rules that prescribe what people should and should not do given their social surroundings and circumstances. Norms instruct people to keep their promises, to drive on the right.... (Hechter and Opp, 2001)

New patterns, norms and routines do not follow directly from the construction and implementation of new policy. They are a result of the myriad of practices that take place on the ground.

> ... emergent properties, qualities, patterns or structures, arise from the interaction of individual elements; they are greater than the sum of the parts and may be difficult to predict by studying the individual elements. (Mittleton-Kelly, 2003)

> What will actually happen in our organization will not be determined by any one plan. It will be determined by the interweaving of them all. That means individuals can do what they like but they may not be able to accurately plan the future that comes about. (Stacey, 2003, p 35)

They can be imagined as well-trodden pathways through a social and organisational terrain. The patterns describe the paths that are created, the places that they lead to, and the ways in which they are constructed. Like a river that gradually changes its course, patterns gradually change in response to the different ways in which they are used. A footpath through the forest (perhaps generations old) can be transformed rapidly if it is used for mountain biking. Sometimes new paths are formed as people start to take different routes. Equally the forest can die or grow. Red squirrels may be replaced by grey ones. Rhododendrons may start to dominate the ecology. Power then has a major impact on what paths can be travelled and what paths are created.

> Power is an aspect of our relating to each other. We can't survive without being in relationship with each other, and as soon as we enter into a relationship with anyone we are being constrained by them and we are constraining them at the same time. We cannot be in relationship without constraining each other. And, paradoxically, at the same time, we are enabling and being enabled. So when one moves to a way of thinking that we're calling complex responsive processes of relating, one places power at the centre of what one is trying to understand. (Stacey, 2003, p 31)

This is essentially a Foucauldian interpretation of power. Foucault's work has underpinned a considerable body of contemporary systems thinking (Flood, 1990; Davilla, 1993; Brocklesby and Cummings, 1995; Valero-Silva, 1996; Midgley, 1997; Vega, 1999). Foucault sees power as constantly in motion, multi-directional and systemic in its patterning:

> The multiplicity of force relations immanent in the sphere in which they operate and which constitute their own organization; as the process which, through ceaseless struggles and confrontations, transforms, strengthens or reverses them; as the support which these force relations find in one another, thus forming a chain or a system, or on the contrary, the disjunction and contradictions which isolate

them from one another; and lastly, as the strategies in which they take effect, whose general design or institutional crystallisation is embodied in the state apparatus, in the formulation of law, in the various social hegemonies. (Foucault, 1984, p 92)

There is not on the one side a discourse of power and opposite another discourse that runs counter to it. Discourses are tactical elements or blocks operating in the field of force relations. (Foucault, 1984, p 101)

Power is a perpetual negotiation that is supported by the crystallisation of particular discourses, which are then embodied in institutions. The social hegemonies that Foucault speaks of are the social norms that I spoke of earlier. Power flows through networks. According to Clegg (1989, p 154), Foucault sees power as 'a more or less stable or shifting network of alliances extending over a shifting terrain of practice and discursively constituted interests'. He adds that 'points of resistance will open up at many points within the network. Their effect will be to fracture alliances, constitute regroupings and re-posit strategies'. These points correspond to the spaces of opportunity that I refer to in the next chapter.

Systemic patterns are often holographic in nature and reveal themselves in local contexts. When you are working in multiple sites these holographic insights create resonances across the system. Sometimes we find them in a recurring phrase or in the telling of stories. In our work evaluating the Welsh Assembly Government's (WAG) Communities First programme it took us some time to discern that in the early years of the programme, the underpinning 'theory in practice' appeared to be one of community regeneration rather than capacity building, despite the fact that the theory of change which underpinned the programme depended on an extended period of 'capacity building'. This meant that significant impacts of the system regeneration projects were being privileged at the expense of community development. One explanation of this pattern is that it represents the aggregation of the practices of people whose former careers had been in regeneration, and whose habits were being transposed into a different terrain. Patterns of this sort can be discerned by looking for resonance across systems.

Some other examples of local social norms are drink driving, the 'school run', smoking, teenage pregnancy, a culture among boys at school where it is un-cool to achieve and dropping litter in the street and in front gardens. Negatively perceived social norms are variously interpreted as deviant, self-harming and anti-social, but of course multiple interpretations are possible. It is quite possible to view teenage pregnancy as a very positive thing, and it is the failure of policy makers to even recognise social norms, let alone try to understand them, that so often puts policy at odds with local communities. What this means is that:

> To understand the whole ... requires an appreciation of constitutive meaning, social practices and actions taken. Interpretative thinking is systemic in outlook because it helps all involved to "see" people's lives as a whole by uncovering what is meaningful to them in terms of social rules and practices. (Flood, 1999, p 55)

In 1999 the World Bank's Poverty Group produced a report entitled *Can anyone hear us? Voices from 47 countries*. This highlighted the serious neglect of social norms in policy development and implementation:

> After fifty years of development assistance, it is clear that policies and projects are not implemented in a vacuum. They are formulated by bureaucrats and planners and implemented by people with a particular mindset in a particular culture, and with particular social norms, reinforced by metaphors, stories, proverbs and films. The power of social norms has been overlooked ... technocratic fixes will continue to be defeated by social norms. (Narayan, 1999)

In our work with Bristol Sure Start projects we explored the implications of one group's conclusion that domestic violence arises not only as a result of power relations between individuals, but also as a result of what is seen to be acceptable within a neighbourhood. Providing refuges and advice was seen only to have a marginal effect on the substantive problem. It was believed that changing the social norms would have a major impact.

I strongly believe that there is a need to radically refocus attention on the importance of local social norms, and that if interventions do not attend to local social norms, many policy initiatives will fail to win community support, rendering them unsustainable. A couple of examples serve to illustrate this: changing norms with regard to trust in the medical profession has had a major impact on the take-up of the MMR (mumps, measles and rubella) vaccination; embedded perceptions about child safety have limited the development of child-minding services in some Sure Start areas; in some communities (particularly where there have been generations of long-term unemployed families) dependancy cultures have severely limited the potential of education, training and employment initiatives. Conversely, significant success in improving rates of breast-feeding has been achieved through buddying schemes that have supported women to challenge local social norms. I would also argue that while people may have relatively little opportunity to alter their material circumstances, by challenging and changing social norms, they could significantly alter the impact of that deprivation on their lives, thereby enhancing their quality of life.

Top-down interventions which have focused on public health issues such as binge drinking, smoking, unsafe sex, eating habits and so on, and more recently on criminal issues have had very mixed results. Systemic action research offers the opportunity to develop bottom-up interventions in relation to local social norms.

Conclusions

Social and economic problems are highly complex and affected by multiple factors. When these factors combine they do not produce predictable outcomes. To understand the dynamics of change we have to look at them in their context and find ways of making visible some of the systemic connections that affect them. This opens up the possibility for interventions that shift outcomes in the direction that we desire. We can never predict the detailed outcomes but we can make judgements about the direction of travel when we can see more of the picture. Despite this, things will not happen as we expect, so we need a process that allows us to change course flexibly and quickly. Systemic action research is a vehicle for that. In the next chapter we look at ways of working with complexity that can underpin the systemic action research process. It is important to keep in mind that most social and organisational change work focuses on what is visible, yet as we have seen, change emerges from the spaces in between, in the interrelationships and in the discussion, and it is mediated by complex power relations. This means that it vital for us to focus on the informal as much as the formal system – to make central what happens in the corridors, the pubs and children's play spaces, to directly engage with social norms and to surface flows of power.

THREE

Working across systems

In this chapter I want to explore how an understanding of systemic change can offer strategies for action research facilitators, and for organisations that seek to embed action research into their decision-making structures. By tuning into systemic patterns and to the constellation of local interrelationships, we are able to spot small opportunities for action that may open up unimagined possibilities for larger change. Improvised strategies of this type are dependent firstly on opening multiple spaces for exploration and acting on opportunities as they emerge, and secondly on skilfully weaving them into a coherent narrative. This enables us to be strategic about our interventions in a way that will maximise their impact. In this chapter I want to make three strong assertions about how to work most effectively within systems. These are to:

- explicitly adopt an improvisational approach to change
- organise around the principle of parallel development
- develop strategies for working with resonance to enable judgement about meanings across a system.

Improvisation

The social and organisational world that we live in is quite different to 20 years ago. Public services are no longer delivered by single government departments. Governance has transformed government, it involves the complex interrelationship of multiple agencies and multiple stakeholders and is characterised by extremely rapid change, in some cases almost permanent change. In order to work effectively on this terrain we need an approach in which 'planning and anticipation give way to improvisation' (Weick, 1998), one that develops iteratively and builds on what emerges. In this section I want to look at some principles of improvisation that can be used to support working with the sort of complexity described. I will draw heavily on theatre improvisation and in particular on the work of Keith Johnstone (1981).

Improvisation does not just happen. Ensemble does not just emerge. Conversation does not 'automatically' open up new spaces for action. Theatre improvisation teaches us important principles that need to underpin strategic emergence. I want to explore three in particular here:

- accepting offers
- seeding small interventions into opportunity spaces
- re-incorporation.

Accepting offers

It can be helpful to envisage the inquiry process as a series of opening doors. Until we go through a door we do not know what is on the other side. Once through the door our experience and perceptions cannot stay the same. As we enter each new space, new possibilities emerge. When we see a new door it represents an opportunity. A key principle for the theatrical improviser is not to block offers to enter these spaces. Clearly in a social and organisational context we cannot say yes to everything, but we need to develop an orientation to accept offers. Imagine a performance with two actors on the stage:

Sharon:	Shall we go to the park?
Bill:	No I'm feeling a bit ill.
Sharon:	Shall I take you home to bed and make you a nice cup of tea?
Bill:	No, it's all right, I'll be OK.
Sharon:	What exactly is wrong with you?
Bill:	Nothing really.

The problem here is that Bill is blocking the story from developing. If Bill had said yes to the park, we might have been transported to the park and new possibilities would have opened up that we could not see from where we were originally standing. Similarly if we had gone back to Bill's bedroom, other possibilities may have opened up. This scenario is very common in social and organisational settings. Suggestions are made, but there are always reasons for not pursuing them. Improvisational learning entails taking risks in actual contexts of performance and practice. Let us now look at a real organisational scenario.

Joanne is the director of a medium-sized voluntary organisation that provides housing support for older people. For some time she was unsuccessful in persuading users of this service to involve themselves in the management committee. Quite unrelated to this dilemma, she was offered charity funding to set up an arts project for tenants. Quilting proved to be of interest, and eight older women tenants/service users became regular participants. They became very close friends and the group kept going after the funding ran out, as it had become the centre of their lives. Through this collective activity, they often shared other concerns about their housing support. Joanne would drop in regularly to these group sessions, enabling her to learn about their views through a different kind of relationship with the women. Slowly, she was able to seed the idea that they might be represented on the management board of the organisation, so that they might contribute to meeting their own and other people's concerns more effectively. Because of the success of this project, Joanne has now secured funding for eight different arts projects for tenants in this project. This has both strengthened connections across the organisation that were previously weak, and taken the organisation into new areas through wider participation of tenants in spotting opportunities for connection and collaboration through the board and across the association that otherwise might have been missed.

Source: (Burns and Taylor, 1997)

New doors are opened by virtue of this organisation taking a major strategic step into the arts, despite this apparently having little to do with its core function. By doing something in one arena, there was a fairly quick impact on another apparently different arena. The example illustrates the potential of emergent strategy development as unpredictable possibilities arise.

Seeding small interventions into opportunity spaces

One of the most obvious things about an effective improvised performance is the interdependence of the actors, both with each other and with their environment. If everything that happens in a field changes the whole configuration of the field, then it is self-evident that it is not only the actions of individuals that count, but the actions of all of those around them. This interrelatedness has an important bearing on power relationships and the ways in which we work with power. Augusto Boal's *Theatre of the oppressed* (Boal, 1979) illustrates how minute shifts in position and unexplored choices in situations of apparent powerlessness can have a significant impact.

This is another important aspect of systemic thinking that was present in the thinking of Kurt Lewin. He was instrumental in developing the idea of force fields (Lewin, 1952), which tells us that because everything is connected, then interventions in response to problems do not have to be direct responses to those problems. A substantial impact can be made on problems by changing something away from the point of focus. His force field model suggested that a range of small interventions could be as powerful as a single powerful action. Complexity thinking has taken that a step further indicating that very small actions can have major effects by shifting the focus of attention and intention, triggering different choice paths. These might occur as a result of bringing into visibility options that did not appear available before.

I used to illustrate this point to students using a small theatrical example. Imagine a stage in which a dramatic performance of 'Romeo and Juliet' is taking place. The drama is intensifying. The audience is gripped as the two central characters command the centre stage. Suddenly, out of the corner of their eyes, the audience begins to notice the face of a small boy peeking out from behind the curtains at the side of the stage. He is apparently 'irrelevant' to the performance, yet in no time at all the whole audience is looking at the little boy. The performance goes on as before, because the actors have not noticed him. When they do notice him they do not consider his presence significant to alter their actions, but he has already had an impact within the wider field, rendering their performance irrelevant. There are a number of significant issues here. An account of the performance would see the action of the boy as 'external' to the performance, yet he is central to it. The act that is taken was tiny but incredibly powerful.

Susan Weil has used the metaphor of logs in streams as a purposeful way of identifying where the small but significant spaces for action lie within a system. Picture in your mind a huge Canadian river in which logs are being driven downstream. At certain points the logs interlock in a configuration that impedes their progress down the river – the proverbial log jam. The log driver cannot take all of the logs out of the water and put them back. Nor can he move all of them into flowing straight lines. But he might be able to move one or two logs that would unlock the blockage. By identifying system dynamics and mapping systemic patterns we might be able to identify the small log that is blocking the stream. The log jam is another example of a systemic effect, discussed in Chapter Two.

Now let us look at some further examples from Kenya. These also show how tiny changes can have impacts that go well beyond what was anticipated, and illustrate that while the outcomes cannot be determined, an understanding of the wider system within which issues are situated can enable us to identify small entry points for deliberate interventions. Selline Korrir, a peace and conflict resolution adviser with SNV, recounts the stories.

Conflict between the Kikuyu and the Pokot in the early 1990s

"In 1991-92 when Kenya was changing from a one-party to a multi-party system there was a lot of resistance from the ruling government, and this called for pressure from both the international community and also from the civil society nation wide to push the government in power at that time out. The President, Daniel Arap Moi, went round the country telling how a multi-party system of governance would lead to ethnic clashes and so ... the politicians aligned to the ruling party met and decided to incite the communities against each other. So in 1992 and 1993 there was very bad ethnic violence. People, neighbours, who had been co- existing for years and years – all of a sudden one night they wake up and start slaughtering each other....The incitement was politically instigated. It was like a government against its own citizens. Its own people. But using the issues that were already dissatisfying within the minds of the people to manipulate people to fight. And one of the issues is that of land.

So one of the districts that was really badly affected was West Pokot district where the minister, then the minister of energy went down to his community and made sure that the Pokot community evicted the non-Pokot community, and it became one of the hostile districts really. Nobody was allowed in. No information was allowed to trickle out. No meeting was allowed – completely!... I could not call any meeting with the men. Not to the youth because everything we did, every step I made was really being trailed.

So what I did was I decided to start getting information through women when they are trading. So each time I met a woman informally I would just strike a talk as I bought the vegetable that I actually did not need, but this helped me to get the information and build a relationship for the work I was to do. And many times though I'd think that they had been told "Just talk your language. Don't even say or accept that you understand Swahili, and anything you are asked say 'I don't know'" and that went on for a long time. And after about two months of just trying and not giving up I ended up going to the market and asking the women, and the women started talking about how they are missing basic commodities that were being provided by the Kikuyu community, that were actually the main business community in West Pokot at that time.

So we started now counting our losses. How did the displacement affect you? You can't get commodities. The salt and of course others. So I took the issue of the business of salt as an entry point, and I just held onto it so tight. And I just said this is what I am going to do. This is what I know will give us the space now to have the dialogue, and so I started inquiring. How do you get salt now that the salt is an issue and you are not able to buy it, and all the shops are closed? And all of the sudden you discovered that you chased away the communities that were really valuable to you. How do we use that to ensure that the communities understand their losses? How do you get the salt now? They said we really struggle and we risk to go to areas where we can get killed to get salt.

So we said let us gather a few and talk and what we need to do is agree not to struggle anymore and don't risk your lives for salt. Just do without salt at home and when your husband asks you why is there no salt. You say the Kikuyus went away and the shops were closed. If they ask "Where is the milk? Why is it that this tea is like this?". Say that the Kikuyu who were selling milk went away. Why is it that you have not sold the commodities that we were selling because then they were selling them to the Kikuyus and non-Pokots. How come that you are not selling the commodities that you have at home? The Kikuyus were buying. They are not there any more.

And so we said that, and we agreed and we had the first meeting of only five women and we agreed that the issue of salt be used more, so when they went they kept on saying. I can't afford salt. I can't access salt because the Kikuyus are no longer there. And so later on we came back and followed up. It was being done in a very secretive way so probably I'd need to meet around somewhere just under a tree and we asked the feedback. How was the feedback? They said "Our men they keep quiet and they are not answering anything". Inside them what is going on. If you look at the way they are behaving – their facial expression, what goes on in their mind? I think they are starting to feel. They are starting to feel by us not struggling to get what they should have, they started feeling the loss. So what do we do? We can now try to get a space with the men to start now asking. So we decided to go to the men and raise the issue of salt again.

Understand these days salt is a rare commodity. We realise that there is something we did that we didn't think about. We didn't know that when the Kikuyus go we would miss some commodities like salt in our homes. These days we eat food without salt. But you see the men according to them before … they didn't want to think about any loss. Because according to them land was an issue. They thought the Kikuyus were invading the land, and if they went away they would occupy the land, which later on turned out to be impossible.

So we used the salt issue around this and we started asking do you think this is something we can talk about now that you feel that this is a loss. Maybe we could get one elder and another elder from this village and maybe just do it secretly and then maybe we could talk about it, and that is where I got my entry point. So I got an entry point with the women, and getting now feedback from the women, and got an entry point now with the men to start now talking about the loss, and after talking with the Pokot men about the loss now it opened a space for a dialogue between the Pokot politicians (civic leaders) now, and the Kikuyu and the other non-Pokots who had been evicted. And that it is how we started now having forums to discuss the issues. How do we go about the issue of land? How do we go about the issue of the lost properties? How do we go about the issues of making resettlement – helping the people who have gone away to resettle back?

And I mean it was amazing. It was just amazing. Of course the government didn't want people to talk with the people themselves, and I and my organisation at that time was seen as an inciter, because you are helping people to understand the issues that they are not supposed to understand. And it was really tough. So it was the small interventions of using just the salt issue and the issue that people were really passionate about. It was very powerful. If someone asks me the story of my life in West Pokot I end up crying, but later I end up again smiling because looking back to see the changes that have developed, the awareness that has been created, and the shaking of hands of those Kikuyu who didn't want to shake hands with Pokots. I mean. It is a real powerful thing."
(*Source:* Selline Korrir, Interview July 2006)

Football: A route to conflict resolution in Mount Elgon

"I remember in Mount Elgon. It again was one of the worst areas that was affected. The first time we ever went we were faced with arrows. We are here in the vehicle and trying to get down and all of a sudden – young men, youth armed with arrows and bows setting to shoot at us … and then a few with guns. They are telling all we want is our land and next time you come back carry your own "genesa" – coffin – carry your own coffin because we will kill you and put you inside that coffin and I thought "my god". This was terrible. I mean it's more like voluntary work, but so risky – you know.

There were only three of us at that time. But it was very interesting because when we got the smallest opportunity. It was just through a shop. When it was so hostile we decided let's just go to the shop, the nearby shop and ask if they have tea and then we can sit. So in the process of sitting we started up a dialogue with this man who was selling tea, and asked what is happening? And the good thing was we had one person who was coming from that community among the team. So we got the confidence. So we worked to make sure there was somebody from that community to be able to lessen the risk of being attacked.

The real problem is now the youth. The youth have been incited. The youth have been armed. So if we could find a way of just helping the youth to come out of the dangerous state where they were in, we might find a way forward. This is what the man said out of our small discussion. So we asked him "Is it possible to get a youth here?". He said if I call one here, you buy the tea because they are very hungry. So it was fine. So we started talking, "how are you?", just trying to create a rapport and then we asked him if he would mind having a cup of tea and he say "yeah" and he drunk his cup of tea, and tried to find out who we were, and we explained. It took a lot of time explaining who you are. You should never be in a hurry in such a situation, because if you are in a hurry you leave suspicion. So we stayed there until midnight. For people just to feel that these are not really dangerous people. So we managed to talk over tea, over lunch, and walked out a bit, and came back to take tea … and the youth said "maybe these youth are very idle that's why they are being misused by the politicians, being dragged, being armed, with the bows and arrows and guns to kill for a cause not known to them". Maybe we start engaging them and maybe just bring one ball – one football. It will make a difference. Well. I wasn't too sure. But we say well it was coming from him let's try it.

So when we went back to Eldoret the following day we carried a ball with us. We were bouncing the ball, and tossing the ball, and then the youth started coming. And then we had a quorum, and we started talking, just laughing, telling stories and using proverbs and finally they said "bring a team from the community [that they ejected from the area] and let us one day have a match".

That is a good entry point now. I thought. Quickly we do things very quickly. After two weeks we had organised for a football match. And I'm telling you those two teams are the teams that actually torched each other's houses. We didn't know, but that team from the Sabaot community that was the team that was really used to cause pain on others. So they played and the day ended.

So we didn't know until we got the feedback. In the evening they went back home. And the story in Mount Elgon especially in the Sabaot community. They said you know today we played. You know the way they say it. The language is much interesting. But the translation is "My feet and the feet of the man that I almost killed touched each other today". And when they touched each other I said I think there is no reason to kill again. Because according to them it is even a taboo to interact with the enemy. With the enemy you've finished, and if at all you get a chance to interact you don't have anything to do with them any more. And we didn't know that that was so powerful, until we got now from the chiefs – the local government representatives at a local level. Telling us you didn't know what you did. You didn't know the impact. They kept telling us the story of how for the first time their feet touched with the enemy's feet and from there they started again."

Source: Selline Korrir, Interview July 2006.

So what can we learn from these two stories? What I have described as opportunity spaces, Selline calls entry points. Senge talks about the same thing when he talks about 'points of leverage' (Senge, 1990). To be able to see possible entry points by understanding the field is a crucial part of the action research facilitator's role. It is often only after the action research process has been underway for some time that the entry points become visible. In the first story a major conflict that resulted in the slaughter and displacement of communities was resolved by engaging with the issue of salt. This appeared to have little to do with the substantive issue, but it was within the field, so it could be harnessed as a lever for change. A small change in the field led to a major systemic impact.

The football example is interesting for a number of reasons. First, Selline acts on the embedded 'knowing' of the boy. The strategy does not seem to have much going for it yet it proves to be the key that unlocks the conflict. Second, it highlights the importance of human contact – that *doing* together might provide the foundations for *thinking* together and *deciding* together. This connects to the notions of 'saying yes' and opening doors that we explored earlier. It is crucial for action research facilitators to take this in. Learning through action is not just about the action. It is as much about doing the action and learning from the action together. Implicit in both stories is a challenge to the assumptions that underlie the situation, and in both, taking time to build trust was a crucial part of a successful process that could not be shortcut.

Re-incorporation

Improvisation is essentially associational, in that one thing leads to another. But it is not free association in the sense that whatever is new entirely supplants what was there before. Good improvisation tells a story. A story cannot be constructed by random associational leaps; it needs to have a narrative structure. One of the keys to that structure is what Johnstone (1981) calls re-incorporation. This involves not only connecting what is happening now with what happens next, but connecting what happened before with what happens next. There always needs to be a cyclical process that moves back as it moves forward. It can be depicted a bit like this.

Figure 4: Typical Action Research cycles – connecting observations of action back to the inquiry that generated it in order to move forward

Each time we drop back to connect up bits of the story that happened before and bring them into the future. Sometimes we need to reach right back.

Figure 5: Systemic Action Research cycles – looping back to connect the past to the future

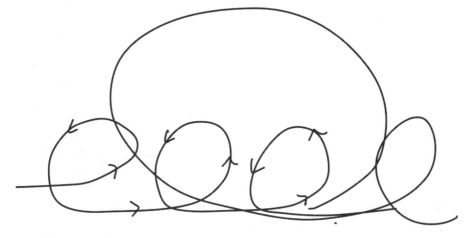

This can be illustrated through children's stories. In my experience it is not a happy ending that children expect from a children's story; it is the weaving of different elements from the beginning of the story into its end. Take a simple story like *Snow White and the seven dwarfs*. Once the seven dwarfs are introduced into the story, they are part of the story, and we are now interested not only in what happens to Snow White and the prince, but also in what happens to the dwarfs. Stories that hold our attention should be seen not as linear texts but rather as a series of spirals in which previous elements of the story become integrated in ever more novel ways as the narrative progresses. Organisations and systems can be seen as stories layered on stories all interweaving with and changing in relation to each other. Improvisation in a whole systems learning process is even more complex than this, because here we are required to work with multiple narratives and multiple stories, and the opportunities that emerge when they converge (either deliberately or serendipitously).

One of the problems with contemporary organisations is that they try to impose change without reference to the characters, the embedded cultures, the narratives that went before. 'Performance targets' for example might have some merit, but because the new has not been woven into the old they appear disconnected from reality. In Chapter Two I recounted the story of NGO interventions in relation to FGM. Unless these NGOs can connect the narrative to the story lines that are already running they are highly likely to fail.

Parallel development

Since the early 1980s I have steadily moved away from a focus on group consensus toward the idea of parallel action. I have begun to see how creativity emerges more through travelling alongside and interacting with difference than through premature integration. I will illustrate this with some personal political stories.

In 1986 I joined an international peace camp in Faslane, Scotland. People came from all over the world and organised into affinity groups. Proposals for action quickly emerged. Two seemed to be garnering support. Experienced facilitators managed a complex dialogic process for deciding between the two. One was to carry out an action at Coulport military base; another was to disrupt the Edinburgh Commonwealth Games. The Coulport initiative had less support but almost no opposition. The Edinburgh action had passionate support and passionate opposition. The only consensus that could be arrived at was the least controversial, and so the decision was made to support the Coulport action. The dialogic process was sophisticated; the facilitators were highly skilled. The process was recognised by all to have worked, but in the end no action resulted because motivation was not there. I wrote in a journal at the time 'the commitment to consensus was at the expense of desire'.

Across nearly two decades of work on participation and participatory governance other concerns have been growing. We built neighbourhood forums and committees; we developed participatory forms of consultation and user engagement. But why were they so empty and unrepresentative, so divorced from the communities they were supposed to serve? Why did so few people want to be on them? I began to re-think the possibilities of participation, arguing more recently that the foundations for meaningful community engagement lie in the day-to-day acts of participation in community life, not in elaborate community decision-making processes (see also Chapter Nine, this volume). Communities gain power and open up possibilities through doing. The limitations of dialogue and consensus as the legitimation for action has become a constant refrain. This is a view that is echoed in the writings of others:

> ... We are suspicious of approaches to AR [action research] that seem to privilege the homogeneity of communities or consensus-based decision making, believing that such approaches open up great potentials for co-optation and coercion. (Greenwood and Levin, 1998, p 12)

In 1998 Margaret Thatcher introduced the Poll Tax. First Scotland and then the rest of the UK rebelled. A movement of 10 million non-payers was built and the tax was eventually abolished. I was part of that movement. At the time, of course, I was just doing it, but I was also witnessing the unfolding of something that has directly impacted on my understanding of learning and change. The campaign was not won because everyone was united. On the contrary, arguments raged about what was the best strategy. The campaign was won because people – each one – did what they believed in, what they were passionate about and what they did best. Some people wrote letters to their MPs. Some people graffitied cars. Some organised in anti-Poll Tax unions to build a non-payment campaign. Some took their arguments to the courts and used many imaginative strategies to evade the bailiffs.

> The activities of those who were not prepared to break the law were not undermined by the actions of the few who chose to throw fire bombs. Likewise, those who chose to leave Trafalgar Square peacefully were not tarnished by those who chose to fight back against police attack. The occupation of the courts didn't prevent those who wanted to argue legal technicalities, and those who chose not to attend meetings but to take action on their own, didn't undermine the collective decisions of those who met in the Anti-Poll Tax Unions. The Movement was not damaged by this diversity, it was strengthened by it. (Burns, 1992)

These very different people could never have agreed on a strategy. Yet without *all* of these actions the movement would probably never have succeeded. The letter writers reinforced the rioters and vice versa. They were systemically connected. Their contradictory actions unknowingly reinforced each other but not in a linear way. In this post-modern world where good participatory practice is characterised by multiple voices I began to see that voices were not enough. Change was resulting from the self-organising patterning of multiple and parallel action streams. Learning through parallel *action* opened the space for possibilities still further.

There are some important things to observe about this process. First, that sustained action can only be maintained where people can act in the service of what they believe in and are passionate about. Second, that strategic convergence tends to emerge, but it should not be prematurely constructed.

Change is fired by the passions of people who are motivated to act on what they believe in. More people will do more things, more insight will be generated, and more possibilities will emerge where passion is at the heart of the process. In other words it is not enough to say that we learn most effectively through action; we also have to create the conditions under which action is most likely to be taken and sustained. This connects to the discussion that follows on resonance. Where there is strong resonance people will be attracted to a line of action; where there is not they will fall away however strong the intellectual argument for it is.

Consensus can be coercive. It reminds me at times of the principle of democratic centralism that was such a strong feature of the small parties of the Left (Socialist Workers Party, Militant etc) whose modus operandi was to extensively debate an issue, then through debate construct an analysis to determine the 'correct' line of action. Once decided, everyone (without exception) had to implement it. Not only were these policies often wrong, they resulted in hundreds of activists enacting policies and practices they did not agree with. They gradually became de-motivated and left. This pattern can so easily be replicated in inquiry groups. The alternative is to 'let 1,000 flowers bloom'. Then in enacting what we are motivated to develop, we discover whether they are working or not. If our approach does not seem to be working, but something else is, we naturally gravitate towards it. This is what happened in the anti-Poll Tax campaign. As the non-payment strategy grew, more and more people clustered around it. So not only did we see a systemic relationship between the different strategies, we also saw the emergence of a dominant strategy that had attracted support in its enactment (not in an intellectual debate about its merits in relation to other approaches). The key learning from this process is that:

- multiple story lines opened up possibilities for action that may not have appeared if just one path had been opened up;
- multiple tracks proved to be mutually re-enforcing even though they appeared to be contradictory;
- multiple perspectives and approaches ensured higher quality work and sustained motivation across the spectrum of activities, because people focused on what they were good at and what they were passionate about.

This thinking is reflected in some recent social intervention theory. Weil et al (2005) argue that multiple interventions are crucial:

> In the multiple intervention model, the idea of step-by-step cause-effect linearity is relinquished. It is replaced by the idea of non-linear sequencing whereby all elements are interconnected and mutually constitutive – a relationship which privileges not one single element,

but relates them to each other in an interactive and multi-causal way.
(Weil et al, 2005, p 218)

These observations have important implications for participatory practice because they highlight the need for multi-stranded, multi-stakeholder processes running in parallel.

Resonance

In this section I will argue that the evidence to underpin action needs to be focussed more on resonance than representativeness.[1] There are real problems with the idea of representativeness in both research and social action, not least because what is purported to be representative rarely is. Can a young person really represent the experiences of all of the other young people in an area, a disabled person the experiences of all disabled people etc? That a process (or a sample) is representative tells us who was there (who was included) but not who has power, and what they care about. Often people only find out what they care about by engaging in action and seeing how they feel.

An improvisation emerges, as we discussed earlier, because one thing leads to another, and people join in with the action that is emerging. It does not wait for formal legitimation or permission to proceed because it is deemed representative. Accountability does not lie in the fit of a line of action to the strategic plan or the formal authority of an individual to act. Representativeness cannot be determined on the basis of the statistical support given to a proposition. It lies in the willingness of people to 'open doors' and walk through them, and the willingness of 'participants' to support a line of action because it makes sense of the reality that they experience. Just as in theory, market accountability lies in the aggregation of individual decisions to buy a product or not, in improvisation fields, movements are built from the aggregation of individual decisions to support courses of action that resonate with their experience. Accountability lies in the process of clustering itself. This does not mean that formal processes are unimportant, just that they should not be used to inhibit action.

When I use the word 'resonance' I mean that:

- people 'see' and 'feel' the connection between things
- they 'know' that it is related to their experience
- they are 'energised' and motivated.[2]

Working with resonance is an important element of systemic inquiry design. Resonance enables sense making, and change occurs where there is resonance. One of the working principles that we have been exploring at SOLAR is that where systemic inquiries converge, within a large-scale project there is massively increased energy for change at the points of convergence. This is because people are already mobilising actions, and because there is a much greater visibility across the system. This may enable larger-scale systemic intervention to take place that would not otherwise have happened.

The possibilities for testing resonance do not necessarily exist in day-to-day interactions. Something may have a powerful connection to something else that is happening in a completely different part of the system. The participants do not know there is a connection. Action research facilitators can see the connections but they do not yet know if there is a resonance. They need to design spaces within which resonance can be tested. One way of doing this is to test emergent ideas and interpretations through large events (see chapters four and six). Another is through the collection and analysis of narratives. Stories give us insight into the complex dynamics of specific situations. But on their own they can easily be dismissed as anecdotes that are only relevant to the local situation from which they came. If we put them together so that people could connect stories and see whether there was a resonance with their own experience, people would start to see the world differently, and new possibilities for action would emerge from their collective understanding of their situation.

Conclusions

Effective sense making and sustainable change within complex systems will be dependent on *improvisational change strategies.*

Parallel development may be a more constructive framing for change processes than either top-down planning or consensus-based planning.

Resonance may be a more useful concept than representativeness for both identifying issues of concern and possibilities for mobilisation.

Notes

[1] There are multiple roots for our work on resonance within SOLAR. Susan started to work with the idea of resonance through her encounters with field theory. My shift toward ideas of resonance came from observations of the anti-Poll Tax movement where it became clear the shifts of energy and activity signalled by strong resonances denoted a much greater accountability than formal representative structures. This provided a challenge to much of my earlier work on participation and local democracy.

[2] Clearly these criteria have to be viewed critically. They do not necessarily indicate that something is right, only that it is supported. People might cluster around fascist ideas in the same way. Equally a sense of belonging can re-inforce reactionary norms ('he is one of us'). The indication of support is more powerful than representation because it is active and based on activity driven by sentiment.

FOUR

Some systemic action research projects explored

The aim of this chapter is to give a feel for the way in which real action research projects can emerge and evolve across a wide social and organisational terrain. Because of the depth and breadth of each of these projects, the examples focus mostly on design. It would be impossible to do justice to the complex issues that each explored, although I do look at some of the detail of the Bristol Children's Initiatives (BCI) project in Chapter Six. In this chapter, I explore the two forms of systemic action research that I typified earlier: *large system action research* which characterises a number of SOLAR projects, and *networked systemic inquiry* which describes the shape of many of the PhDs that Susan and I have supervised.

Large system action research

Four systemic action research projects are highlighted here. First, the Melbourne inquiry into psychiatric care facilitated by Yoland Wadsworth. Second, a project that worked across Early Years initiatives in Bristol. Third, a national programme evaluation of a capacity building initiative involving 142 programmes across Wales, and finally, a whole organisation inquiry into vulnerability with the British Red Cross.

The four large systemic action research projects outlined here have been shaped quite differently. They have many aspects in common, but each is defined by a particular strength. The Melbourne project is particularly characterised by its refusal to be diverted away from users as its driving force, and the way in which its insights gradually had greater and greater systemic impact. The Bristol project was unusual in its complexity and the extent of its multiple strands. The Welsh Assembly Government (WAG) project was notable for the extent to which the action research was structurally embedded at a strategic level, so that insights from the ground could lead within weeks to major strategic decisions being taken. The British Red Cross project illustrates the way in which the involvement of hundreds of stakeholders (mostly staff), in multiple large events, enabled learning and innovation to travel directly through the organisation. We might aspire to a project that held the strengths of all of these, but projects like the phenomena they are engaging with are context specific and can evolve in unpredictable ways. It is perhaps better to hold them up as examples of what is possible if the right spaces and moments open up.

This chapter tries not to paint a glossy picture. It shows how each of the projects evolved, and offers the reader some insight into what worked, what did not and why. It explores the way in which different components of action research need to interact, and how different approaches to action research can suit different purposes. It also explores some of the design problems that have emerged in large-scale action research projects.

Melbourne Understanding and Involvement (U&I) project (1989-96):[1] a user-driven inquiry scaled up to impact strategically

One of the most important large system action research projects was the Melbourne U&I project on acute psychiatric services carried out by a mental health service user organisation between 1989 and 1996. It was commissioned by the Victorian Mental Illness Awareness Council and was supported by Yoland Wadsworth and Merinda Epstein. The aim of the project was to engage multiple stakeholders in a co-researching process that would change practices, procedures and structures in order to facilitate a better experience for service users experiencing mental illness. Activist consumers in a disability resource centre initiated the project.

It was here that the agenda began to be constructed. The project started small; one of its first activities was an exit survey. A social worker enabled some more traditional research to start in one of the wards. Action research was started in the form of a collaborative dialogue between a small group of consumers and staff within a major public psychiatric hospital. The figure opposite illustrates the first phase of the study.

Here iterative cycles of dialogue moved sequentially between staff and consumers. This illustrates an important design feature which is that co-researching and co-generation of knowledge does not mean learning together all of the time. Often it is crucial that groups deepen their own

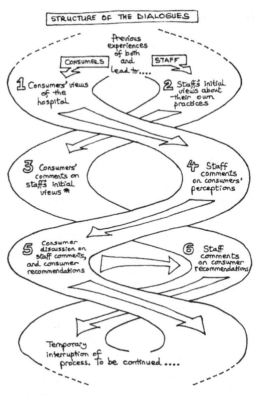

STRUCTURE OF THE DIALOGUES

Previous experiences of both CONSUMERS and STAFF lead to....

1 Consumers' views of the hospital

2 Staff's initial views about their own practices

3 Consumers' comments on staff's initial views *

4 Staff comments on consumers' perceptions

5 Consumer discussion on staff comments, and consumer recommendations

6 Staff comments on consumer recommendations

Temporary interruption of process. To be continued ....

* Time did not permit this material (at 3) to go to staff (at 6). Instead consumer discussion and recommendations (at 5) went to staff (at 6).

Reproduced with thanks to the Victorian Mentall Illness Awareness Council, Melbourne.

understandings before they are brought into relationships with others. In a long-term systemic action research process, time is made to build these different processes in when they will be most beneficial.

The project eventually 'scaled up' into much wider spheres, extending outward to people who were running other wards, then to the whole hospital, the medical director and the area mental health service, and finally into the arena of state and federal policy. By the end of the process more than 30 separate inquiries had been initiated as part of an integrated whole. A sense of the scale of this project can be gained from a footnote to Wadsworth and Epstein (1998):

> The project inquiry group (the "we") comprised a core research team of three consumer researchers and a research consultant: an "inner inquiry group" or collaborative committee of around a dozen (half staff and half consumers) which later became a collaborative QA seminar of about 30; a broader inquiry network, which included 60 staff and consumers who took part in the interviews, discussions and small subprojects and later expanded to around 200 people strategically located throughout the state and also the national mental health system; plus a self run group of 12 to 15 consumers who were acquiring experience as paid consultants in a range of different capacities (as interviewers, librarians, committee members, policy commentators and so on), both within the project and then increasingly called on by other services at area, regional and state government levels. (Wadsworth and Epstein, 1998, p 357)

Despite its strategic direction of travel the research always took its directions from the consumers' intentions to change the (often) damaging acute psychiatric in-patient experience. Thus the systemic picture that it generated was driven by the consumer perspective, even though many other stakeholders were involved:

> The model is ... not constrained to the acute setting, but instead is system-wide, both because what happens in acute and continuing care has repercussions that reverberate system-wide beyond the "hotspots" and also because there remain the same needs for continuous attention to service development and quality improvement as a result of consumer feedback and collaborative planning in community settings. (Wadsworth and Epstein, 1996, p 176)

Summary of the U & I model

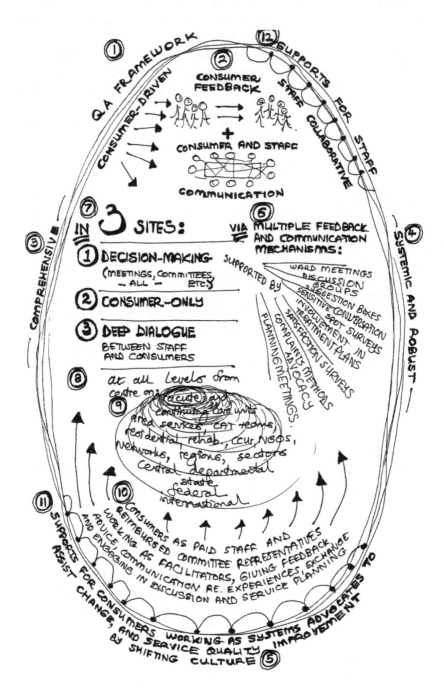

Source: Wadsworth and Epstein (1996), reproduced with thanks to the Victorian Mentall Illness Awareness Council, Melbourne.

Wadsworth and Epstein summarise the key design elements of their project as follows:

> Numerous methods (up to 14 or more) — enough to ensure every consumer who wants to can give feedback and find a place in the process for communication with staff.
>
> Several different "sites" for the operation of most of the different methods — including consumer-only sites, staff-consumer "deep dialogue" sites, as well as all sites of ordinary decision-making.
>
> Many elements of resourcing of infrastructure (10 or more) to support the programme of methods across the different sites (including consumer-staff dialogue consultant facilitators, and small grants of funds available to be used by consumers to support their own processes, and mutual support arrangements).
>
> A philosophy or set of principles to effectively guide the effort and keep it "on track", and involving a multiplicity of staff and interested supportive others selected or agreed to by consumers (eg community visitors, external self help group people).

Yoland Wadsworth's keynote address to the 2005 World Congress of action research in the Netherlands gives a more visceral sense of the whole that these action researchers were working within, and the way in which they were working:

> ... we had an experience of working in and with what, for all the world, felt like a giant moving living system — all the while weaving and ducking, knitting and intervening, observing and responding to the surging, retreating, moving, swirling living forms; stepping back to reflect and then going in deeper, like a deep tissue remedial masseur seducing painful muscles to give up their load; finding the spaces to draw breath, finding the hooks on which to hang activities, clearing away the log jams and oiling the rusty patches; sometimes working alone, more often in pairs or small groups, and sometimes all together; small cycles within larger cycles within very big cycles; shaping old things into new things, new ideas, conclusions, new concepts and plans and skilfully grafting them onto old strong practices — new procedures, new job descriptions, new kinds of ways of doing and being; then carefully watching them — did they "take" and become part of the human ecology of "the way we do things round here"? Or did they default and decay, and need to be re-examined and reworked?
>
> Sometimes it felt like building Edgar Schein's "parallel processes", or cycling alongside practitioners and consumers miming new actions; sometimes it felt like

building Vygotsky's "scaffolding" to allow new ideas to be sketched on a blueprint and then "built in" as new practice; sometimes it felt like Michael White's narrative therapy as we nursed the "wounded care bear" to recover its good intentions and revise some of the iatrogenic language of the existing story; sometimes it felt like we were getting out the ruler and measuring just how far the changes had come, how different the new practice was on the graph from the old practice. We became fully engaged as "whole (individual) beings" with "a whole (social organisational) being". The deeper we were involved, the better we understood it; and the better we understood ourselves, the better we were able to step into the turbulence, the chaos, the conflict and rigid structures, and the silences and defences large and small. Everything was data. Every thought and response of our own or others' told us something more about the giant living system we were part of and working with.

The feeling that she conveys and the principles that underpinned this work are similar to those that have characterised many SOLAR projects.

Bristol Children's Initiative (BCI) action inquiry project (2000-04):[2] a multistranded cross-city inquiry process

The BCI action research project was centred on two Sure Start programmes[3] and the Bristol Children's Fund.[4] These delivered services and support to young people in some of the most 'deprived' neighbourhoods in Bristol. It involved parents and

Figure 6: Bristol Childrens Initiatives project – emergent design

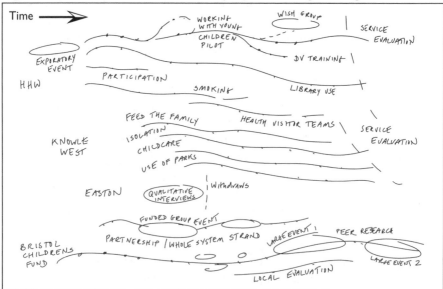

organisational stakeholders from a wide range of public services. It was designed as an evaluation process but become a multi-stranded action inquiry process.

An evolving design

In 2000, when I was working for the University of Bristol, I was asked whether I would be interested in evaluating the Hartcliffe, Highridge and Withywood Sure Start programme (HHW). We discussed the possibilities of doing something a little more innovative than a traditional programme evaluation. A highly structured evaluation programme was being put in place at the national level, but the government Sure Start Unit was initially fairly permissive about the sorts of local evaluations that could be commissioned. The main requirement seemed to be that they delivered evidence that could be used to support the development of the programme. This perspective changed over time, with significant consequences for our work, but it initially allowed the space for something innovative to emerge. In this context, the primary aim of this work was to engage with the more complex and difficult issues that needed long-term, in-depth and multi-agency exploration, rather than focusing on the things that we already had a good idea of how to change.

Our early thinking suggested that we would need an action research facilitator for around a day-and-a-half a week. We did not think that we would find someone with the experience we needed to work for such a small proportion of the working week without paying consultancy fees. So we explored the possibility of expanding the process to other local projects and splitting the cost. We held a city-wide meeting of Sure Start projects and the Bristol Children's Fund. All of those who were present were excited about a different approach so we agreed to proceed as a consortium. HHW was ready to go first. The others still had a lot of basic setting up to do so would not be ready for about a year. We agreed to put our initial focus on HHW and gradually taper down our involvement with them. We decided that in each of the Sure Start programmes we could facilitate four inquiry streams. The programmes would determine their own inquiry themes. While there was nothing stopping the different areas choosing the same themes, there was a feeling that if areas focused on different themes we would be able to enhance cross-project learning.

Most of the work was carried out through an inquiry group process. This involved regular meetings with multi-stakeholder groups. The work began to settle into a pattern where the groups met every two months. The action research facilitators normally worked with the group in the morning (9.30am–1.00pm) and then returned to the office to record the meeting. Of course it was never quite as neat as this but this was how we structured it. We settled on this pattern because we needed at least half a day to do this work effectively. Also parents could only come to three-and-a-half hour sessions in the morning as their children needed picking up from school from 3.00–3.30pm. The other important factor was that there needed to be a good space between meetings to ensure that actions could be taken and to ensure that all those who needed to attend were able to.

Eleven main inquiry streams had been initiated by the end of the process. In Hartcliffe, Highridge and Withywood four inquiry streams were launched. They selected the focus for these groups to coincide with the four national objectives of Sure Start: emotional and social development, health, play and learning and strengthening families and communities. Domestic abuse was chosen because it was perceived to be an endemic underlying problem in the community that substantially affected local children's emotional and social development. It was also a live issue in the community and attracted significant parental involvement; in contrast the selection of smoking cessation was more top-down, linking to a major Sure Start target indicator. The management team wanted to do some cross-cutting work on participation so this became the third inquiry theme, and the final one focused on library use. This was because in an area where there were over 1,200 families less than 50 had taken out loans from the library over the past year. The management team, in conjunction with the local Sure Start implementation teams, chose the inquiry starting points. There was no real inquiry process that underpinned the selection of issues, although we did do a training day that highlighted issues such as the need to focus on local social norms. One of the early lessons that we learned was that a generic inquiry process to identify starting points was crucial.

In Knowle West four entirely different inquiries were set up, and the selection process was oriented towards cross-cutting issues that were identified by key workers. One called 'Feed the Family' focused on nutritional problems in the area. The others focused on the use of parks, isolation and childcare.

In Easton we started the process with a series of generic interviews across the neighbourhood with community groups, voluntary organisations and statutory organisations who worked with Sure Start. We decided that a better way to initiate the groups would be through an exploratory inquiry process underpinned by qualitative research. This proved to be a really effective grounding, but unfortunately before we had really got underway Easton Sure Start pulled out of the programme.[5]

Our work with the Bristol Children's Fund took a slightly different tack. Unlike the Sure Start programmes they did not deliver services directly, but funded around 40 projects to support children. Some of these were in geographical areas of high deprivation; others worked with particular client groups such as children on the autistic spectrum, homeless children etc. We started our work with them at a strategic level, initially focusing on the extent to which they could work effectively as a whole system, and then more intensively on approaches to children's participation. We also did some inquiry-based work on local monitoring and evaluation.

As the inquiries began to take shape across the projects it became clear that we were coordinating a highly complex process involving many parallel and interlocking inquiry strands. Although the group-based inquiry was at the heart of the process we used lots of other methods to support it, including:

- collection of stories to illustrate different childcare scenarios
- two large event processes with children
- peer research by children
- interviews with stakeholders
- quantitative and qualitative data analysis
- collection of practice data by health visitors and midwives
- hanging out at drop-in sessions to get a feel for the issues.

Examples of how the inquiry process worked

In Chapter Six I discuss the way in which a whole inquiry stream on domestic violence played out over two years. In this section I want to offer a few vignettes that illustrate the nature of the inquiry process and the ways in which insights can be generated that might not emerge in any other way. The following examples illustrate some different ways in which challenges to assumptions within the inquiry process open up possibilities for change:

> In one group the discussion moved to the issue of local play facilities. The group mentioned the Millennium Green playground that was the only playground available for families in the area. One member of the group said that she had never been in there because it was attached to the school, and she thought it might be part of the school, and if it was part of the school it was not for her. She was expressing feelings that would not have come out in an interview or a questionnaire. Yet her information was vital. This is an example of how we need to tap into our wider senses in order to make sense. In response to her expression of ambiguity the group put a big sign on the playground saying that it was open to the public.

> The Hartcliffe group working on library use was talking about working with parents and children together in the library. One of the professionals told a story about how since childhood she had found it difficult to choose fiction. This made it very difficult for her to show children how to do it. So the inquiry re-focused on what support adults needed to support children to do what they (the adults) had not been able to do themselves. One of the particular successes of this group concerned the issues of registration. Young people would not borrow from the library because their parents would not sign up to the library service. They would not sign anything official. Perhaps they did not have identification, or they did not want to give their

details to the state, or they could not write. Whatever the reason there was a hostility to registering. The group wondered why the Sure Start programme itself had found it so easy to register people. In fact virtually every family in the area with young children was registered. People were happy to register with Sure Start because they saw it as a local group that was there to support their children. They did not see it as an arm of the state. After much inquiry the group opened up a dialogue about whether it might be possible to take Sure Start registration as library registration. This was resisted at first because the library had citywide procedures for checking people out. But the difficulties were worked through in dialogue, and a Sure Start registration became a library registration. This is a real example of partnership that defied the restrictions of established organisational systems. There were other hard challenges to the library service. It was feared that by opening up the library too much there would be too great a risk of books getting stolen. Yet at the heart of the inquiry was the fact that so few young people were reading books. Was it better for some books to be stolen and even more books to be read, or for books to be secure and unread? This sort of challenge is hard to work with because it goes to the heart of what a library service thinks that it is supposed to do and supposed to be.

In one of the groups a participant described how she had given up smoking at the point when her relationship had broken down and when her whole life had changed – 'If I could live without him, I could bloody well live without the cigarettes'. This opened up a discussion about our life course and our life expectations. There was a resonance within the group around the idea that it is often when we are fundamentally re-evaluating our whole lives that we will make the change. This suggested that the best time to work with people may be when they appear to be at their weakest rather than at their strongest. This early conclusion was not seen as truth, just as a new departure point for inquiry.

One of the difficulties of institutionally supported inquiry is that if the inquiry is genuinely open it can clash with pre-existing (often national) targets that define the activities of the organisation. While the Sure Start has to meet targets aimed at reducing teenage pregnancies a local inquiry group might be more concerned with how to ensure that teenage mothers have good pregnancies, good births and good lives.

These are just a few fragments. What is important about them is not that they have arrived at the right answer, but that by challenging assumptions they open up new ways of seeing things that in turn open up new possibilities for action. We may only discover if something is the right solution some time after the event, when it has been enacted and time has passed to enable some judgement of its impact. In Chapter Six I explore in more detail some other exciting ways in which assumptions were challenged that led to innovative action. In the meantime let us look at what can be learned about the overall process.

What did it achieve?

The BCI project achieved very mixed outcomes. Let me take the four Hartcliffe groups as an example. I think the domestic violence group was very successful. It opened up multiple inquiry streams, involved multiple stakeholders, developed a sophisticated analysis that it then moved to action. It also found ways to extend the boundaries of the group way beyond its own membership. The library group produced some very powerful positive outcomes (see also Chapter Six), but its potential was not fully realised, because it never really got to grips with the underlying question 'What is a library in the 21st century?'. The two other groups were more problematic. After doing some good work on accessibility, the participation group hit a brick wall because it was too abstract, and the smoking group had a series of very insightful meetings that failed to develop into action. Our work with the Bristol Children's Fund work had similarly mixed outcomes. The strand on partnership working and developing a whole system perspective failed to build a real momentum at senior management level. The work on children's participation, on the other hand, galvanised a large number of people, across a large number of projects, and culminated in a series of successful participation events involving young people from across the city. To some extent this variability can be put down to our learning about how to do action research (there are many things I would do differently now), but it also points to the nature of action research. Because it is dialogic, embedded in complex realities, engages with power, and is situated in particular contexts (and so on), what happens is always uncertain. This means that sometimes it will produce outcomes that wildly exceed expectations, perhaps unlocking deeply entrenched problems. Sometimes it will enable things to develop quietly, as through time and dialogue new insights can be generated. Sometimes it will facilitate the coordination of relatively straightforward tasks, and sometimes it gets stuck and nothing much happens at all.

It is important to remember that some of the impacts of these inquiry groups will be invisible, because they take place outside of the arena of the action research process itself. Two examples spring to mind. The first was the smoking cessation strand of the HHW BCI group. This appeared at face value to be unsuccessful because it failed to move beyond a deep discussion to action. Yet, one of the members who was the smoking cessation lead for a primary care trust said that the discussion had profoundly changed her outlook on the issue, and consequently her practice. The effect of this cannot easily be assessed. The second was the impact of the whole process on the development of children's services for Bristol. As a result of the ground-level inquiry work we were invited to engage with the *Every Child Matters* working group to feed into issues about the role of community-based children's initiatives within the new Children's Trust. How much influence this had is open to debate, but again it points to effects that may lie outside of the immediate boundaries of the project.

One thing I can assert confidently is that an enduring legacy of this project was how much we learned about how to do systemic action research. Some of the specific learning is reflected in the section that follows, but the broader messages underpin a great deal of what is written in this book.

Learning about the process

So what did the BCI project teach me about process and design?

First, we learned from an early stage that it did not make sense to choose inquiry themes to fit what was already there (for example, the structure of the organisation, established organisational priorities, national targets). It had seemed like the right thing to do at the time, because an action inquiry approach was resource intensive, and could not deliver evaluation across all of the activity areas of the Sure Start programme. We thought that if we did it this way, depth evaluation of one priority area could be attributed to each of the key programme streams. This would allow us to meet the needs of formal evaluation processes. But a top-down definition of the problem led to real difficulties in maintaining participant motivation. In some cases the theme was too abstract (for example, participation). In others, as we identified above, the definition of the problem was not necessarily shared by the participants.

The way in which inquiries were framed was important. Building on the sentiment of appreciative inquiry (Ludema et al, 2000), it was important to ensure that at least some of our lines of inquiry were entirely positive. The domestic violence group, for example, asked questions like 'Beside the law, what stops people from engaging in destructive actions? What are the social elements that hold boundaries?'. This allows learning about what works and enabled communities to think about what already exists that is of value and could help us.

Close to the end of the project, we learned the importance of having a detailed overview of the whole programme before delving too deep into the work of the inquiry groups. Two years into the process the political context was shifting. The government's evaluation noose was beginning to draw itself around the projects and it became more and more clear that the projects would have to deliver some traditional evaluation. We agreed to carry this out both to keep the space open for more innovative work, but also because we felt some obligation to these projects who had 'put themselves on the line' in order to do something different. The work involved producing a report for both the Knowle West and HHW Sure Start programmes (Burns et al 2003; Boushel et al, 2003). These reports included detailed descriptions of each of the services, qualitative data on change that had resulted and a quantitative analysis of service use. This produced some fascinating insights into who was using what and produced patterns that hinted at the how and why. While it would have been virtually impossible to generate meaningful data of this sort much earlier on in the process I am convinced that the inquiries would have benefited hugely from it. What it gave us was a detailed map of the whole, within which to connect issues that were emerging from inquiry strands. There is a real danger that action research is seen as an inquiry-based alternative to data analysis. In my view the data often provides fertile ground for a multi-stakeholder analysis.

One of the core purposes of this inquiry process was to genuinely engage parents and professionals in meaningful dialogue. The extent to which this was achieved was mixed. Some groups struggled to maintain the interest of parents. In others two or three parents stayed involved over a period of years. Parents were not always best engaged through the long-term inquiry process. Sometimes they were involved through:

- dialogues in drop-ins
- large events and conferences
- parallel self-help groups
- engagement with project workers.

What is significant is the parents who were there were genuinely *of* the community, and although not 'representative' in the democratic sense, were representative in that they had fairly typical life histories of people in the area. Normally in participatory processes it is hard to sustain the commitment of parents who are not already long-term community activists. The inquiry process in Hartcliffe, Highridge and Withywood maintained the active involvement of more than five committed parents who were genuinely representative of their communities. A similar number of people were involved in Knowle West groups (particularly in the large events). Through the Bristol Children's Fund even more parents were engaged. This may seem a small number but they were seriously engaged and absolutely not the 'usual suspects'. The Sure Start family link workers can also be seen as part of the wider picture of local participation. They had been recruited from the local estate because they had local knowledge and insight and were trusted locally. When these people were involved in the inquiry groups another strong set of indigenous voices was present.

We also learned some important lessons about the commissioning and managing of the process. A city-wide group of project coordinators was set up to oversee the project and make links across it. This had the potential to be an inquiry group itself and it did begin to connect up issues across the projects, but these links were fairly embryonic. The project revealed many potential areas for cross-city working. We managed to act on some of the possibilities, but missed others. For example, in the groups on domestic violence and smoking a parallel discussion emerged about the value of buddying. People giving up smoking, for example, might have more chance of sustaining their abstinence if they were supporting someone else to give up smoking. Both groups explored the possibilities of setting up buddying systems, but a more strategic look at this issue might have generated more activity. Similarly, the Hartcliffe participation and domestic violence groups, and the Knowle West childcare group all raised the issue of fathering and the roles of men on their estates. If the project management group was also working as an inquiry group we might have built on these interconnections more effectively.

Having said this, the task of this group was already complex. The project was managed by four agencies and three accountable bodies. The research team was initially based in the University of Bristol, then at SOLAR in Northampton, and then with SOLAR in UWE. We failed to appoint an action research facilitator the first time around, and the second action research facilitator became ill within a few months of starting the project. Because of the budgetary cycle of the projects, there was a staggered start that was probably the main reason for the early departure of the Easton Sure Start programme. The evaluation requirements of the government changed radically from the start to the finish of the project, making the project vulnerable. While projects had made a three-year budgetary commitment, they still faced severe budgetary constraints, and this made it difficult to sustain commitment to an innovative process. To some extent this governance process only mirrors that complexity that we were working with. Nevertheless it serves as a reminder that the 'governance' of an action research process needs to have time and attention.

All of this raised important questions about when is the best time to engage in inquiry, and the nature of the inquiry that you engage in at a particular time. As part of our process evaluation one programme manager expressed the view that we might have got the timing wrong:

> ... she felt that one of the difficulties was that we have projects which were moving so fast to create the future ... because they had to create them from nothing, you know 50 services. A capital programme for all of these different sites and whatever.... The action research process could have been more effectively integrated say 3-4 years into the programme rather than 1-2 years into the programme because their capacity to deal with change when they were already dealing with change was quite limited. So that might be part of their resistance in a way to try to integrate more change, because you're layering change on change then. (Burns and Daum, 2004)

Perhaps you need to have been going for some time before you can really get an in-depth enough picture. I am not sure. The counter-argument is that if you build inquiry into the process from the start then you are able to constantly challenge your assumptions and learn from experience as you go. I think that what that requires is that the action research process is embedded into the decision-making structure of the programme itself, rather than being something on the outside that 'reports' to the decision makers. Perhaps if the strategic decision making of the Sure Starts themselves had been created through an inquiry process, informed by the local action research groups, then the learning would have become more embedded. We came much closer to achieving this in the Welsh Assembly project outlined below. Similarly, while the BCI process was intended to be an evaluation process, we never really succeeded in getting it to fit the formal evaluation requirements. It grew organically as a multi-stranded inquiry process constantly opening up potential, but also raising anxieties because it was not always fulfilling the formal requirements. The evaluation of the Communities First programme more closely models how action research processes can be developed explicitly to meet evaluation criteria.

Evaluation of the Welsh Assembly Government's (WAG) Communities First programme (2003-06):[6] a major national programme evaluation

In this section I explore an action inquiry process that evolved to underpin the evaluation of WAG's Communities First programme.[7] Described by the Welsh Assembly as its flagship programme, it was very much in the media spotlight and operated in a highly politicised context. It was conceived as a 10-15 year programme, with £83 million set aside to support 142 neighbourhoods in the first three years. Each project had an employed coordinator. Some had quite large teams. Their first task was usually to build a formal partnership of stakeholders to support their work. The projects were seen as catalysts for community-based regeneration, and their work centred on capacity building; networking with a view to influencing mainstream programmes; local needs identification; levering larger-scale regeneration monies into neighbourhoods; and managing some capacity building services. Their power lay mainly in their capacity to influence, and in growing new forms of distributed leadership that could exert their own pressure for change.

Communities First was not only large in itself (in the sense that it encompassed 142 programmes); there were also a myriad of grant recipient bodies that were part of the organisational architecture. Furthermore the success of the programme depended on significant changes within external agencies and institutions (including, for example, local authorities, health boards and the police). These all had to be built into the learning system. Situated within the Communities Directorate of the Welsh Assembly, the programme was administered by a core team in Cardiff and five regional implementation teams. It was supported by a

Figure 7: Communities First Evaluation – emergent design

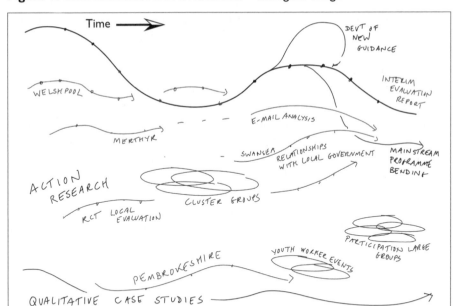

£2 million annual support package carried out by a myriad of voluntary agencies. Unlike most other UK regeneration programmes it was highly non-prescriptive, which gave it great potential for innovation, and it was underpinned by strong community development values. Its long time frame meant that its engagement was not distorted by the need to deliver immediate outcomes.

The evaluation was initially comprised of three parallel stands: an action research element that involved three local action research projects, case studies of 30 partnerships, and household surveys in each of those 30 areas carried out by a social survey company. SOLAR was responsible for the action research part of the programme. This was designed to link emerging insight from the ground to the core decision-making processes about the programme. It aimed firstly to test whether the detail emerging from localities was shared across the programme, and secondly to develop innovative ways of engaging with problems and issues. In each area we planned to carry out exploratory interviews; support a peer research process built on themes that emerged from the interviews; organise a sequence of multi-stakeholder conferences structured around the peer research outcomes; and then set up inquiry strands to explore in more depth the key questions that had emerged. When we designed the evaluation, we felt that the depth of insight gained through the inquiry processes in three areas would complement the snapshot data from the case studies and the survey-based data across the whole programme. This would give a more complete picture of the whole and enable us to explore the detailed dynamics of local change as a result of extended engagement. As we will see our perception was to change over time.

The action research process began in the middle of 2004 in Welshpool. The area was chosen because it was relatively isolated and did not have a strong history of regeneration. We wanted to get a feel for how the capacity building process might be developing in relatively virgin soil. We quickly discovered that more basic capacity building work was needed prior to any meaningful action research being possible and decided that the best approach was initially to 'work alongside' the coordinator. By working alongside we meant (a) visiting regularly and acting as a sounding board; (b) helping to facilitate some group meetings; and (c) helping to develop some of the early capacity building. So we learned by 'doing with'. We started a similar process of working alongside the Pembrokeshire programme that was a special interest project focusing on youth. We also planned to work on the Gurnos Estate in Merthyr (in the heart of the Welsh Valleys) using the original action research design. Merthyr had one of the highest levels of Communities First investment, a long history of regeneration and community development and a very experienced coordinator. Following discussions with him we concluded that the most effective approach was to focus on the 'mainstream programme bending' issue.[8] We worked with the detailed information that he provided about his relationships with other agencies. This helped us to understand the blockages that the programme was facing, and to grasp the nature of the coordinators' role, particularly in relation to mainstream programme bending. So our approach to each of the first three action research areas had changed within a few meetings.

The evolution of our research design continued apace. Following early conversations with officials within WAG, we were able to add a systemic action research group at the centre. All of the main players involved in the management and governance of the programme attended, including the head of the Communities Directorate, the head of the Communities First programme, all of the officers based within the Welsh Assembly, the leads of the five regional implementation teams and two representatives from the Communities First Support Network (CFSN). The group met for a whole day every six to eight weeks and considered this event to be a crucial part of their policy development and implementation process. The creation of the WAG Action Research Group marked a shift in the focus of the evaluation so that instead of three parallel strands (case studies, survey data and action research), the action research process became a hub through which learning about the programme was analysed and acted on. The meetings maintained a consistently high attendance. They discussed key issues, rethought policy, identified possibilities for action and reconstructed guidance. The sorts of issues that were covered included: communication; the role of the implementation teams; support services for Communities First; unpacking the distinction between regeneration and capacity building; relationships with local authorities and grant recipient bodies; equalities; guidance to partnerships; embedding local evaluation; intermediate outcomes; overarching partnerships and coordinators; and responses to national evaluation findings.

These issues were initially generated through the case studies and the local action research studies. But we needed to know how widespread the concerns that were raised were. To achieve this we set up three cluster groups (of *rural* partnerships, *valley* partnerships and *urban* partnerships).

Cluster groups are based on a large group process where between 20 and 100 or so people are brought together to test the significance of issues that have emerged elsewhere in the learning system. They may also open up new issues in their own right. These can be developed later through new stakeholder inquiry groups. In this way the cluster group becomes a validation process for emerging evidence, a place in which new issues are made visible triggered by the connections made in the group and a space within which systemic patterns can be identified. In this case, their purpose was to:

- find out whether our perceptions about major issues were accurate – including corroboration of the emerging view about the deficiencies of the programme;
- establish what action people wanted to take in response to them;
- build relationships with coordinators so that new inquiries could be built later;
- identify what coordinators thought would be good indicators of success;
- explore differences in their workload patterns;
- map the patterns and interlinkages that were emerging across the whole programme;
- explore widespread assumptions about the basic foundations of the programme (for example, was it a regeneration programme or a capacity building programme?).

More than half of the coordinators attended one of the three events, and the amount of data that we generated was huge. Importantly we were able to corroborate some key concerns. For example, there was a major concern about the effectiveness of the support network (CFSN). After the events the situation was completely unambiguous and we were able to confirm that the messages we had been getting through one-off stories in different localities amounted to a bigger systemic pattern.

One issue that emerged in both the central group and the cluster groups concerned 'the relationship between Communities First partnerships, and local councils'. Although WAG funded the programme, the money was being channelled through local 'grant recipient bodies' (mostly local councils) who also acted as employers. Cluster group meetings had highlighted difficulties in the relationship between some local councils and Communities First partnerships. It was clear that action needed be taken to strengthen relationships, but it was not clear what it should be. So we moved to set up a strategic action inquiry group involving key stakeholders on this issue. The emergence of this process reflects a widening of the system boundary with the realisation that learning confined to the WAG and Communities First projects would not be enough. We also set up an action inquiry group of coordinators in Swansea to work specifically on this issue.

The development of this group echoed a shift in our work which was already starting to shape our work in the localities. Having worked with some neighbourhoods in detail, it became clear that we needed to focus more on thematic work across neighbourhoods with small groups of Communities First programme coordinators. In Rhonda Cynon Taff we brought together a group of experienced coordinators to explore the process of embedding local evaluation (in ways that could capture the complexities of activities and the intangibles that we knew were crucial to the coordinators' effectiveness). We extended our work on youth issues much wider that the Pembrokeshire Communities First programme once we realised that funding for youth-related work constituted around 40% of the Communities First programme. We wanted to get a wider picture of what was needed to build capacity for youth through Communities First, so we organised two national events for youth workers and their coordinators. This process also gave us another lens through which to view the programme as a whole.

The final element of the action research involved workshops to explore the nature of community participation. This was partly in order to map a baseline for future evaluation and future inquiry. We had agreed with our research partners that rather than spend a lot of money on household surveys which were unlikely to identify any change within the life time of the evaluation, we would concentrate on 10 areas where we would produce a detailed baseline of quality of life, social capital and community participation. The former would be generated through the Index of Multiple Deprivation data (IMD), other data and survey material. Social capital data at individual level would be generated through a household survey, and the community participation baselines would be generated through interviews and a group-based assessment using the *Making community participation meaningful* framework that I had developed with Marilyn Taylor and others (Burns et al, 2004a). This last element contained an element of action research as the profile that was generated through a participative process could be used to enable communities to reflect on future action to enhance participation in their areas. It provided data to underpin a neighbourhood-wide action research process. The baselining process has been important in establishing the complex relationship between the programmes and local participatory activity. The dialogue allowed us to identify far more than the formal groups that fed into the formal structure.

The outcome of all of this activity was a dense network of action inquiries:

- multiple session inquiry streams in Welshpool, Swansea and Pembrokeshire;
- five half-day meetings with the coordinator in Merthyr (mainly exploring mainstream programme bending issues);

- five half-day sessions with a cluster of Rhonda Cynon Taff coordinators working on embedding local evaluation;
- three full-day cluster group meetings and an extended analysis;
- nine full-day action research sessions with the core WAG group;
- two full-day sessions with youth workers and coordinators with a specific youth brief in the North and South of Wales;
- a further half-day with a group of coordinators working on mainstream programme bending;
- 10 full-day community participation sessions as part of the baselining process.

Some of these started in an open-ended way; others were charged with problem solving. Most identified new issues that in turn opened up new inquiries and catalysed new leadership. As the network of people involved in the evaluation process widened, the process became more participative and more accountable.

The action research process became a key vehicle for driving the policy and implementation decisions of WAG. Given the extent to which the action research process has become embedded it can be regarded as part of the programme itself. This is highly unusual for any government programme.

The impacts of all of this work were fairly immediate. By the time we had completed a three-year interim report we were able to document a long list of changes that had already come about:

- Identification of a major information gap about partnerships leading to decisions about evaluation, restructuring CFSN, and coordinator meetings etc.
- Agreement to formalise regional coordinators' meetings to ensure an effective forum for information exchange between partnerships.
- Agreement to embed action research into the core decision-making processes for the programme.
- Clarification of the programme vision. The programme is now unambiguously articulated as a capacity building programme. The group defined the programme as 'an internally funded capacity building programme leading to externally funded regeneration and mainstream programme bending'.
- Recognition of the need to comprehensively rewrite the programme guidance.
- Identification of the need to strengthen the resources in the central implementation team led to a decision to recruit a new Senior Executive Officer
- Acceptance of the principle that some partnerships will fail. Clarification of the characteristics of failed partnerships. Agreement in principle that partnerships could lose funding. Need for further work on criterion for deciding when a programme stops getting funded.
- Decision to re-profile CFSN's work in order to make it more generic and proactive.

- Exploration of the ways in which WAG might need to intervene to support a bottom-up permissive programme. Recognition that because it wanted to be bottom-up at times WAG was too hands-off.
- Acknowledgement of lack of success in developing minority ethnic work (has contributed to a more active engagement in facilitating solutions to the Newport conflicts).
- Identification of a need to identify, develop and finance a conflict resolution for the programme.
- General shift in perspective to mainstream programme bending after clarity that little was happening here: 'need to establish what we want to bend and why'.
- Agreement to explore the possibility of extending overarching partnerships to other areas to support mainstream programme initiatives.
- Identification of intermediate outcomes for the programme.
- Agreement that local evaluation needed to be embedded in all partnerships.
- Agreement on the need to negotiate a performance assessment process for coordinators with grant recipient bodies

(*Source:* Tarling, Burns and Hirst 2006)

Some key learning from this project

As we can have seen above, one of the great strengths of this sort of process is that it demonstrates achievements as it goes along. This is important because evaluation processes often struggle to show their own value. Here the evidence of success lies in the action that is generated. The other major strength of this design was the way in which information generated in parts of the system was able to inform activity in different parts of the system. The extent to which the process became embedded in the management of the programme was exemplary.

There were also a few weaknesses. The first derives from the scale of the process and the timescale. As we moved into the third year it became clearer where we needed to focus our strategic energy. As I indicated earlier we began to open up new inquiry groups around, for example, issues of mainstream programme bending, but these groups never really had time to become embedded and do the work that they needed to. This takes me to my second point. This is that processes of this sort are very difficult to maintain after the end of an action research project. While the external facilitators are there to 'hold' the process, government organisations like WAG have demonstrated amazing levels of commitment to the process, but when our contract ends and the day-to-day work pressures continue to mount, that commitment can disappear very quickly. This raises fundamental issues about sustainability that we tried to address more systematically in our next big project that involved action research on vulnerability with the British Red Cross.

Rethinking Vulnerability: systemic action research with the British Red Cross (2006-07):[9] a highly networked organisational design

SOLAR has been working with the British Red Cross on a project called Rethinking Vulnerability. This section, which describes the shape of the project, is a co-written text written by Susan and I as a precursor to future publications.

The Red Cross is a large organisation with 3,000 staff and more than 30,000 volunteers. With its headquarters in London it is organised into the four territories across the UK. It is primarily known for its work in relation to disaster response and first aid but its many other services include, for example, the provision of wheelchairs, stress relieving massage and skin camouflage.

The British Red Cross had carried out a review of vulnerability some 10 years earlier but could see that its outcomes had not embedded themselves into the organisation's practice. In the meantime the world had moved on. New issues were emerging such as, for example, the influx of huge numbers of refugees, the spread of AIDS and an increasingly ageing population. They wanted an action-oriented approach to help them re-think this issue and at the same time improve their capacity to respond to vulnerability, while increasing their profile within the UK. Susan's core design built on our different experiences of large-scale systemic inquiry, and we jointly edited the final submission. The design that we offered (and which was successfully tendered for) was organised into three main phases.

In Phase One participants explored the issue of vulnerability and established a baseline of understanding about both vulnerability and the position of the Red Cross in relation to it. Phase Two involved using the insights generated to explore the implications for the organisation. Phase Three involved planning for a change process through which those implications could be operationalised.

Phase One began with 12 full-day inquiry groups (comprising perhaps 10-20 people each). These explored vulnerability in relation to the Red Cross in a fairly general and open-ended way. They identified recurring concerns and questions, tensions and possibilities within the organisation. Some of these groups were

Figure 8: British Red Cross Vulnerability Project – emergent design

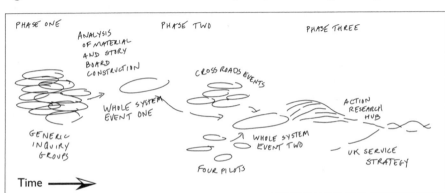

'slice groups' that mixed people across sections and status. Others were sectional groups (for example, management, volunteers, frontline staff). The inquiry groups generated stories, ideas, narratives and commentary as well as observations from the action research facilitator team. Over the summer of 2006 Susan spent a month analysing transcripts, notes and outputs from these inquiry groups, interview data, records of group meetings and organisational documents from over the past 10 years. She then organised the data and the analysis thematically and visually into seven storyboards for the 'whole system inquiry' event planned to mark the end of Phase One. Each storyboard was distinguished by a key theme, which signalled a systemic tension that seemed to warrant further organisational learning and inquiry. Each theme was underpinned by three questions, supported by quotes, metaphors from the inquiry group work, visual images and excerpts from documentary texts. This material also brought into view the espoused intentions and values of the organisation and how these related to 'reality' as experienced by different stakeholders. Susan describes the storyboards as a 'research gallery of living knowledge'.

> **'Storyboards offer a** way of "playing back" key resonances and tensions in a complex system (Boal, 1979). The juxtaposition and connections across the boards enable participants to glimpse a "dynamic whole" – a picture which comprises issues that they will recognise, but also the interrelationships and patterns that are hard to grasp in everyday life. Through conversations focused by these storyboards, people can surface taken-for-granted assumptions and world views that influence how they make and evaluate the effectiveness of their choices. They can thus become more inquiring about the unintended impact of their choices in relation to values and strategic aspirations (Weil, 1998). This re-presentation of data is intended to support a more systemic consideration of what issues may need to be foregrounded for action and further inquiry at the expense of others. People often feel validated in experiencing this "playback" of patterns that may be difficult to express or name.. By becoming more aware of these patterns they can feel empowered to make alternative choices.' (Susan Weil)

People at the whole system inquiry event worked in small groups with the material presented on the storyboards. This enabled them (and us) to assess its significance for different stakeholders, and its wider implications for the organisation.

Following the whole system event the steering group selected four pilots, one per territory, on the strength of their capacity to engage with the key organisational learning questions identified from Phase One, and on their potential to do innovative work that would help the organisation to push the boundaries of its current thinking and practice:

- The Easington (Durham) pilot aimed to test out the extent to which vulnerability was linked to area deprivation; whether the dynamics of volunteering were different in areas of deprivation; and why it has been perceived to be difficult for the Red Cross to set up services in places like Easington.
- The Swansea pilot was further developing a programme of supported discharge from hospital for people who were homeless. One specific aim was to 'develop more diversity within the recruited volunteer population'.
- The Milton Keynes pilot focused on how they could empower and support Black African women with HIV to self-assess their needs, and better access and influence the services they required.
- The Dundee pilot worked in partnership with another charity involved with young people of addicted parents. Its focus was on 'empowering young people to act with confidence in times of crisis'.

Each was allocated a dedicated facilitator from the SOLAR team who would support the pilot over a period of six months. In addition to the pilots, Phase Two had three further inquiry strands:

- a series of 'crossroads events' that were located across the four territories and that brought people together to discuss emergent issues and insights from the research, and to consider their implications;
- ongoing work with project commissioners, directors and the steering group;
- other 'informal pilots' relating to strategic issues that had emerged during Phase One.

The work with the pilots began with a two-day workshop. Participants were struck by how much connected them when they worked together in cross-pilot groups. They were encouraged to record their initial thoughts on the choices and actions they had in mind for their pilots, the assumptions and knowledge that informed these choices, intended and possible unintended impacts, drivers for their pilot and best outcomes. After an introduction to action research, they met with their support facilitators to review their individual 'data' and to prepare a joint after dinner presentation for invited guests. They were already living a key principle in this work of keeping boundaries open and involving people as 'critical friends'. The next day, we introduced them to questions about policy, practice and partnership. We explored with them the relationship between crisis resilience, response and recovery, and we worked on the implications of a shift towards outcomes and impact rather than outputs. From here, with the support of their facilitator, they went away to begin their action inquiries with others in the organisation and with their community partners.

Crossroads events were hosted in each of the four territories, and offered the opportunity to update people on strategic insights that were crystallizing across the project as a whole, and to pursue specific issues that were emerging. Variations of an open space approach were combined with regular updates on the research, 'whole system reviews' and future scoping activities. A budget was secured to enable the pilots to be represented at all the events, and SOLAR team members each attended at least two of these events. This helped to keep the learning across the project knitted together.

At the same time we were working on a framework through which people across the organisation could review and make critical choices about current activities and work that they might want to develop in the future. This was structured around six strategic filters designed to ensure that the Red Cross focused its work directly in relation to its core values and priorities.

A critical turn in the project came during Phase Two, when we proposed that there be no 'final Phase Three' for this project. We felt that it would be more effective to stream the action research work into the development of the new UK strategy that was being coordinated by the Director of UK Service Development. We would support her work through an action research 'hub'. This work was to be underpinned by the collective thinking that was done at the second whole system inquiry event, supported by project recommendations that had been developed beforehand.

The second whole system inquiry event enabled mixed groups to engage thoroughly with the learning from the pilots. The pilot teams offered presentations, and prepared storyboards that tracked their six-month journeys, and identified key organisational learning outcomes from their work. Following participants' dialogues around the storyboards, small groups were invited to identify future scenarios that they would expect to result if the Red Cross were to embed the implications of this work into concrete changes. In the afternoon they worked in seven 'development stream' groups:

- leading and managing change
- achieving flexibility within corporate boundaries
- learning from experience
- moving from activity outputs to outcomes
- implications for volunteers
- flexible finance
- external communications and fundraising.

The whole system inquiry provided an opportunity to scope the way forward for streams. Group members were asked firstly to identify their own recommendations, and then to reflect on recommendations that had been drawn out of Phases One and Two of the project. We hope that this thinking will frame the ongoing work as it becomes mainstreamed into the organisation.

Some learning from the project

One of the greatest strengths of this process is that it was entirely inquiry based and did not have to 'pretend' that it was something else. So it was not constrained by being constructed as an evaluation or formal research project.

The storyboarding process continues to prove effective. In the early stages of a project, it was time intensive for the project team. But by the time of the second whole system inquiry the pilots themselves were constructing the storyboards (see centreplates 4 and 5). The act of constructing the board became part of their learning process. By bringing insights together through storyboards, and validating the learning that has taken place at each stage, the work that follows can build on what has already been achieved, rather than constantly returning to the original questions.

Perhaps the most exciting part of this design was the way in which it involved so many staff and volunteers. Over the 18 months probably more than 500 were engaged in some way. This meant that learning could travel directly, through conversation (both formally and informally), from those who were involved, to others in the organisation. Having said this, there was much greater involvement of staff than volunteers in the whole day events. The Red Cross' more conventional volunteer forum mechanism was used to conduct quite an extensive consultation with volunteers at the start of the project, which meant that a good proportion of volunteers knew that a project was afoot; nevertheless a major ongoing challenge for the organisation will be to extend the conversations that have begun more deeply into the volunteer base. User involvement also remains a challenge. Some service user involvement was undertaken as the project developed, especially in the pilot projects, but as yet this has been relatively limited. This is not entirely surprising, as the evidence of much of our other work suggests that it can take more than a year to build meaningful relationships with local people and groups. This highlights one of the downsides of a project that ran over a relatively short time period. Having said this, increased user involvement may in the long run prove to be a major outcome of the project, particularly if it achieves its aim of working with more people who are vulnerable to crisis.

Because the project spanned just over a year and most individuals were only present at one or two groups, the early work had to focus on developing a breadth of understanding, enabling us to see systemic patterns and dynamics. Some participants were able to engage with a large number of different events and therefore developed a deeper understanding of what was emerging; others only 'touched' the process in a single event. Consequently, the success of the programme has been highly dependent on the capacity of the enthusiasts who have been closely involved, to take insights back into their own work settings and to open up discussions in the localities. In the long term the future of the process will be dependent on the development streams and the UK strategy hub sustaining their leadership way beyond the life of the project, and on the embedding of learning and action inquiry across the organisation. Only time will tell if this happens.

The shape of large system action research

Yoland Wadsworth describes her work with the Melbourne psychiatric services as an octopus with tentacles stretching into multiple domains. I would describe the BCI model as a vine that grows and roots where it touches the ground, each time spawning a new but connected growth. A close colleague described our Welsh Assembly work as an organic process which was held together by a spine and a bone structure. Each of these metaphors conveys a growing multi stranded process.

Networked systemic inquiry

In this section I want to illustrate what we now call 'networked systemic inquiry', the shape of which I can illustrate though a number of PhDs I have supervised over the past 10 years.

Linda Gordon's PhD (Savoury-Gordon, 2003) focused on the spillover effects of a worker buy-out of a major steel plant. She wanted to understand whether and how changes in participatory practice in the workplace impacted on workers' lives outside of the plant. This immediately extended the canvas out from the plant and required a multi-stranded inquiry process that incorporated workers, families, community representatives, aboriginal people and so on. Unusually Linda was working in parallel with another student, Gayle Broad, who was exploring worker participation in the plant itself. While these were independent pieces of work they were in many respects intertwined, and the way in which each of their research paths opened up was influenced by the other.

Alison Gilchrist's work (Gilchrist, 2001) focused on community development and networks. She was a few years into the work when I inherited her supervision. When I first looked at her work I could not quite see how all the bits connected. There was a reflective analysis of a festival against racism that she had been involved with. There was a personal inquiry into her own community development practice, her history as an activist and her role within her own local community. There was an inquiry process with a group of community workers. Each intrinsically offered insight into the core issues, but layered into the analysis were the patterns that emerged from the interrelationships between them.

Marina Prieto Carron's work (Prieto Carron, 2006) was an inquiry into female workers in Central America and corporate codes of conduct. This work involved what was happening in the corporate boardroom, the operation of supply chains, work practices on the ground, international activists engaged in dialogue across the web and so on. How could she understand the oppressions created from globalisation without somehow bringing all of these things into a whole? How could the informal data that was so crucial to what was happening be weaved into the analysis? How could insight generated in a highly political context move from one part of the system to another without causing damage to those from whom it came?

All of these students were building an inquiry from fragments, drawing insight from the interrelationships between them and then testing the resonance of what emerged in yet further inquiries. Since then I have been supervising a small group of SOLAR PhD students who are explicitly adopting a systemic approach to inquiry. Here the emergent patchwork design is even more pronounced. Let me give a flavour.

Alan Taylor began his inquiry looking at toxicity in voluntary and other values-based organisations. He wondered why it was that organisations that professed strong social values often seemed to be destructive environments to work within. As the inquiry has unfolded it has shifted its emphasis towards an exploration of the implications of hetero-normativity, sex, and the body in organisations. Again the work has traversed multiple terrains including, among others: reflections on the voluntary organisation within which he worked for 15 years, resonant conversations with colleagues, friends and other professionals, a piece of long-term consultancy in East London and a personal reflective inquiry.

Anne Archer has been exploring the notion of 'being with difference' as opposed to managing diversity or equal opportunities. The patches in the collage have included learning about 'non-verbal communication and being' through interaction with her horses, an inquiry into her relationship with her boss, a senior partner, and an exploration how difference affects corporate life. The context for her work has been a leading profesional services firm where she has held senior human resources roles.

Susan Ballard started her inquiry into mobilising collective will in response to climate change with a local inquiry in the village of Bromham that was exploring a proposal for a waste-to-energy plant linked to a sustainable housing development. Another inquiry stream relates to a game she has been developing with the New Economics Foundation. Recently she has carried out work for Hampshire County Council into 'champions for change' and has been working in government departments at ministerial level. In parallel to these pieces of work she has been carrying out a 'first person' inquiry into her own 'will' in relation to a wide variety of issues.

The form is akin to the creation of a living collage (see Chapter Six). As their lives unfold and their central inquiry develops so they spot more sites for inquiry that connect. Common to all of these inquiries is a combination of:

- intentional navigation
- serendipity
- the researcher as central to the emerging inquiry.

Sometimes we learn most by discovering completely unexpected connections or connections that we may only have a hunch about. This suggests that within an inquiry process we need to allow space to juxtapose things where the connections are not obvious. One linking thread that will always be present is the action research facilitator him or herself. If an action research facilitator is at the hub of their inquiry rather than neutral to it, then almost by definition different pieces of their inquiry become connected by him or her. Traditionally, even where emergence is supported through, for example, snowballing techniques, the 'linear logic of progression' is that *one thing leads to another*. This is important but it should not obscure another dynamic, which is that *one thing connects to another*. This dynamic highlights the need for action research facilitators to explicitly engage with the interrelationships between things which means looking not only at the subjects or objects of activity but at the spaces in between.

If an action research facilitator is working on a consultancy project, has an inquiry group running, and is engaged in an internet dialogue, and so on, and they see connections between them and connect them in action, then they are actively creating the terrain on which their research is played out. If the system is in the mind of the inquirer (see page 119 for more details) then the choice of what 'system' to look at is a choice about what sets of connections and interlinkages to focus on. The research embodies the journey of the research facilitator because it is a 'life journey', not just a 'research journey'; it is connected by life choices. So not only is their legitimacy in the 'participant' status of the researcher, it is difficult to see how the research could come into existence without the researcher at its heart.

Conclusions

This chapter has outlined different possibilities for the design of systemic action research. In the next chapter I try to pull out some of the underlying design principles. It should already be clear from the examples outlined above that these could be applied in different ways in different contexts. Some designs are highly structured, others much more organic. Some of them emphasise long-term 'deep' inquiry over time by small groups that build out, others have extended rapidly across a whole organisational network. In each the boundary critique around what *should* be worked with, and what *could* realistically be worked with will be different. The decisions about both initial and emergent design cannot be based on a formula. Each requires judgement, diplomacy and an attunement to what might be possible in a particular social and organisation constellation. This requires action research facilitators to develop particular skills that are quite different to those of consultants, community development workers or traditional researchers. I explore these in more detail in Chapter Seven.

Notes

[1] 'The popular project title of "U&I" was an acronym of the full name "Understanding and Involvement", which itself was playing on the dialogic mirroring of the "you" and "I" with either standpoint being occupied (interchangeably) by professional staff and service-using consumers.' (Yoland Wadsworth)

[2] Matthieu Daum was the main action research facilitator. I facilitated some of the groups and managed the project. Dianne Walsh carried out the qualitative and quantitative research that supported the action research.

[3] A third Sure Start programme was part of the initial consortium but it later withdrew.

[4] The UK Sure Start programme was modelled on the US Headstart program. It involved the funding of extensive programmes to support 0- to 3-year-olds in the most deprived communities within the UK. They were 'rolled out' in five phases, eventually leading to around 500 programmes. These in turn paved the way for the development of less intensively funded Children's Centres in every ward in the UK. The Children's Fund was a government programme for 5- to 13-year-olds. A central unit was established in most major cities and large towns through which perhaps 30-50 neighbourhood or issue-focused projects were funded. These were usually selected following bids from local voluntary and community sector groups and a few statutory services.

[5] Our perception was that this happened because the action inquiry consortium was created before some of the Sure Start programmes (including Easton) had been set up. They were brought into the process by their 'accountable body', the local primary care trust. When they were up and running, and in a position to discuss the action research work with us, we discovered that because neither the staff nor the committee had been directly involved in the creation of the consortium, there was no real support for the process.

[6] Roger Tarling (CPC) managed the wider consortium. I directed the action research strand of the programme. Barry Percy-Smith, Dianne Walsh and I facilitated the groups. Other members of the team were Andy Hirst (CPC), Arwel Jones and Marilyn Taylor (UWE).

[7] Some of the text in this section is drawn directly from Burns (2006a). Thanks to the American Evaluation Association.

[8] 'Mainstream programme bending' is a phrase used in contemporary government circles. It refers to an intent that locally based pilots and programmes should have a significant impact on the ways in which mainstream services (for example, health and education) are delivered.

[9] Susan Weil directed the British Red Cross vulnerability project. She and I guided the overall direction of the project, in close collaboration with Nick Starkey and Margaret Lally (British Red Cross). The project was supported by a team of SOLAR action research facilitators: Jackie Draper, Clare Hopkinson, Cathy Sharpe, Alan Taylor and Dianne Walsh, Jocelyn Jones facilitated some of the early inquiry sessions. Liz Lloyd, from the University of Bristol, developed the underpinning conceptual and theoretical frameworks and supported the process with policy analysis and research. Jeanette Iles provided generic support to the project.

FIVE

Some design principles for systemic action research

Despite the diversity of action research designs represented in the previous chapter, there are a number of underpinning characteristics that need to be reflected in most systemic action research designs. The seven that follow are among the most important:

- an emergent research design
- an exploratory inquiry phase
- multiple inquiry streams operating at different levels
- a structure for connecting organic inquiry to formal decision making
- a process for identifying cross-cutting links across inquiry streams
- a commitment to open boundary inquiry
- The active development of distributed leadership.

An emergent research design

By now it should be clear that the way in which we do our work needs to echo the ways in which we observe change taking place in the world. Given our critique of centralised planning it would be odd to apply the same planning principles to systemic action research. So, just as emergence characterises social and organisational change it must also characterise our action research design.

Wadsworth (2001) describes the way in which her study evolved:

> The research commenced in a single hospital ward and then – in order to research and develop improving things for any single inpatient – found itself following the threads of that single inpatient's experience out to the rest of the hospital and to the sub-regional area mental health service, then to a regional level, and finally connecting to state-wide and federal mental health service systems. These interconnecting elements of a service system were in turn connected to wider communities of interest (such as non-government organisations, family, friends, and carers, self-help groups, the churches, the professions, unions, teaching institutions and so on) and finally contextualized also within a diverse society (of different individuals, multiple cultures, workplaces; industry, commerce, homes and local communities). In this way it found it needed to achieve – or contribute to – a "critical

mass" of culture shift and widespread or whole systems organisational change if it was to make a difference in any single service–user's life. (Wadsworth, 2001, p ix)

In the previous chapter I described the way in which the Welsh Assembly project design emerged (see also Burns, 2006a). An emergent research design means that although we can specify the methods that we are likely to use, the broad structure of the research, its possible progression, and maybe some limited milestones, we cannot provide detail on the content of the research, and we cannot specify in advance all of the methods we will use. By not doing so we allow ourselves time for the research to develop iteratively, and at each stage to assess what is necessary for the next stage. At the beginning of each new stage we need to ask ourselves:

• How is it all going? Are there any issues arising that need attention?
• Are we still 'on track' with our underlying research purposes?
• Do our underlying purposes need to alter?
• What new questions do we need to ask?
• What new inquiries do we need to open up?
• What new data do we need to collect?
• Which new organisations and people do we need to involve?
• What new action do we need to take?
• What practices and methods do we need to use at this stage?
• Do we need to produce any outputs or feedback from our work at this stage?

This process of unfolding the unknown is not always easy to justify to commissioners of research who are expecting defined outputs, related to specified resources, on a clear timeline. The best way to respond to this concern is to explain the reasoning for the approach, and then show what sorts of results have been achieved in other projects. It can also be helpful to point to the deficiencies of traditional approaches.

Implicit in this idea of emergence is time. Time allows us to reach a depth that episodic research and inquiry cannot.

> I mean if these issues are entrenched then it's not through one meeting that you are going to have an effect on this, you know, a meaningful or significant effect, you might start chipping at it ... in one focused group. (Mathieu Daum)

> ... "holding the systemic picture" and understanding enabling and disabling patterns – while under pressure to act – often requires a number of cycles of enquiry before the shift to insightful action becomes meaningful. (Weil, 1998, p 50)

If we take dialogic, deliberative and inquiry-based processes we can place them on a timeline. Generally the shorter the time frame the less space there will be for the emergence of key issues, and time to work with them. This pattern is represented in Figure 9 below. On the far left-hand side of the figure are traditional consultation methods that rely on a direct response to questions. Here emergence is precluded. Focus groups allow space for dialogue, but time is limited and the questions are predetermined. There is no space for new questions to be asked, new evidence to be collected, time to reflect, or action to be carried out in order to deepen understanding. As we move toward the right we bring into view one-day events such as 'open space', which allow for emergence in the construction of the agenda, but where time for exploration is highly limited.

Figure 9: The duration of dialogic, deliberative and inquiry based processes

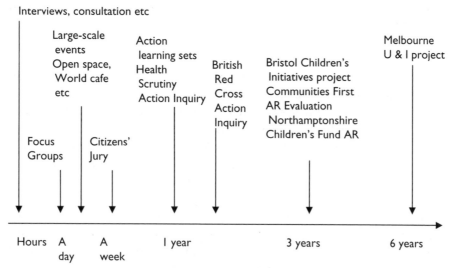

Note: The Health Scrutiny Action Inquiry was a year long process in which SOLAR worked with six Thames Valley local authorities to explore how to make the 'health scrutiny' process effective. The Northamptonshire Children's Fund Project was a three-year inquiry which supported the evaluation of the Children's Fund projects. The Melbourne U & I project; the Bristol Children's Initiative project, the Communities First evaluation and the British Red Cross vulnerability project are all described in Chapter Four.

Citizens' juries enable greater deliberation, encourage a variety of different voices to be heard and enable relevant evidence to be assembled. But again, the framing of the issue is predetermined and action is not part of the process. Action research is a longer process. It is possible to complete straightforward strands of inquiry within a six-month time period but most 'short inquiries' will be at least a year in duration. Typically depth inquiry strands may last two to three years, not least because as we discuss in the next section, time also needs to be given over to establishing what are good inquiry starting points. Ideally inquiry processes will become embedded and self-sustaining but even without this inquiries can extend for as long as six or seven years with external facilitators. The Melbourne U&I project is a good example of this.

An exploratory inquiry phase

How the action research emerges and where it emerges from is crucial. Some attention needs to be given to starting points. Given that one of the explicit purposes of action research is to challenge assumptions and test what is important, it is usually a mistake to structure a large system inquiry around predefined organisational or managerial objectives. This is over-linear and is likely to turn the inquiry group into a task group as participants move too quickly to identify solutions to predefined problems without first establishing what the real issues are. It is also far less likely to be sustainable as it does not derive from the passions of people on the ground. So establishing stakeholder resonance is also important when identifying starting points.

There are a number of possibilities for starting:

- *Initiate a generic inquiry process at the beginning of a programme to explore key issues.* In the BCI project I think we should probably have started with an open-ended dialogue rather than structured our inquiries around programme themes. The Hounslow Children's Health inquiry (see page 118 and page 178) is an example of this (Percy-Smith et al, 2003; Percy-Smith, 2007). Here peer research identified the key starting points. These were tested in relation to service providers in a large event. This provided a foundation (which was never realised) for inquiries at major disjuncture points between the children and professionals. In the British Red Cross project we structured this in as the whole of the first phase of the research. Mixed inquiry groups generally explored perceptions and experiences of vulnerability in relation to the organisation of the British Red Cross. By the end of the process we had identified a range of key issues to work on. These included the 'strategic positioning of the Red Cross', 'how to identify people who were susceptible to crisis but vulnerable because they did not have the resilience to cope with it', 'recruiting a different demographic profile of volunteers', and so on. They were tested for their wider resonance in a whole system inquiry event, and then the action research was ready to explore some key areas in depth.
- *Engage directly with what is already happening.* In our planned project with an acute hospital trust I facilitated a number of training development days that had already been requested from the training department by various clinical and management teams. I also carried out interviews with a wide range of managers across the trust. Because these entry points were spread across the organisational terrain it was possible to quickly discern underlying generic patterns that could become starting points for the inquiry process. From a

full-day session on disaster management, for example, we identified 24-hour working as a crucial issue.

- *Start in a few areas where there is a manifest passion for action and grow the inquiry.* This might more closely correspond to the Melbourne mental health research. Here, the issues are already bubbling. People are motivated and can carry the inquiry process into other arenas.

The best starting points may not be the most obvious ones. An open inquiry into the lives of young people is likely to offer more than one that starts with health issues defined by professionals. An organisational inquiry into vulnerability might best start with personal experiences of vulnerability. A Sure Start evaluation might best start with an exploration of local social norms. Open starting points within clear but loose boundaries are probably the best way forward.

Multiple inquiry streams operating at different levels

In earlier chapters I highlighted the need to build a systemic picture to work within. There are different ways of doing this. One way is to start in a particular local place and build outwards from there. This is what happened in the Melbourne U&I project. Here the systemic picture that is built is rooted in the original inquiry – a process that Wadsworth describes as 'scaling up' (Wadsworth, 2005). An alternative approach that has characterised most SOLAR inquiries is to build from multiple starting points. By initiating multiple exploratory inquiries we are able to cast many different lenses onto the terrain. To illustrate this I will briefly relate a piece of exploratory inquiry that I carried out with SNV on HIV/AIDS in Kenya.

The SNV team mind mapped the many different issues that were emerging in relation to AIDS. We started to explore their interrelationships on the flip chart as shown below. One way of mapping is to follow the trajectory of the individual, but if we rely on this then we miss an understanding of the structural patterns that are inhibiting solutions. We need to consider different individuals in different contexts at different times. This means that multiple maps need to be generated even to get a starting picture of this issues. Below I have reproduced just one of these maps. Here some clear lines of thought emerged around potential inquiries.

The mapping starts to tell the story. In Kenya HIV/AIDS is concentrated in the cities and along the roads. Anti-retroviral drugs are brought into clinics. These depend on people taking them every day. If they are not taken regularly, HIV can accelerate into full-blown aids very quickly. Transport is a problem so this forces people to live where the clinics are, which further concentrates the problem in these neighbourhoods, breaking down their social and economic infrastructure. A policy and implementation strategy focused on the provision of drugs to individuals can fail to engage with the cumulative systemic impact of those multiple interactions. AIDS is one of the major priorities for international

Figure 10: A rough cut at systemically mapping AIDS/HIV in Kenya

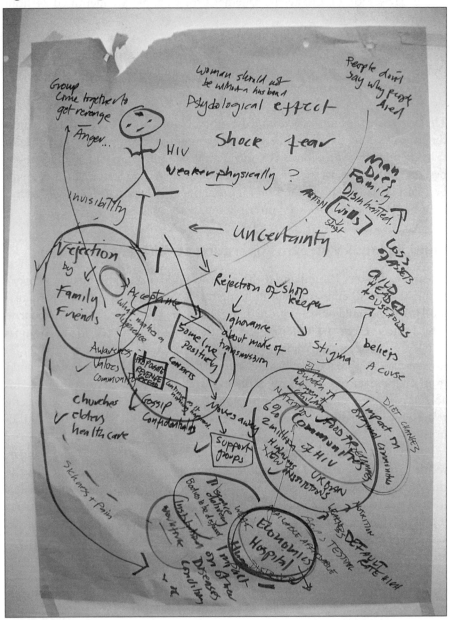

aid organisations. This has led to the prioritisation of AIDS treatment in hospitals, distorting the balance of care in a country where malaria is still the biggest killer. The economics of hospitals can be fundamentally affected by the activity of the aid organisations. There is a slightly gruesome entrepreneurial subculture emerging around the disposal of bodies that presents dangers as well as economic opportunities. There are now many child-headed households as a result of AIDS that generates a huge range of social and economic implications. Culture is important. The lenses through which AIDS is viewed are incredibly varied, and there are many different beliefs that inform those perspectives. Some believe that it is a curse; others see it as a symbol of moral degeneration; others are simply frightened.

When we start to tell the story we juxtapose many different narratives, some of which flow from each other, others that appear not to. As we talk we begin to see the connections, we are in a position to cluster issues and see what is missing. We can start to get some depth about some of the issues recorded on other flip charts. In this case as the stories unfolded I circled different sections of the map.

- life trajectories of individuals
- rejection by family and friends
- emergence of communities of HIV sufferers
- impacts on the wider health system
- child-headed households.

Each of these might be starting points for inquiry strands. It is evident from this early mapping that in order to get a working understanding of the systemic dynamics at play it is necessary to open up inquiries in different sites. We might, for example, initiate one inquiry strand in the hospitals, another with a group of children carers, and another within a neighbourhood with a high concentration of HIV/AIDS sufferers. As these inquiries unfold and action is taken, the need for new inquiries emerges, and so the process moves on.

Through the process of inquiry the starting questions will often change. An inquiry into domestic violence could transform into an inquiry into the roles that men play in this community. It could equally spawn tributaries. Later it might connect with other inquiries. The inquiry process can be seen as a fruit tree that is growing new branches. Sometimes the tree is pruned and branches are cut off to focus the energy of the tree. Each season the tree produces fruit that seeds new trees. Multi-stranded inquiry processes can thus take different forms:

- parallel inquiries that may later converge on the ground or in a strategic inquiry process;
- sub-inquiries that emerge as inquiry streams in their own right;
- emergent inquiries where a new issue arises out of an existing one;
- braided and collaged inquiries.

These are illustrated in the figures that follow. In the figures the lines represent main strands of inquiry, the hexagons represent meetings and the stars represent convergence points.

In Figure 12 an inquiry on domestic violence has grown two new branches. These now become new inquiry groups. Their composition may be largely the

Figure 11:The inter-relationship of emergent inquiry processsess

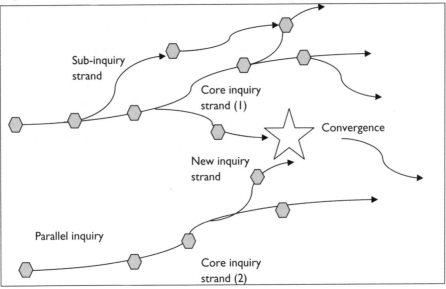

Figure 12: Inquiries evolve

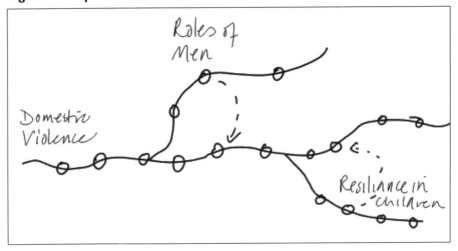

same or mostly different, with only one or two people holding the connection to the main trunk.

Running in parallel to this group is an inquiry into childcare (see Figure 13). This too has spawned two branches. There is a point at which the two inquiries converge. Both groups are working on the role of fathers in the community. This is a high energy point that could lead to a new group on fathering. Where patterns and issues converge across inquiry sites there can be a powerful explosion of energy and newly kindled enthusiasm.

Figure 13: Inquiries converge

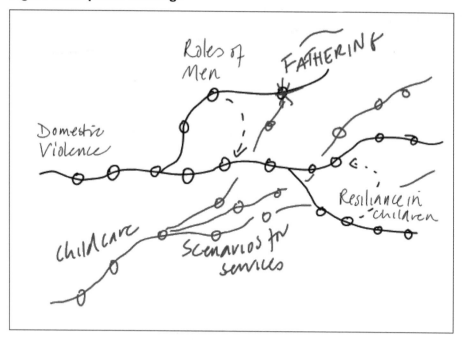

A key role for an action research facilitator is to have a view of the whole, 'to broker these connections', and to support the development of emergent inquiries. As the inquiry system grows more and more inquiry streams will be initiated or emerge. It will begin to engage more and more people and will start to pick up all of the important disjunctures within the governance terrain.

In Figure 14 we can see multiple inquiry streams. Some have started later, some have merged, some have split to form new inquiries. A few of the strands have converged. Others stay independent but are brought into relationship with each other where important connections can be made. Now the process becomes more complex. More strategic groups need to emerge to make sense of, assimilate and discuss issues and activities that are emerging from the ground. This may mean that we need to introduce large events into the process. Sometimes we bring together people from similar settings into these events. In our work with market and coastal towns in South West England we met each year with stakeholders from nine towns. In our evaluation of the Welsh Assembly's Communities First programme we brought together all the urban initiatives, all the rural initiatives and all of the Welsh Valley projects.

So, as I articulated in the introduction to this book, in addition to the system thinking that underpins the approach, large system action research is characterised by a multi-stranded learning system where the interrelationship of emerging inquiry strands gives meaning to the wider patterning of the whole system, and reveals possibilities for system change.

Figure 14: The shape of a multi-stranded inquiry process

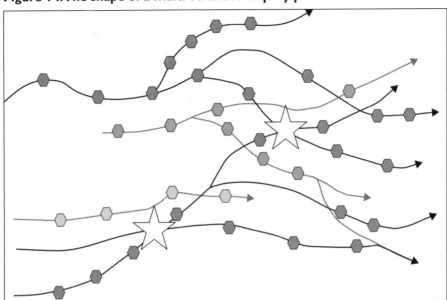

A structure for connecting organic inquiry to formal decision making

One crucial lesson about the design of a whole systems process came from the BCI project and was built into the Welsh Assembly project. This is that while the inquiry process is organic in form it needs to connect to the formal structures that are relevant. The dialogue that follows between Mathieu Daum (MD) and I (DB) reflects the difficulty of focusing on the inquiry streams and leaving the overarching learning architecture until later.

> MD: I don't think we can think of the role of the facilitator independently of the structure of the project ...

> DB: ... or the politics of the project ...

> MD: ... and also the politics, to give you an example, I think the project originally was structured in such a way that the contact between the research team through the research facilitator and the institution funding it, was only in each of the action research groups, with a ...

> DB: ... sort of dotted line, to the programme manager ...

MD: ... yeah, exactly, a kind of verbal agreement that, this, we would keep each other in touch, but ...

DB: ... it wasn't formalised ...

MD: ... there was no formality or formalisation and I think this is crucial because, I mean, we then encountered the issue half way through it when we realised that it's important to connect to a senior management team when we offered them a more formalised entry in there which then they refused. (Burns and Daum, 2004)

By the time we needed to engage the senior decision makers, an image had already been built of a series of semi-autonomous groups that would generate insight and take action. If they generated actions that were controversial or would have wider implications for the whole project then they would need to go to a strategic decision-making forum for approval. In retrospect I can see that we saw the role of the strategic levels as (a) legitimation and (b) troubleshooting. By the time we had built the Welsh Assembly project our conception had changed. The strategic levels had to be co-generators of change. In order to secure this, it needed to be made clear from the start that they would not just be working on local or tightly defined thematic issues; they would be working with these issues in order to engage with wider systemic patterns. The model below (Figure 15) is a simplified version of the action research structure for the WAG project. On the ground stakeholder inquiries were taking place. These were resonance-tested

Figure 15: Structure of the Communities First action research process

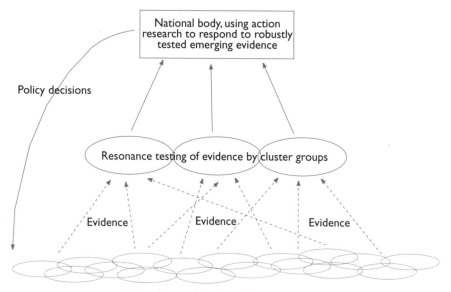

Action Research by Local Stakeholder Groups

in a variety of forums (including cluster groups) and then strategic level inquiries were embedded in the programme management group.

A rather different example of the way in which formal structures enable action based on informal relationships to be more effectively mobilised comes from the anti-Poll Tax campaign. This also shows how systemic inquiry can be embedded into everyday political organisation. I lived in Easton (a poor multicultural area of Bristol, whose many people lived harmoniously side by side, but who often did not communicate across cultures). Talking to your neighbours about your financial situation was culturally taboo. A major non-payment campaign was emerging, but people feared taking part because they felt they would be on their own. We decided to speak to as many people as possible in every street in our neighbourhood. Every door was knocked. We asked them the question: 'If you knew that 80% of the people in this street were prepared not to pay the tax (because they knew that 80% of the street also would also not be paying) would you be prepared not to pay?'. When we had been around all of the streets we went back to the houses and told people the results. Because people knew what everyone else was thinking they were prepared to act.

Through this process hidden patterns of intention surfaced, but the survey was not neutral. Intentions were formed as a direct result of the survey. The anti-Poll Tax unions provided a formal structure within which opinions that were forming in a fragmented way could be brought together, crystallised, and acted upon.

A process for identifying cross-cutting links across inquiry streams

One of the more difficult challenges of this work is to link insight across multiple learning streams in order to spot systemic patterns. Sometimes these are embedded within the fine grain of a written account. An inquiry may have as its focus domestic violence but within the conversation crucial commentary on a range of other issues may be present, for example, the role of fathers; how social norms are embedded, leadership, childcare and isolation...

In traditional research, stories and dialogue that are not directly related to the substantive inquiry are easily 'discarded'. In systemic action inquiry we are able to take those insights into new inquiry processes. We need to both track the path of an inquiry stream and to connect cross-cutting issues that emerge as fragments in different inquiry streams.

Take the following scenario that is a collage of a number of different projects that we have facilitated. Imagine that there were inquiry streams on 24-hour working, library use, childcare and domestic violence.

Figure 16: Following threads which are seeded *across* multiple inquiry streams

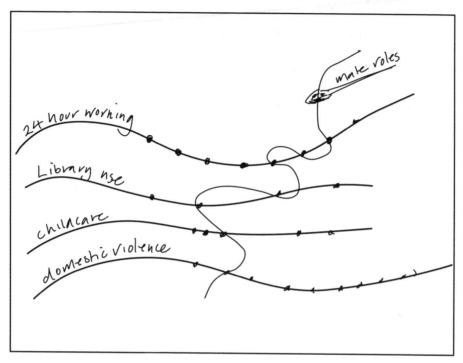

The inquiry stream on 24-hour working may give us a glimpse of the impact of shift work on family life. The library use group might be exploring why men do not take their children to libraries; the childcare inquiry obviously has the role of men in childcare as a core theme; the domestic violence thread could be exploring male roles in a local community. What emerges is a cross–cutting inquiry thread on male roles.

Similarly some men may have raised the issue of staff safety on night shifts; this might connect to a discussion about threats to library staff when a cafe was introduced to the library; the childcare group might be discussing how to 'handle' children when they are violent; and the domestic violence group has been talking about the risks to professionals of intervening in domestic conflict. Again there is potential for a cross-cutting inquiry thread on responses to violence.

The example that follows is a real one from the BCI project. This excerpt is from a note of the BCI domestic violence action inquiry:

> One thought was that sometimes professionals are worried about asking about violence because of an assumption that it will generate it: ie if you don't talk about it, it can remain quiet, but if you start

asking about it, it will become uncontained. This works then as a collusion with the violence, through the idea that if we don't hear it, it doesn't exist. (Bristol Children's Initiative Hartcliffe Highbridge and Withywood action research notes, DA 17 January 2003)

Now listen to these notes from an entirely different inquiry focusing on health:

'If people raise a difficult issue we note it.'

'I sometimes don't ask certain questions because there is nothing I can do about them.'

'... sometimes we know what the problem is, so we avoid asking what we know.'

Here an issue is emerging across inquiry streams about how professionals are dealing with difficult issues. It may only have been a tiny fragment within each of the substantive inquiries but juxtaposed against what is emerging in other parts of the system it may have enough significance to justify its own inquiry process. We can now look for evidence to support or refute the existence of an underlying pattern. Even if there is an underlying pattern the issue may not be crucial enough to justify the resources that would go into a new inquiry, but fairly often an issue will be identified that is crucial.

There is an important issue to bear in mind. This is that the new issues that I have described may well not emerge in parallel. It may not be apparent when the issue of male roles emerges within the domestic inquiry stream that there will be a 'fathering' issue that needs to be connected to. This will only become clear later. This makes it even less likely that the connection will emerge through either a text search or data coding. In a traditional piece of research the first statement probably would not be coded because on its own it feels insignificant.

Maintaining open boundaries within the systemic action research process

There are two key reasons why it is critical to maintain open boundaries. First, because in the real world things constantly change. People change jobs, they suddenly become passionate about things, or lose interest. New people emerge who are important, and so on. Second, because action research is about action, and action requires leadership. Leadership is another one of those things that emerges and if we close the boundaries of inquiry we often close ourselves to the people who might drive the change that we aspire to. Thus one of the key differences between a systemic action research approach and a cooperative inquiry process concerns the boundaries of the group itself. This extensive quotation from Peter Reason's introduction to a special issue of *Systemic Practice and Action Research* gives a clear picture of how these boundaries are constructed:

> One key characteristic of co-operative inquiry is that the group, which is typically closed to new members for the duration of the inquiry, offers a safe space within which inquiry can flourish. The group is usually drawn together through a series of exploratory conversations and meetings, and at some point, which often has symbolic significance, the boundary is drawn so that "now we know who 'we' are", as McArdle puts it, and members can engage in the processes of inclusion, control and influence which constitute group process ….
>
> Creating a boundary creates safe space but also a boundary issue: if some are "in" then others are "out" and the transition back across the boundary to share the learning with others needs to be managed carefully. As Mead tells in his account, the police leadership inquiry group offered a transformational space for its members, but, he adds, "we are still struggling to communicate the benefits of a collaborative approach to a wider police audience". Charles and Glennie from the beginning have to create a safe space for their inquiry group within the complex and pressured field of child protection. The midwives inquiry group that Barrett and Taylor write about appears particularly successful in making a space for themselves *and* establishing the Early Mothering Group as a recognized part of hospital practice; this may be because they were willing to open their group boundary at an appropriate point. (Reason, 2002)

One of the problems with this approach (which is quite similar to that which faces action learning sets) is that if the learning takes place within a closed group it is very difficult to take it out into social and organisational settings. Large system action research works with the notion of open boundaries. This does not mean that anyone can drop into the group. Rather it means that there is an expectation that the group will change because the social and organisational context within which the group is trying to do its work is constantly changing.

The active development of distributed leadership

As I mentioned in the previous section effective systemic action research requires us to build strong networks of distributed leadership. A study commissioned by the National College for School Leadership (NCSL) highlighted the following as the key definitional elements of distributed leadership.

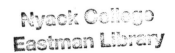

Firstly, distributed leadership highlights leadership as an *emergent property of a group or network of interacting individuals*. This contrasts with leadership as a phenomenon which arises from the individual.... What is most distinctive about the notion of distributed leadership is summed up in the second of the meanings identified by Gronn, namely *concertive action*. Contrasted with numerical or additive action (which is the aggregated effect of a number of individuals contributing their initiative and expertise in different ways to a group or organisation), concertive action is about the additional dynamic which is the product of conjoint activity. Where people work together in such a way that they pool their initiative and expertise, the outcome is a product or energy which is greater than the sum of their individual actions....

Secondly, distributed leadership suggests *openness of the boundaries of leadership*. This means that it is predisposed to widen the conventional net of leaders, thus in turn raising the question of which individuals and groups are to be brought into leadership or seen as contributors to it. This openness is not limited merely to the extent to which the conventional net is widened within a particular community. It also raises the question of the *boundaries of the community within which leadership is distributed*.

Thirdly, distributed leadership entails the view that *varieties of expertise are distributed across the many, not the few*. Related to openness of the boundaries of leadership is the idea that numerous, distinct, germane perspectives and capabilities can be found in individuals spread through the group or organisation. (Bennet et al, 2003)

They argue that it is the first of these that distinguishes distributed leadership from other forms of leadership. I have found this synthesis helpful and would interpret its resonance with our work as follows.

Leadership opportunities are emergent properties of systems. Understanding systemic patterns enables leadership opportunities to become visible. These opportunities need to be taken up by those best placed to act on them. Thus leadership in this context is most likely to be vested in people who have a driving passion for an issue, are highly respected by peers and or colleagues for their work, and who sit at the heart of cross-boundary networks. They are often not formally designated as managers or decision makers, but they may be managers in one sphere taking the initiative in another. They are people who make things happen irrespective of status.

The creation and development of distributed leadership is an essential part of large system action research. It is not only a positive by-product but a crucial element in the development of the networks that drive the process. Effective action inquiry is based on relationship building that is in turn built on trust building. Leaders that emerge from the process will be able to open doors that no external facilitator will be able to open.

Conclusions

What we have described here is the construction of a learning architecture that can hold considerable complexity. The complexity arises from the uncertainty inherent in emergent process; the need to hold multiple inquiry strands in relation to each other; the maintenance of a research terrain in constant flux; a changing profile of research participants; and so on. A myriad of systemic effects, some visible others less tangible, will emerge simply as a result of the unfolding of these complex processes. But we can also more deliberately fashion strategic opportunities from the possibilities that arise out of the relationships between action inquiry strands. To do this the complexity has to be 'held', 'facilitated' and 'channelled'. This is why the systemic design principles articulated in this chapter are so important.

SIX

Practices of systemic action inquiry

The approach to action research that we have been developing at SOLAR is built on a learning architecture of parallel but connected action inquiry streams. I have illustrated how these might emerge and what shape they might take in the previous chapter. In this chapter I want to look in more detail at what the individual strands look like. The chapter focuses firstly on dialogic inquiry, secondly on visual inquiry, and finally on embodied inquiry. These give a flavour of some of the practices we use at SOLAR, but they should not be regarded as the only way of doing this work.

Dialogic inquiry processes

Facilitated action inquiry streams

Action inquiry processes may start with a few people in conversation, or in an exploratory action research meeting, or in a large event. They may be concerned about a specific issue, dilemma, or problem or have an open-ended question such as 'what are the health issues for this community?'. As discussed in the previous chapter, some starting points are better than others, but it may not matter as long as we have time, flexibility to change tack and multiple entry points into the social and organisational arena. The only thing we have to ensure is that there is a real passion for the work. Before moving to action, an inquiry is likely to go through an iterative process similar to that articulated by Wadsworth and Epstein (1998), where the inquiry:

- allows issues to emerge
- surfaces different perspectives on them
- builds a systemic picture to contextualise them
- goes deeper
- surfaces the undiscussables.

Once action is initiated new insight will emerge, which will trigger further inquiries.

An inquiry group may run for just a few months or a few years. It may stay with a single core group but more likely its membership will expand and change. It may continue to work on the issues that it started with, but it is just as likely that the group will realise that the underlying issue is something else or that there is a need to split the group to enable sub-inquiry strands to emerge. Each session is recorded and written up. Actions are identified that will be carried out between group sessions. Typically a group might meet 10 times over two years.

In the early stages of inquiry, emergent understanding will be strongly supported if space is created for stories to be told. A story can be a brief account of something that happened, or a complex interwoven tale. If we rush to inquiry before we hear people's stories we often miss crucial understandings. Embedded in each story is a process that helps us to understand the complex interrelations between things. Stories hold an emotional content that cannot easily be accessed through official accounts. When we are telling a story we use the words that mean something to us. Often it is those specific words that provide a key to what the real issue is. Working with stories is messy and complex because they do not easily fit into categories. Working with stories across a large system is even more complex because we need to find a way of connecting them without losing their essence. So we need to:

- create spaces in which people feel able to tell their stories
- identify the patterns that connect the stories
- develop forums within which their wider resonance can be assessed.

The stories combined with other information provide a context for discussion. The discussion helps us to ask the right questions. A considerable amount of time can and should be focused on this in the early stages of an inquiry group. It is likely to be far more productive to find the right question to ask than to rush to find answers to the wrong question. So what does an inquiry process actually look like? Over the next few pages I explore in more detail two inquiry stands from the BCI action research project. Both were part of the HHW Sure Start work.

Domestic abuse inquiry stream

I want first to look at the domestic abuse action inquiry stream. There were many things that went wrong in the BCI action research process, but this one mostly went right. I will describe what was done, how it emerged, how it was recorded, how it was acted on, and some of the things that we learned about how to do this sort of work. Inevitably it is only possible to offer a flavour of a group that met regularly over two years with lots of action interspersed.

The domestic abuse action inquiry stream had a core inquiry group that met for 13 half-days over more than two years. It also created a sub-strand that held more than five meetings over the same period. It was regularly attended by the manager of a family link work service, a midwife, two social workers, the Sure Start children's services team leader, the police domestic violence liaison officer, a counsellor from the local family centre, two health visitors, a counsellor and family centre manager and the safe community partnership officer. The group also worked closely with local women who had been victims of domestic abuse. As the group progressed it involved more people – for example, child psychotherapists.

The first few meetings were entirely exploratory and quite eclectic in their focus. People told stories of their own and other's personal experience and explored scenarios that arose from that experience. They started with a general unravelling of the issues and how they were being played out in HHW. This list from the action research stream review gives an idea of the terrain that was covered in the first few meetings:

- People do not see it is an issue. It is linked to cultural norms in the community. Domestic violence is the norm
- There is pressure from extended families to stay in the relationship
- Controlling partners
- Children do know what is happening
- Children's rights versus adults' rights
- Sometimes it is difficult for staff who are facing the same issues to confront them
- Isolation, bus fares etc
- People might not want to talk to people in their area
- Addiction/collusion/choice
- What makes it hurt enough for people to want to change?
- Maybe working with children is the best way forward
- Is it easier to break the cycle in some places than in others?
- How powerless are men without jobs without the family to retreat to?
- What kind of role models are there around for boys and young men? Gazza versus Beckham?
- Housing: why are women removed? Could we pilot an alternative?
- How to reach men and change culture; if you individualise men and see them as having the problem they will not look at it.
  (Daum, 2003b)

The group was aware from an early stage that it did not have enough hard information on the extent or nature of the local problem. It also identified the need for new people to be involved. The local police officer responsible for coordinating domestic violence was invited to the second meeting. Police figures showed domestic violence accounted for around 1% of their caseload. The midwives and health visitors felt that that this could not represent the whole problem since it actually featured in around 30% of their caseload. They agreed to go back to their files and check for domestic abuse, and they asked their colleagues to do the same thing.

Here a field-based peer research process was initiated to provide supportive data to the inquiry stream. In systemic action research it is important to understand that neither the inquiry process nor the analysis needs to take place entirely within the confines of the inquiry group. Some of the best inquiry is facilitated by the group but takes place in community and practitioner settings.

By the time we reached the third meeting we were quite sure that the issue affected 30%-40% of households. This meant that the group was dealing with a population-level problem rather than one confined to individuals and families, and this opened up new lines of thinking. If domestic violence is as much about 'what is acceptable within this community' as it is about the relationship between two individuals, then how do we make effective interventions in relation to local social norms? Discussions took place about role modelling, the wider role of men, public awareness campaigns, and so on. One of the early activities of the group was to carry out a survey in order to get more information and to try to understand the situation better. This illustrates the way in which an inquiry group can use traditional research data in support of an inquiry process. These excerpts illustrate how the survey responses enable inquiry questions to be formulated and explored:

> 'The survey still showed a lot of fear about social services taking kids away. This is the immediate association people make. This echoed X's experience of a visit she made this morning to a family where there is domestic violence, and where one of the fears the mother had was that her kids would be taken away.

> 'Surprisingly, when asked to talk about what domestic violence meant to them, women often mentioned stories of women hitting men, bringing out the old image of the woman holding up a rolling pin etc.... X mentioned how that went against her assumptions that domestic violence is primarily about men hitting women, which she assumed would be shared by the women she interviewed. We spent a bit of time talking about why these women, in different group interviews, often brought up this image of women hitting men. Was it because talking about violence to women felt too close for comfort, and they didn't want to go into it, but rather deflect the conversation from it? Was it because women's violence towards men does take place in this community, more often than we might presume? How much should we take their comments at face value? Do we need to rethink our conceptions of violence in the home?

> 'X then wondered if they had mentioned financial control as a form of domestic abuse. It seems that they didn't, and that they didn't bring up sexual abuse/violence either. They primarily talked about physical and emotional abuse.

> 'How can we create a space to work with women who express "he beats me but I still love him"?'
> (Daum, 2003b)

By the time the group got to the third meeting it was beginning to identify areas of possible action. Three key areas emerged out of new questions:

How do you reverse the norms of re-housing?

It is usually the woman who has to leave the family home in domestic violence cases. This is mainly because if the man knows of her whereabouts she could be at further risk of violence. The inquiry group explored in depth the implications of this. As a result of leaving the family home, women's social networks were destroyed and they were left isolated in a place they were unfamiliar with. Children were uprooted and also lost their networks. What if it were possible to work with the housing department to set up an action inquiry process around a project to reverse this? The implications could be assessed through action.

> 'We revisited the housing issue: women feel that it is good to have the choice, but women may not want to stay in the house where the man knows she lives. In fact, the legal situation is complex, especially in the case of a married couple. Even if they are separated (but still married) the man is allowed to be in the marital home. This can open up the way for intimidating and abusive behaviour, theft, etc in the story shared with the group the man didn't do all of these: something stopped him. Beside/beyond the law what else stops people from engaging in destructive actions? What are the social elements that hold the boundaries? What role do neighbours play and how can we engage them as a resource?' (Daum, 2003a)

We can see from this text that while the focus in this moment is 'housing', other important issues are being asked. What are the things that stop men becoming violent? How might we think about neighbours within the wider systemic picture? And so on. It is easy for these questions to get lost when the focus is on something else. A key role for a systemic action research facilitator is to ensure that these insights are retained, and seeded into other inquiry arenas (see Chapter Five, page 96).

How do you break the generational cycles of violence?

The group started to explore generational cycles of violence. They asked 'If domestic abuse is locked into a repeated generational cycle where would we break it?'. After much discussion they started to explore how it could be broken with young children under the age of four. They knew they would be breaking new ground by working directly with children who were so young. A sub-stream of the main inquiry group was set up to work out how to do this in a way that was both ethical and safe for the children. They brought in new people. They had to answer difficult questions like 'How do we get the consent of parents to work with their children on domestic abuse when the abuse is not disclosed in the first place, but we know it is happening because of things the children say?'. It was not in any case likely that the parents would want their children talking about these issues with outsiders. 'We'd like to work with your children to explore how they cope when you are beating up your wife' was certainly not an approach that was likely to get very far. The group decided to pilot the project with an existing group in a local family centre:

> The group looked at accessing existing resources and soon developed a partnership with an existing weekly session working specifically with children with a range of internal and external behavioural problems. It soon transpired that the referral pool for that group, and for the one the AR [action research] wanted to set up was mostly overlapping; this facilitated the extension of the group's focus to explicitly include children coming from abusive households. This process has been highly successful, for many reasons:
>
> • it demonstrates collaboration across agencies as opposed to competition and ring fencing;
> • it shows that you do not have to set up yet another group; that thinking about existing resources and transforming their focus can bring about a win-win situation;
> • it demonstrates, in action, the long-term preventative ethos of Sure Start.
>
> The existing group works using a very specific methodology, which has been shown to enable children to express and 'work through' difficult psycho-emotional experiences that they cannot express in other settings. This initiative was set up with a view to send other Sure Start workers at this group as assistants, so that they could learn the methodology and would be able to help it being transposed to other settings within HHW.
>
> While clearly not able to do everything it identifies as important, the AR group has also been thinking about the importance of working in schools to educate the generations who are just about to form relationships. It has been identified that domestic violence is highly present in couples aged 16-24.
> (Daum, 2003b)

How do you provide comprehensive training for professionals?

These were deep questions with the potential to have an impact in the long term. But there were also more practical questions to answer, like how were all of the people that needed training on domestic violence issues going to be trained? What would the training need to cover, how would it be funded? and who would deliver it? The group put a lot of energy in exploring training needs and working out how they could construct a comprehensive cross-agency training programme.

While these three major areas for action were prioritised, many other issues were also explored. For example, the action research group was keen to explore a line of thinking that was developing around the idea that:

> 'Supporting may be more beneficial than being supported.' (Daum, 2003a)

Interestingly this thinking was also emerging in Knowle West. As I indicated earlier, I think an opportunity to build a city-wide inquiry on this and other issues was wasted because we did not really build the infrastructure to enable this.

The group also spent considerable time exploring how to involve victims of domestic violence in the process. There was a feeling that this needed to happen in parallel with the 'professional' group (this echoes the decision made in the Melbourne mental health work). Initially it was thought that the best way to involve parents was to support a parallel parents-only action research group. This shifted to a local advisory group made up of 'survivors'. This in turn shifted when a local self-help group, WISH (Women Involved in Self-Help), started. This group worked independently but fed into the work of the action research group.

> 'X invited to the meeting two local women who want to set up their own domestic abuse support group. They are part of a group of six women, who didn't know each other but were on the same course: one of them said "if I won the lottery, I would set up a refuge". The other five all got really enthusiastic and since then they have been trying to make something happen.... The idea of the group is refining: support/drop-in group, there on the off-chance if someone wants to talk, campaigning locally, giving advice, buddy system.' (Daum, 2003b)

As we can see the group was working on many fronts. Its agenda evolved iteratively through the inquiry processes. Early dialogue, storytelling, systemic mapping and collective information gathering enabled a dynamic picture of the issues to be built. This generated further lines of inquiry and suggested possible actions. A small number of these were prioritised. But new ideas and possibilities continued to be generated, and these were 'held' within the main inquiry stream. Some of the larger actions formed their own tributaries. Over time these seeded new insights back into the main group. Because new lines of inquiry were being generated the group could continue for as long as it was held to be useful. This is a real example of the concepts described in Chapter Five.

Figure 17: Domestic abuse inquiry stream

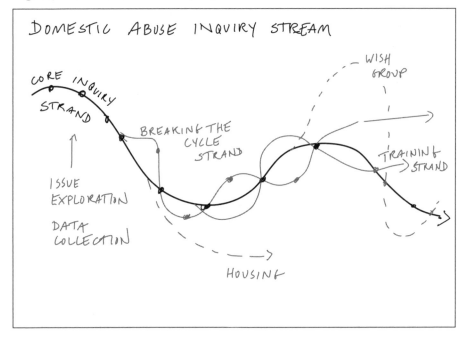

Library use action research stream revisited

This section reproduces the final reflections on the library use group produced by the action research facilitator. This is a process already described in Chapter Four – that account was based on notes of supervision sessions with Matthieu Daum. This account has a different style and emphasises different things. Both accounts have been included in the book so that the reader can see how significant the write up of events is.

> ### Summary of library use action research strand
>
> This action research strand, looking at increasing library use in a particular disaffected part of Bristol, stemmed from a particular desire to place the emphasis on young children reading and borrowing books as part of Sure Start Objective 3 on play and learning. It attracted 10 people throughout those 18 months: enthusiasm was stronger at the beginning, but had faded towards the last six months of the project.

The task of this action research was deceptively complex: how could we generate a renewed interest for the local library, and translate it into renewed activity? This was the first dimension of this complexity: the context, both local to the area, and national/cultural. Locally, the area has a lower than average literacy and school achievement level, hindering a community relationship to its library. At a wider level, libraries, just like churches, are institutions in crisis at the beginning of the 21st century; part of the challenge then, beyond the local context, is set in the question: 'How can the library, as an institution, adapt to the tremendous changes in its environment, the complexity of the transformed needs of the population it serves, and the proliferation of new media currently available and widely used?'.

This contextual set of challenges was never really worked with directly in the action research; however, a lot of work was spent initially thinking about how to draw various groups into the library and how to combine and enrich their activities with those of the library – in other words, a development-through-symbiosis model. This could include bringing in fathers groups, schools, having a Sure Start base there, storytellers, crèches, space for childminders, grandparents etc.... The three most daring ideas linked to this were: making structural changes to the building for access to the garden; commissioning a community art project; and setting up a cafe (a private business). Only the art project – which is linked to outside alterations – was followed through. The other two, which would have involved internal alterations, were clearly resisted, and eventually dropped.

It seems clear that the action research generated positive outputs and outcomes that could not have been reached without it, that is, without a facilitated process that brought key stakeholders together and provided them with the space to think about and envision a future situation. Among these positive outputs and outcomes, were:

• increased request for use of rooms by local groups: a 'by-product' of the action research;
• a mural aimed at promoting a more attractive picture of the library, which was set up as a big consultative and inclusive community project;
• an innovative partnership between HHW Sure Start and the library to send Sure Start registration details to the library and therefore automatically register families for the library;
• increased stocks and resources: books, cushions, but also computers, leading to increased use of the library to do homework;
• a 're-launch' of the children's area that went very well, and kept the library alive in the community.

However, a year after the last action research meeting, the picture remains mitigated. There is no noticeable increase in joining from Sure Start children (the system described above is not yet operational), but there seems to be an increase in older children joining and borrowing. The mural was an achievement, but nobody apart from staff seems to notice it.

Data gathering about key parameters in the library are still not easily available; however, all seems to point towards no noticeable change in the borrowing rate of children's books for 0- to 4-year-olds. However, borrowing from the Sure Start book loan scheme is proving successful, so overall borrowing of books in the area is on the increase. The new library project has stalled due to complications with purchasing land, and planning permission has yet to be granted; this means that the current library needs to continue to find ways of surviving in its current environment.

The fairly mitigated outcomes seem to be linked to the difficulty in the group to engage with internal changes, metaphorically, but also practically. The emphasis was on the superficial, the resistances were against depth. This is evidenced by:

- the difficulty experienced by the group, and in particular the library staff, to pursue the idea of having a cafe on the premises;
- the eventual refusal to commission the structural changes (despite funding from Sure Start) that would open the library up to the garden and to many unknown possibilities;
- the discomfort and avoidance of working with the difficult issues around the question: who is this library for? In particular, the possibility that for this library to be able to cater for young children, it may also need to cater for teenagers, with all the prejudices that then get evoked;
- the refusal to look at setting up a crèche on the premises, despite offers from HHW Sure Start to staff it;
- the dominance of a data system that is in itself a major obstacle to being able to know the internal state of the library (that is, who borrows, what, where, how often, etc...);
- the incapacity for the library to advertise what happens within it: the low attendance to storytelling, for example, could be linked to the fact that Sure Start did not know (when) it was happening. But there were many other examples;
- the reliance on 'the new library' as an escape from working with the issues facing the current library.

As mentioned earlier, processes of transformation at a systemic level here seem to resonate with processes of transformation at the individual level: it is easier to engage with what is at the surface, but much more difficult to engage and work with the internal issues and challenges. This is echoed by the attendance pattern, where those on the periphery of the system were present and involved at the beginning, but towards the end only the library staff and the Sure Start Children's Services manager were present.

The change in action research facilitator may have coincided with a receding enthusiasm in the topic, or triggered a different response from participants linked to the style and the understanding of the role of facilitator. This could be explored in another discussion. More importantly to note, however, is that throughout the 18 months, the group at its fullest was made up of nine women and one man, plus one male facilitator. This composition can only have an impact on how the group worked, especially with regard to leadership and followership. Some interesting illustrations took place in the last two to three meetings; faced with the junior library staff's recurrent objections as to why this or that could not be done, because of this or that regulation, the facilitator moved from trying to lead the process of change through motivating, reflection and action, to challenging those often self-created obstacles by expressing his anger and frustration. This in turn provoked anger from the library manager who expressed it at the following (and last meeting). What resulted from this heated exchange was the opportunity to refocus on what they really desired in terms of change; that session was acknowledged by all as (one of) the most productive meetings of them all.

Review of the Library Action Research group at HHW SureStart 30/01/04

These 'after the event' reflections by the facilitator might be quite different to the views of participants. This firstly, raises the question of whether there is a mechanism in place to record multiple interpretations session by session (or in summary later in the process)? or should this be one of the core roles of the action research facilitator? Secondly, it highlights the importance of looking back at what has actually been achieved. It is very easy to produce a long list of outcomes from action research without any evidence that they have changed anything. Thirdly, we can see that some things that appeared to be entirely unsuccessful may actually have been successful but that success is not immediately visible, because the outcomes were displaced outside of the core arena of the work. Here we can see that there is no impact on library borrowing but there is a significant increase in borrowing from the Sure Start programme. Did the library group catalyse action elsewhere, or were we asking the wrong question? Perhaps the best route to getting young people reading does not lie with the library at all.

> '**It is important** to acknowledge that as well as wanting to change, a system may also want to not change; to resist the possibility of finding themselves in a different, even improved, situation. Paradoxically, the familiar, even if not satisfactory, remains more bearable than the (idea of the) unknown. Linked to this, there is also the question of process: whilst we may want to reach the outcome we are working towards, we may not want to go through the unsettling process that gets us there.' (Matthieu Daum)

Large-scale events

Sometimes we develop action inquiry through large event processes. In systemic action research these will be interspersed between and run alongside inquiry streams. Their role within the wider design is varied depending on the process. They can be used to:

- open up new inquiry questions and clearly frame the questions that need to be explored in an ongoing inquiry process;
- test the resonance of issues emerging from the ground (for example, from other inquiry groups or other research);
- enable a group to visibly move forward together. When you can only see a few people's responses to issues you may not have enough information to give you confidence to take action. Large system processes can enable this;
- collectively interpret and analyse data from earlier inquiries;
- generate substantial new data in a short period of time. We have often asked people to go through a structured process where they assess things that have happened, write down stories, create collective maps etc. A one-day event has produced more data than might be achieved through six months of interviewing;
- bring systemic patterns to the surface;
- bring people together in unusual combinations.

In designing large events we have borrowed from a variety of approaches including 'open space' and 'world café'. Harrison Owen invented open space technology between 1985 and 1989 (Owen, 1992). He noticed that the most important conversations actually took place in the coffee breaks and other informal time, so he tried to develop a process that was akin to a permanent coffee break. This process can work at different scales involving just 20 people or hundreds of people. An open space event typically starts with a defined theme that might be general (for example, leadership) or more focused (how might we work with 'vulnerability'?). An open space session invites people to stand up and name a conversation that they would like to have. They name the issue to the group, and then write it onto a chart with sessions and times marked on it. Owen's process illustrates the power of serendipity and interconnection, and stresses the quality of the conversation, rather than the number of people participating, or the importance of the participants. According to Owen, 'the right people are the people who are there'. A high quality conversation can be had by just two people, as long as they are discussing what they really want to discuss. If people are no longer stimulated by the conversation, the process encourages them to find another conversation that they are stimulated by – 'the law of two feet'. By encouraging participants to work either on issues that they have identified, or on issues that have been identified by others but 'speak to them', powerful connections can be made between people who have shared concerns. A depth of insight can be reached, which would be unlikely in a traditional meeting or conference.

'World cafe' is another interesting approach to large system events developed by Juanita Brown (2001). It involves arranging a large room in a cafe style. The event takes a key theme. Issues are then discussed table by table. Each table has a white paper tablecloth, and as the conversation unfolds, participants are encouraged to write, draw, make connections and so on, on the tablecloths. At a specified time people are asked to move tables. One person remains on their original table to link the new people to the original conversation. The new people begin to fashion a new but related conversation. The conversations become more connected with each iteration.

> **What is essential** in this work are forms of visual and metaphorical mapping, almost akin to the idea of "live" storyboard creation. In this way, the collective wisdom and patterning across the conversation can be made more visible. So too can questions that have emerged. This then provides the basis for tracking further inquiry, while simultaneously providing a record that helps participants not to disappear the learning that unfolded as the busyness of the day job kicks in.' (Susan Weil)

SOLAR large events have built on many of the principles described above. One example was a piece of work carried out for the Hounslow Community Health Council[1] in 2003 (Percy-Smith et al, 2003). We were given a very broad remit to explore issues of health with young people in the borough. Working through networks we identified 10 young people in different settings (schools, care homes etc) who were in a position to work with other young people in those settings. We ran a series of training days with this group on peer research and then they went back to their setting to explore the health issue. One group made a video, others produced posters and so on. Each produced different sorts of data that were brought to a large event. The large event involved around 80 young people and 30 professionals. The professionals included teachers, health professionals, social workers and senior managers. In the first morning session we arranged five or so young people on a table with two professionals. The young people – all from different settings – had not met each other before. The group opened up a discussion on how they saw health issues for young people. The adults were told that they were not allowed to speak for the first hour. They were just to listen. Many of them really struggled and there was considerable learning in this process itself. We then asked the professionals and the young people to work independently on the issues that the young people had raised. They had to do this graphically (see later in this chapter for some of the powerful issues that emerged through that visual work). In the afternoon we brought them together in mixed groups so that they could engage in dialogue. At the end of the day we constructed a panel of senior decision makers. They were asked what they had learned from the day and what they would do as a result of it. They were also exposed to the group's probing questions. There was one powerful moment that I recollect:

> I recall a half-hour discussion with six young people on sex education.
> We talked about their experiences of sex, how they learned about it,
> how it had been dealt with at school, and why sex education was so
> bad. Later in the day we asked senior managers to reflect on what

they had learned. The Director of Education stood up and gave an honest account of the difficulties they were having in response to drugs problems and then, almost as an aside, said that perhaps they needed to learn from their successful sex education program. I immediately picked up the roving microphone and took it to table where the young people who I had been talking with earlier were sitting. They talked to the whole conference about the disjuncture between their experience and that of the professionals. I now think that we should have secured agreement then and there for the Director of Education and other professional colleagues to continue to work with these young people, in an ongoing inquiry group, to co-construct and enact a new approach to sex education. (Burns, 2006a)

In this scenario the large group becomes a place where those with power become publicly accountable in their responses to issues raised. It can also be a powerful springboard for the next stage of the inquiry process. What is crucial to enable all of this to happen is good preparation, good recording and space to allow parallel narratives to develop before they are brought together. Here it is in the form of peer research. In Chapter Four other large system processes were described that we embedded into the British Red Cross vulnerability inquiry. Here the storyboards bounded the dialogue and offered a platform of raw material to build on.

So large events offer important opportunities to make connections, test resonances, deepen inquiry and open up spaces for collaborative action across stakeholders. But like any other process they also have limitations. Some of these are articulated in the following reflection from Pat Shaw:

The open space event generates a strong temporary sense of community, whereas the kind of work I am describing generates a rather weaker, shifting, ill-defined sense of "us" because conversations are always following on from previous conversations and moving on into further conversations involving others. People are often gathering and conversing around ill-defined issues, legitimation is often ambiguous, motivation is very varied. The work has much less clear and well-managed beginnings and endings. There is not the same sense of creating common ground for concerted action. There is no preconceived design for the pattern of work; it evolves live. We are not necessarily trying to create outputs in the form of public action plans; rather, we are making further sense of complex situations always open to further sense-making and in so doing redirecting our energies and actions. (Shaw, 2002, p 146)

Large events then need to be seen as just one part of a continuous learning process. They are an important space for another type of conversation, but on their own their impact is likely to be superficial.

Visuals and other sensory data in action research work

As I said in the introduction to this book, sense making requires far more than intellectual analysis. It quite literally requires us to use our senses and our emotions. The two brief examples below highlight the significance of our senses and emotions.

> An adult childcare worker described a nursery that she had attended as a child. Her overriding memory was of the *smell* – the horrible smell. In conversation we established that the nursery was probably very well equipped, and the nursery staff were probably very good, but the smell completely dominated this child's experience. In planning these things we rarely take our senses into account. Even when we do the smell experienced by a child may be entirely different to that experienced by an adult. (story from BCI project)

> A number of professionals have inquired of this study, how it is that psychiatric patients could make judgements about the services they were receiving that were valid or rational. The answer to this inquiry is that the psychiatric consumers have points of view which are valid and reasonable per se. A single example may illustrate this basic methodological point. A service user (who a psychiatrist might name as "paranoid") may act fearfully as if the world is hostile. For this person the world is hostile. (Wadsworth, 2001, p 8)

Visual work gives us access to these different forms of knowing. Pictures can be used in a variety of ways. First, they can act as a trigger to connect people to experiences and emotions that can open up lines of inquiry and interpretations that might not have been envisaged otherwise. Second, they can be a representation of the subconscious that can help us to conceptualise a system, understand a set of issues and so on. The way in which people conceptualise or visualise a system has a considerable effect on how they operate within it. We have already talked a little about capturing feelings in words, but often something different is required.

Using images to convey meaning and to open up new lines of inquiry

Visuals can convey meaning and 'different ways of knowing' that cannot be articulated intellectually. They provide a vehicle for 'getting in touch' with deeper feelings and articulating complex relationships.

I have already described the large group process within which the image below was generated. In this section I just want to explore the image. It was created as part of the Hounslow Children's Health inquiry (Percy-Smith et al, 2003, 2007) by three young women and a young man. Before it was created, the young people and the professionals in the room were talking at cross-purposes. Stress had been identified as a major issue. This was a surprise to the professionals and they were keen to engage with the issue. Their initial response was to propose stress-free zones with Jacuzzis. The young people's response was palpably dismissive, as if to say 'don't you get it. We have places to chill out, but always we come back to the stress'. When this image emerged they began to find a common language. The words 'everyone has a breaking point' opened up possibilities for inquiry that were not there before. We could now explore questions like: 'What are the breaking points

This image can be seen in full colour on Centreplate no 1

in your community?', 'What are the things that might tip you over the edge?', 'What can we do to stop people from tipping over the edge?'. The juxtaposition of images on the pages was striking. Here is piece of paper that depicts a beautiful woman, a man with a gun, black men behind a fence – all are experiencing the same feelings of being trapped and stressed. There was of course a great irony in the image that was labelled 'don't judge me before you know me, just listen' as so many of the professionals in the room had found it so hard to do that just a few hours before.

This collage emerged spontaneously, but collage can also be created deliberately. One of its greatest strengths is that it can be used as a collaborative process in which individuals bring their own fragments and connect them with an emergent representation. One way of creating an inquiry collage is for participants to work alone to build their part of the picture, and then to juxtapose their work against the work of others, adding commentary or new images to make connections. Another approach is to co-construct a collage using images and text.

Collage makers juxtapose partially or fully formed artefacts. They may take the whole or just a part. The bits may be ripped at the edges but that could be what enables it to connect. The narrative of collage is not linear. If change does not occur in linear causal lines, then it seems obvious to me that good explanation will not be entirely linear. This does not mean that a linear narrative is unhelpful but that it is only one way of generating insight.

I am struck by how easily my children navigate through hundreds of internet pages and are able to engage with multiple non-linear narratives. A blog, for example, can be read as a temporal narrative tracking the issues foremost in the author's mind. It can be read thematically through threads and hyperlinks. It can be searched using key words for specific meaning. It can be interrogated and and meanings can be elicited directly. It is dynamic, evolving and always moving onto new territory. This process of constantly adding new elements into a collaged inquiry is a central part of systemic action research, and braiding these inquiries so that they bind together while retaining their creative autonomy is a skill which is crucial for systemic action research facilitators.

Susan Weil has made extensive use of photographs in her inquiry work (Weil, 1994). The photographs allow people to connect to a non-intellectual part of themselves. In our British Red Cross project we used photographs to open up the early inquiry groups. We laid out 200 or more photographs for people to choose. They were encouraged to make emotional not intellectual choices. The images acted as a trigger that linked people back to things that had happened to them. Often the photographs would appear unconnected to the subject in hand. A photograph of a train, for example, might connect someone back to feelings of vulnerability when they were evacuated in the war.

My colleague Dianne Walsh built on a technique called "rivers of experience" developed by Denico and Pope 1990 (see also Prosser 1988, and Gave and Walsh 1998) as a way of engaging families in our Northamptonshire Childrens Fund project (Percy-Smith and Walsh 2006). We needed a tool that would encompass families' stories without slicing them up and losing their complexity. The rivers invited participants to identify moments of significant change (critical incidents) in their lives, to help explore ways in which public services could better support individuals and families. They were constructed with individuals prior to inquiry events to ensure that voices of the most vulnerable were able to be heard without requiring their physical presence. Children's Fund workers were the researchers in this process and presented the rivers on the families's behalf (see centreplates 6 and 7).

One of our SOLAR 3 PhD students, Anne Archer, has been doing work on 'being with difference'. She has been trying to articulate the difference between this and other forms of diversity work. Anne works with horses. In one of the group sessions she brought with her a short video; this showed her walking in close synchronisation with her horse and conveyed to the viewers what Anne meant by 'being with'. The image held a depth of meaning that a word-based description could not have done.

Using images to surface systemic assumptions

Individuals have a construction of the systems that they are working with in their mind, and this will not always be conscious.

> System in the Mind [SITM] is the systemic construction – the system – through which every individual represents, in an unconscious way if it is not worked through, his environment. This construction at least influences – but often determines – his relationships, his behaviour, his decisions, his vision of himself and his place in the universe. SITM comes directly from the person's history and his relationships with his original institutions (family, school…). It structures the individual and conditions his relationships with institutions in the here and now. (Gutmann et al, 2005)

> [System in the Mind] is the basic structure through which each individual (person, institution) carries an institution in his or her mind. How he (or she) uses to refer to it, to rely to it, to be mobilized by it. (Gutmann et al, 2006)

We have used drawings to make that system visible. When we uncover the visions held by individuals we may discover that there are underlying systemic patterns that begin to shape a collective systemic picture. To illustrate this process I have taken a segment directly from an inquiry process that we carried out with an organisation that works with children. Participants each did a drawing of how they saw the system of which they were a part. They were then asked to interpret their own drawing. Following this the group discussed the issues that were raised. To preserve anonymity I have not referenced the unpublished report and minor changes have been made to the quotes. The name of the organisation has been replaced by 'our organisation'.

The group saw far more in the pictures than the individuals who drew them. Collective understanding of subconscious meanings emerged in the dialogue enabling a systemic understanding of what was happening to be built.

The pictures give a very vivid image of how people see the organisation. Some of the observations were relatively straightforward, although insightful. The bees represented busyness. Sometimes we equate successful outcomes with busyness. Actually we may all be running around successfully doing things that are not effective. Many of the pictures showed walls between the organisation and the projects. The board in particular is always tightly bounded. It is never depicted as part of an interactive system. One picture showed a bureaucracy feeding a bureaucracy. All power emanates from the centre and even the most powerful are depicted as powerless. Another depicts a labyrinth with money as a goal. Picture A is a building site, where people continue to build to three quite different plans while what they are building is being bombed and knocked down by a ball and

Picture A

[A] Participant's comments: The building is 'Children's Services'. The weekly ball is the 'initiatives' coming from government via the Government Office that change the reality for children's services. The planes are government directives coming over the horizon. The planners are each trying to achieve their own visions and direct things. Our organisation is trying to repair damage and deficiencies while moving towards a final joining up. The management board is trying to assimilate all this and move forward.

Picture B

[B] Participant's comments: The Children and Young Persons Unit/Government Office are represented as serious civil servants in an ivory tower – very disconnected with the services of young people – very distant from the management board.... Our organisation is represented as a bank passing out investment funds to a number of

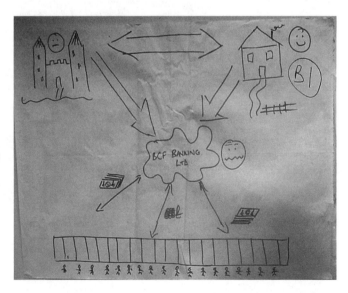

groups requesting a return on investment. There are a large number of funded groups representing a wall/barrier to the management board. The children and young people are hidden underneath.

Picture C

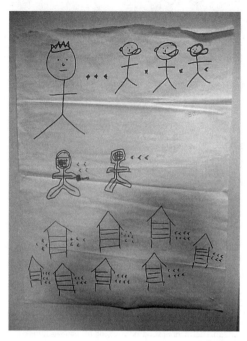

[C] Participant's comments: The beehives hold lots of busy bees who are the funded groups and the children and young people involved with them. Why bees? Because I thought 'busy' activity going on constantly. The bees are looked after by the beekeepers who hold and manage the resources and make the honey. The beekeepers look unfriendly, are they? No, just protective clothing, to help them do their job efficiently and concentrate on gathering the produced good quality honey (evaluation and support from care team). Next are the landowners. They control the resources and affect the beekeeper and the production of the bees. There are a few bees buzzing around representing myself, other funded groups and service users. They do not have much influence but they can sting. Overall the king or government controls everything and he can change his moods. The landowners listen very carefully to what he says so they do not lose control of their land.

Picture D

[D]Participant's comments: How do you get from synchronised swimming to being safe underneath? The boat is full of children and parents wanting a different environment for themselves. Underwater is a new world with enriching opportunities and hazards. The management board has to give children and their families aspiration for this new environment. The management board is made up of half scuba divers and half synchronised swimmers. They look like they are

doing the same thing and dancing the same dance but under water they are struggling and their legs are wobbling all over the place. The scuba divers share the same language, all learned, they depend on each other for their own safety and will only be able to get other partners, children and families into the new environment if they have one common language. Some parents can scuba dive and we need them. The wreck has snakes living in it and there are always sharks around. Sharks are not always dangerous but stop a lot of people diving!! They only need respect! Your task means your underwater time is time limited and you are absolutely dependent on not being alone. You also need to learn a lot about procedures and protocols to stay safe so everyone knows what to do.

PLATE I

This collage was made by young people in Hounslow. It's multi-layered messages opened up the potential for real dialogue between young people and professionals which had not been possible before. See pages 115 and 118.

Source: Percy–Smith, B., Burns, D., Walsh, D. and Weil, S. (2003)

PLATE 2

These two posters were also created as part of our Hounslow project which focussed on healthy futures for young people. The juxtaposition of stereotypical images of female beauty with the gruesome bodies scarred by surgery enabled young people to find a starting point for further inquiry. See pages 115, 118 and 130.

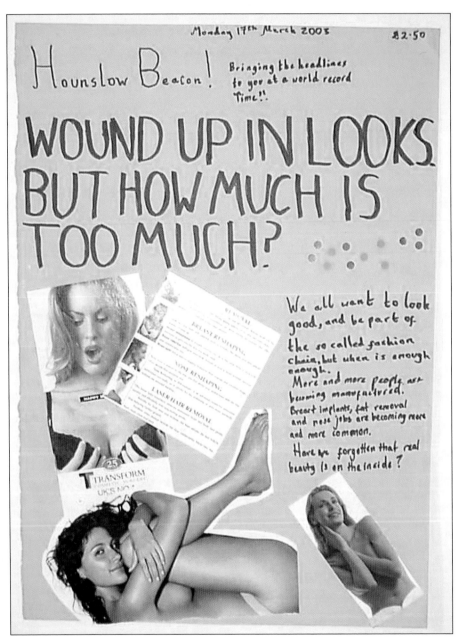

Source: Percy-Smith, B., Burns, D., Walsh, D. and Weil, S. (2003)

PLATE 3

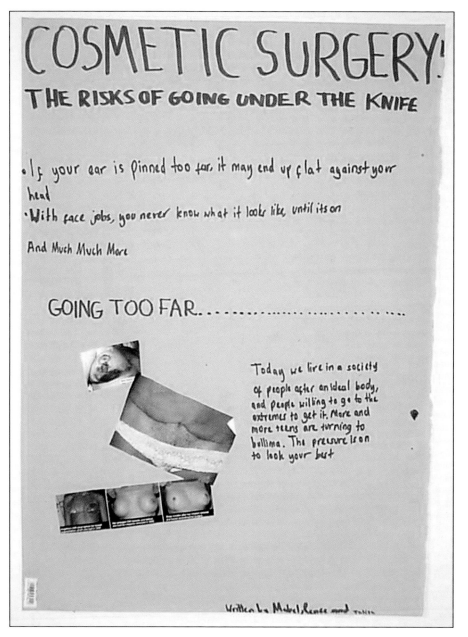

Source: Percy-Smith, B., Burns, D., Walsh, D. and Weil, S. (2003)

PLATE 4

This story board was created by the Swansea Pilot of the British Red Cross Vulnerability project. It highlights key issues and dilemmas providing visual and textual triggers for both resonance testing and new inquiry. See pages 77-8.

PLATE 5

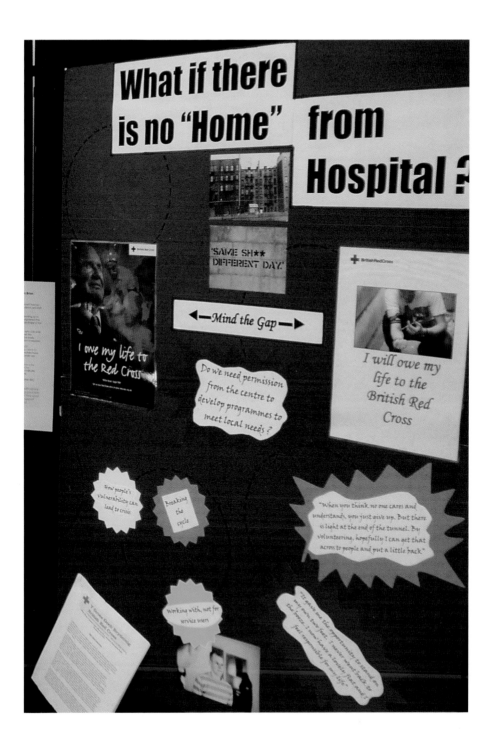

PLATE 6

The 'rivers of experience' posters which are reproduced here illustrate one visual technique which can help group participants to paint a detailed picture of their lives.

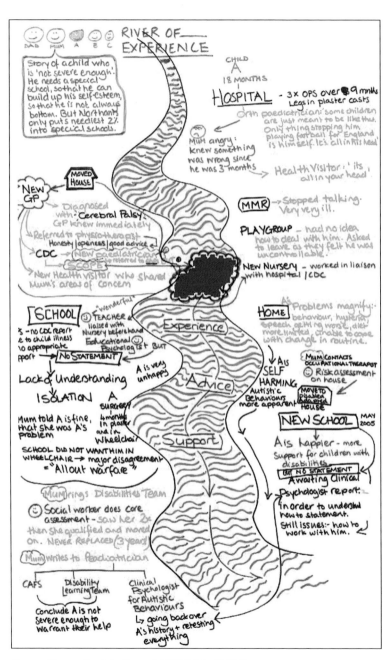

Source: Percy-Smith, B. and D. Walsh (2006)

PLATE 7

When the pictures are brought together a rich collage can be constructed which offers both 'data' in itself and multiple starting points for inquiries which have resonance across the group. See page 119.

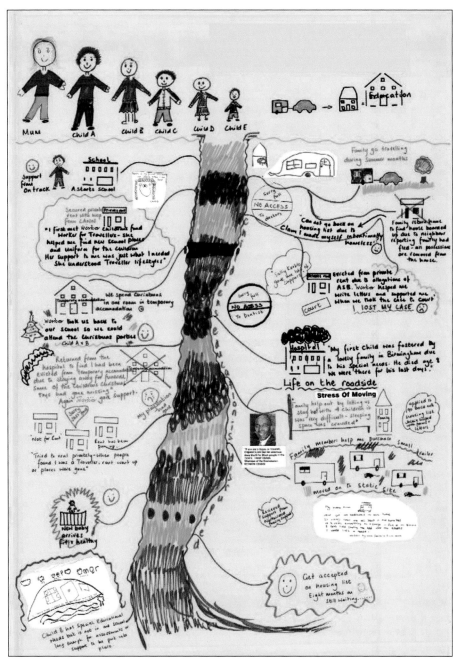

Source: Percy-Smith, B. and D. Walsh (2006)

PLATE 8

The diagrams represented on this page depict the learning architecture of two very different systemic action research projects.

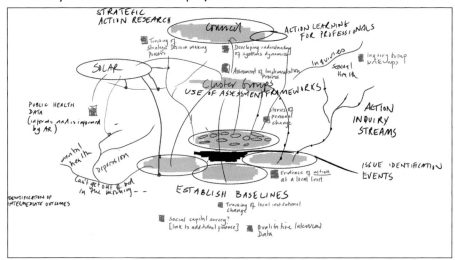

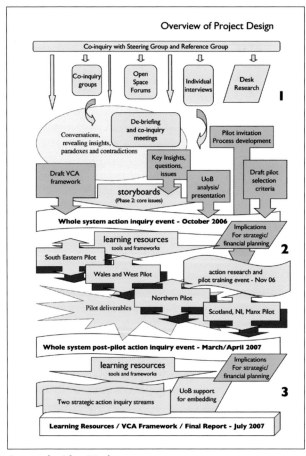

Above: Sketches for a proposed action research project which was to work across four neighbourhood regeneration neighbourhoods.

Left: Initial design of the British Red Cross Vulnerability Project (2006-7). See page 76.

Artwork: Alan Taylor

Picture E

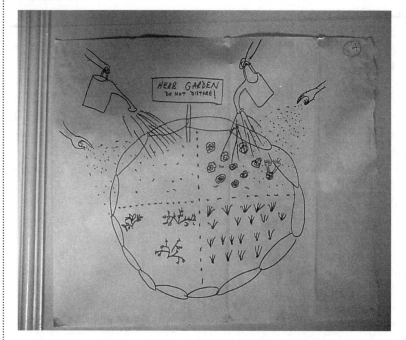

[E] Participant's comments: The herb garden is the statutory agencies all planted in segregated areas of the garden with a 'keep out' message. Our organisation throws seed and water into the herb garden and threatens the stability of the garden. The result will be a breaking down of boundaries and new growth, but the herb gardener may remove the seeds that they perceive of as being weeds. The trick is to choose the right kind of seed, the right amount and to sow in the right areas for growth and to keep watering.
Key questions:
Who controls the water and seed throwing?
Who designs the garden?
Who chooses what quality and type of seed?
Where am I in the picture? A lettuce saying 'come to me'.
Slugs – who are the slugs?

chain. Picture E is a highly structured herb garden where 'good' food is produced for the children. But all possibility of doing things differently is prohibited. There is a strict crop rotation system that will produce things in the right order. The role of the organisation is to seed the garden. It shows a highly segregated organisation, with a meaningful 'keep out' sign....

Because it was also a dominant image in the work we did with the funded groups it is worth reflecting in a little more detail on the metaphor of the organisation as a bank, handing out investment funds. This was expressed clearly in three of the drawings. In Picture C, the honey produced by the busy bees can be seen as the return on investment; in Picture E, the herb garden, it is the salads, herbs, etc that constitute the return on investment (although in that case, the produce may be going to the children). In Picture B the organisation is explicitly depicted as a bank.

The implication of thinking of the organisation as a bank is that it creates a split, where the funded groups are not part of the organisation, but are its customers. Two things follow from this. There is a split in terms of purpose, with the bank's purpose being to make a profit on its money, and each funded group's purpose being to achieve success on the business plan for which they received their loan (the idea of loan is interesting – it implies that it is not a gift/funding and that it is expected to be paid back with interest). The second point is that it takes away any political power from the funded group, left as an isolated customer for which the only connection is one of a customer relationship with their bank. Interestingly, and perhaps paradoxically, by seeing itself as a bank (that is, not as part of the same system as funded groups) the organisation is not only rendering the funded groups powerless, it is also depriving itself from the opportunity of building a strong political force capable of fighting for change within the city's Children's Services. The concept of return on investment brings up a very interesting question: who, in the city, will reap the benefits of the organisation? According to its formal documentation, it is there to benefit children in need, their families and consequently the communities in which they live. The drawings, however, suggest different pictures held in the mind of management board members. In the case of a bank/financial scenario, the bank (at the centre of the drawing) is the first beneficiary of the added value produced by the system; the funded groups, it can be argued, also benefit since the money they have borrowed enables them to go about their business. It is difficult, however, to see how the children benefit. In Picture C, the honey will only be enjoyed by humans: beekeepers, landowners, the king ... the bees themselves (funded group staff and children alike) only go about their repetitive business in the same way as they have done in the last thousands of years. It is unclear, in fact, what the organisation has done to impact positively on their existence: new hives perhaps? In any case, the sense is that the system has been organised primarily so that humans can access more honey.

The pictures also told us a lot about what management board members hold in mind about the children that their organisation works with. In many of the pictures the children are on the outside. It is mostly difficult to differentiate between children and funded group staff. This has a number of implications that may not be obvious at first sight. Perhaps the most important is that children's voices disappear within the wider system as projects are asked to 'represent' their perspective. The children's perspective will be quite different from even the closest of professionals to them. A sense of danger is present in a large number of the drawings – represented, for example, by sharks and snakes in the water. Protective clothing has to be worn to enter the world where the bees (children) live, the building site and the dangerous waters. Children are not regarded as equal citizens and their worlds are regarded as unsafe to adults.

These snapshots of systems that management board members have produced offer very different images of what the role of the organisation is and might be. They raise the question of what the primary task of the organisation is in practice:

- to perpetuate itself
- to keep busy and be seen to be busy (to support constant building work even through it is plain for all to see that it is being knocked down even as it is being built)
- to provide a return on investment
- to 'get stuck in' and jump into the ocean with the recipients of services
- to seed new initiatives
- to provide support.

This work is a good example of the way in which actionable knowledge (Argyris et al, 1985; Argyris, 1993) can be generated that cannot necessarily be proved. Even if all of the participants had agreed on an interpretation, for example that they perceived that places occupied by the children were dangerous to adults, how could we prove that this was actually the case? If, hypothetically, we could, then how could we prove that this systemic metaphor was shaping the construction and development of the system? Despite the lack of proof we are able to highlight interpretations that have resonance. These allow us to ask questions like: 'If this is what is going on, how might we change what we do in response to this understanding?'.

'**The difficulty with** pictures is that they are actually a highway to the unconscious, and as such they can actually scare people, who suddenly discover that despite their best, conscious intentions, they had been engaged, individually and collectively, in something quite different, sometimes even contradictory. The tendency is then to disown or to play down the meaning of what has emerged. A few thoughts about how to get out of that trap. The key is to place emphasis on the systemic, to move away from personal guilt and shame. The picture can then be seen as a personal representation of what has collectively been created, through collective engagement. Another important issue is to remind people that the picture represents their view of how the different, multi-layered elements are being articulated in the creation of what is happening. This is the systemic beyond their organisational system. How they have evolved to respond to the multi-level demands from all the different stakeholders. Then we can start thinking about whether the articulation of the different demands could actually take a different form; one that would better reconcile their initial, authentic, genuine intention with the structuring and organising of their work.' (Matthieu Daum)

When I was working with the SNV team in Kenya we did a similar piece of work. I asked the team to draw pictures of the relationship between their organisation, the organisations that they worked with and the issues that they were trying to address. I have found a number of guidelines useful in the practical application of this work. I am explicit that participants should not produce a 'diagram' of relationships but a metaphorical picture. They are told that they can use words, but that the pictures should come first ('draw the picture then add any words').

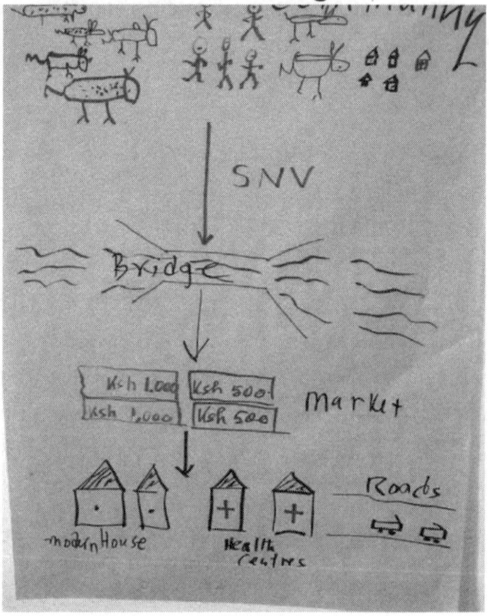

The picture opposite seemed less promising than others (because it was more diagrammatic). Yet it was enormously revealing of the system as perceived by staff. People started by asking why SNV was on one side of the bridge. 'Shouldn't it be in the middle?' 'Shouldn't it be the bridge?' A discussion ensued about SNV's bridging role. About three minutes into the conversation someone said, 'wait a minute, there isn't a bridge'. As you can see opposite what appears at first glance to be a bridge does not actually cross the river. This opened up another conversation about whether SNV depicted itself as a bridge without ever crossing the river.

Picture of SNV and bridge

We looked for systemic patterns across the pictures. We saw in four different pictures:

- a pair of binoculars
- a mirror
- a camera
- a pair of glasses.

All depicted SNV looking on from afar at where the real action was. The picture above shows SNV on the other side of the river. Another showed it on the other side of a ravine trying to throw a grappling hook over to the other side.

SNV had in recent times defined its role as working with meso level organisations (local government, local NGOs etc) and as such it did not get directly involved in the delivery of, for example, services or aid, and consequently was not engaged directly with people on the ground. As a result it could not even see what was going on. The picture below shows SNV in the top left looking toward the cooking pot. They know that something is cooking but they have no idea what

Picture of ravine

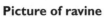
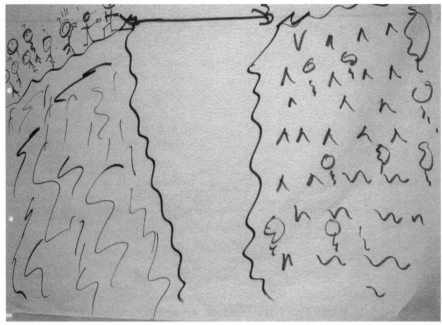

Picture of cooking pot

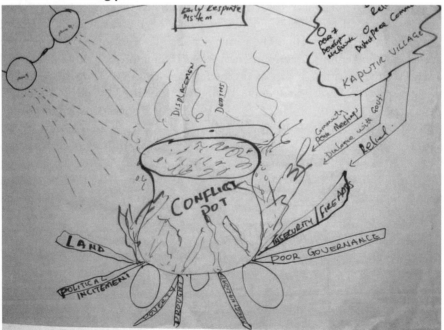

was in the pot. Not only were the contents obscured by distance but also by the steam, and of course the effect of this is multiplied as the glasses steam up. The group identifies the different tools which it uses in an attempt to see what is going on. It concluded that it needed to discard these and 'just see'. It explored what this would look like and the implications for the organisation.

The discussion challenged a core assumption (theory in practice) of the organisation, which was that focusing on meso level organisations meant engaging almost exclusively with meso level organisations. The inquiry moved on to explore the ways in which support to meso level organisations could be directly enhanced by multi-stakeholder work using an action inquiry based approach.

'Remove the glasses'

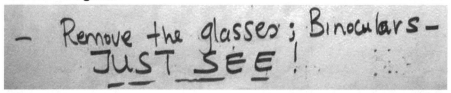

Using images to generate a different sort of evidence

Pictures can generate evidence of change. If a person or group is asked to depict an issue one year, and to depict the same issue the next year, the change may be very visible. In 2001 I was working alongside the Regional Development Agency and nine rural small towns (Burns et al, 2004 *a and b*). We ran a day session for representatives of nine market and coastal towns. One of the group drew a picture of a box. On the facing side of the box we could see the two hands and face of someone trying to climb out. The image depicted the relationship between the group and the Regional Development Agency. The picture not only captures the essence of the situation, it can be used effectively to show change. A year later this group was able to draw people climbing out of the box and to articulate how and why this change had come about. If you show people these two images next to each other, they 'know' what the nature of the change was. If alternatively you asked each group to score the strength of its relationship with the RDA and you conveyed the percentage difference to a group it would mean very little.

Source: Burns (2000)

Mapping connections to bring the wider system into view

Mapping is another helpful way to understand connections between issues and to explore their dynamic interrelationships. There is a strong emergent tradition of this sort of work that includes the drawing of rich pictures in Soft Systems Methodology (Checkland, 1981; Checkland and Scholes, 2004), and the development of mind maps (Buzan, 1991). This can be done on paper or using new technologies.

Dianne Walsh and I have started to develop interactive mind maps to enable large-scale participation. We found that most of the qualitative data analysis software was not appropriate for the job. Information tended to be organised in a hierarchical structure, and graphical material was represented very clumsily. The mind-mapping software was better and we have started to use this as a navigation tool through information generated in inquiries. For the future we are looking at the possibilities of designing our own software. This would have to have among other things:

- the ability to take multiple routes through the data
- a good graphical interface that allowed maximum participant interaction
- the ability to password-protect different parts on a map
- easy integration of images, sound files and video clips
- the ability to label relationships and interrelationships as well as the 'objects' they were related to
- very flexible hyperlinking with both text and icon labels.

Using this sort of technology to support the analysis of data within the facilitation team has been relatively straightforward. More difficulties were raised when we explored with clients the possibility of placing data onto an interactive website. This put into conflict two core principles underpinning our work: the desire, on the one hand, to be as participative as possible, and, on the other, the need to work diplomatically with sensitive information. Systemic action research to explore the development of this sort of process could be extremely valuable to the action research community.

Distilling learning to enable it to travel

Images are crucial to sense making in a participatory learning system. They provide a way of enhancing and accelerating learning within a context where conversational networks are the core conduits for knowledge generation and change. The reason for this is simple. We retain a memory of images. They connect us to the emotion generated about issues, and like a poem they capture the essence of the issue. I remember our Hounslow conference because the images play over and over in my mind. I can see the young woman with the words scrawled across her: 'I may be beautiful but I still get stressed'. I see the pictures of damaged and deformed women's breasts (see centreplate no 3) that those young women cut out to convey the pressures that they were under to have cosmetic surgery. I trust also that those images have stayed in the minds of the participants and have acted as catalysts for change in a hundred unknown arenas. In contrast, I am trying to remember what I learned from the last academic conference I attended. I am struggling to even remember what the papers were about, let alone what they said. So, like conversation, these images *are* the dissemination.[2]

The storyboards described in Chapter Four are another form of distilled learning where text and images are mixed.

Embodied inquiry

Physicality

Before discussing some of the techniques of embodied inquiry that can be used, I would like to say a few words about physicality itself. Sitting in a circle talking will not always be the best way to generate creative inquiry. Informal conversation is generative not only because people will say things that they would not in a formal situation but because they are physically moving. Because they are moving they are animated. If you talk to people in a bus queue or in the queue at a post office you will probably get a different response to the same questions asked of someone sitting down.

In 1989 I was enticed by a juggling friend of mine to spend three months working on improvisation skills at a circus school in Bristol. There I learned about the importance of movement. In moving we see things from different positions through different lenses. Through movement we build energy that feeds creativity. There is a powerful relationship between motion and emotion, and emotion is a powerful driver for both insight generation and change. Momentum lies in action. It is much easier to prevent a stationary bicycle moving than to stop one that is coming at you at 15 miles an hour. Movement is a response to power. It is no accident that social movements are called movements.

Kurt Lewin, writing in 1952, was acutely aware of these issues:

> It is a simple fact, but still not sufficiently recognized in psychology and sociology, that the behaviour of a person depends above all upon his momentary position. Often the world looks very different before and after an event which changes the region in which a person is located. That is the reason why, for instance, a fait accompli is so feared in politics. A change in position, for instance, the locomotion of one group to another changes not only the momentary surroundings but more or less the total setting. (Lewin, 1952, p 137)

Let me tell a story of my local community. This is a story both of 'living life as inquiry' (Marshall, 1992) and of the significance of the physical. I used to live in a terraced house on the edge of a park. Gangs of children used to sit on the wall of the park – hanging out, chatting, drinking, playing football. They were mostly between the ages of 14 and 16 but some were younger and a few were older. They were outside our house because the side street running off the park went up to the chip shop. For the most part they were no trouble, although some of my neighbours started to get annoyed when they played football in the road and smashed a few car windows and a house window. Things started to deteriorate when a woman who had tried to talk to them was singled out and harassed over a sustained period. Graffiti was painted across the wall of her house describing her as a whore. Things got worse. They threatened to burn her out of her house. The fire brigade came round and blocked up her letterboxes. The police were called frequently but we were told that they could not do anything unless we had witnesses to the harassment and were prepared to go to court. The children knew the law backwards, and were always a fraction of a millimetre on the right side of it. Sometimes my neighbour and I were so angry that we went out and confronted them. They just laughed at us. They knew that we could not touch them. The older children watched on as the younger ones goaded us. The whole situation seemed completely irresolvable. The woman who had been targetted planned to move out. My neighbours and I decided to try a completely different approach. Instead of engaging with the young people directly we would go out and sit on the wall ourselves. Every evening from about seven o'clock neighbours from about 15 houses sat outside on the wall drinking beer together and chatting. It had now become our social space. At first the young people were totally bemused. We got the odd comment, but they actually did not know what to do. We were visibly organised but we were not organised against them, so they did not know how to respond. After about five days some of them started to talk to us. After about ten days we had really begun to learn something about their needs. We had some respect for them and they had some respect for us. We continued to meet like this for about a month. After that the level of negative activity significantly diminished. Our physical presence had changed the field and had opened up possibilities that were not there before.

Physical playback as a process of insight generation

Perhaps the best example of transformative theatre work is that of Augusto Boal, which he began to articulate in his seminal book *Theatre of the oppressed* (1979) and later in works such as *Games for actors and non actors* (1992). I cannot possibly do justice to the long tradition of participatory emancipation work that his thinking has spawned, but the essence of Boal's work is a performance that plays out the dynamics of oppression. Having played it out once, it is then discussed (facilitated by a mediator who Boal calls 'the joker'). It is then replayed, but this time anyone can enter the scene and take it in a new direction. At each juncture in the unfolding performance new possibilities for action may emerge. The new performance becomes an expression of what could be. Possibilities are generated subconsciously through the process of improvisation. Once generated they can be enacted in the real world, just as any other inquiry outcomes. Boal's work has taken a number of different forms:

- *Invisible theatre* is a form of guerrilla theatre or public provocation, designed to elicit discussion from an audience that does not know that it is witnessing theatre.
- *Forum theatre* is the best known and most widely practised form of Boals theatre: it is an interactive form used particularly where there is a shared oppression, with a participating audience of 'spectactors' focused on gaining a better understanding of a problem or issue and testing out possible solutions.
- *Image theatre* involves communication through the sculpting of our own and other's bodies.
- *Legislative theatre* is a method in which forum theatre is used as a basis for the formulation of policy, rules or legislation in any body from school to government. (see www.cardboardcitizens.org.uk/theatre_of_the_oppressed. php)

There is a strong resonance with the action research approaches that we have been developing at SOLAR. Playing back a scene, a scenario, or process allows it (a) to be seen afresh, and (b) to be seen from multiple angles by different people. This presents opportunities for action that did not appear to be there before. In work of this sort the inspiration to create and develop solutions emerges in the moment, in the interaction, through a process of improvisation. But the improvisation does not have to take place 'live'. It can be developed as an 'unplanned simulation' in which solutions can be tried in a safe situation before they are enacted in the world.

Constellations work (Mahr, 1999) is another emerging practice that elicits insight from the embodied interrelationships between people. Ty Francis describes constellations as:

> ... a way of looking at hidden dynamics that are "below the radar" of awareness and which can entangle projects and people over long periods of time if not attended to.'(Francis, 2006)

This process was first developed as a form of systemic family therapy, but it is now used in organisations and other settings. By providing a 'living map' of the factors and forces at play in a situation, a constellation provides support for new solutions to present themselves. The physical placing of people in relation to each other within a social or organisational 'field' offers insight into the dynamics of a situation. Changing their position offers solutions.

There are important differences between Boal and constellations. At the heart of Boal's work (and incidentally that of his close friend Freire, author of *Pedagogy of the oppressed*) is an emancipatory and participatory ethos. The 'audience' is a fundamental part of the process. Described as a 'spectactor', there is always the potential for a member of the 'audience' to enter the scene. This is not always the case in constellations work where a disproportionate amount of power can be vested in the facilitator. Some contemporary practitioners such as Albrect Mahr and Vivian Broughton who are using constellations to explore political issues have introduced the principle of co-inquiry into their work.

The reason that I have offered these examples of embodied inquiry practice is to show that by working with our bodies, we can unlock systemic insights that may not be accessible through other inquiry processes (dialogic or visual), and in doing so we can extend the range of our inquiry practice.

We can use many different methods to do action research and combining them will often result in the richest systemic picture.

Action research as a hub for a mixture of methods

So far this chapter has given a flavour of inquiry practices that might offer a different sort of insight into system dynamics. This emphasis should not be taken as precluding traditional research methods. Like others who are developing systemic action research approaches (Midgley, 2000; Wadsworth, 2001) I would argue that it is crucial to challenge the notion that because we are working in a new paradigm then everything has to be based around inquiry groups. If we take this path we are likely to radically limit our field of vision and miss crucial understandings. In large system action research a whole variety of methods are likely to be used. Even more so because the terrain in which we are covering is large, the contexts are varied and political expectations are diverse. We may need to carry out surveys, monitor attendance data, establish local patterns through IMD data, engage in inquiry groups and large events, and perhaps use visual inquiry processes. What is key is that the action research becomes the hub through which analysis takes place and action is constructed. So mixed methods are likely to be a defining feature of systemic action research.[3]

It has long struck me that the police have a highly methodologically mixed approach to inquiry. In their quest to find out what happened, they follow hunches and intuitions, interpret patterns that in some way correspond to situations that they have found themselves in before, make visual connections using storyboards, use hard forensic data and psychological profiles etc. Narratives are a core part of the process. Understanding the complex dynamics of drug trafficking does not require interviews with a representative sample of drug ring participants or even a systematic review of all drug trafficking offences. It is actionable knowledge, and interestingly this sort of real world inquiry does not seem to get serious criticism from positivist science.

I would like to conclude this chapter with a scenario that has been constructed from a real world situation. It illustrates how the integration of methodologies might enable a deeper understanding of issues and the process of change:

Scenario for a 'thematic action research strand' that emerged as a result of both survey and perceptual data collection

Situated in an inner-city neighbourhood with a mixed ethnic and class profile lies a popular local primary school (Greendown), which has a waiting list of at least double the numbers of available places. As a key neighbourhood site it is a good focus for early research.

School roll and educational attainment data is obtained through the administrative data analysis. The neighbourhood observations and survey enable the location of parents and their networks (resulting from school-based interactions) to be mapped. The agent-based modelling and the one-to-one interviews help to build a more detailed picture of these networks. The survey picks up individual parental anxieties about education and records patterns of decisions they have made. This early research suggests that there are issues that could usefully be explored in an action research group. The generic action research picks up a concern that the primary school classes have 33 children in reception but by Year 6 there are only 15 in the class. It appears that many of the 'middle-class families' are moving out of the area when their children reach the age of 9 or 10 or are bussing their children to schools outside of the city.

The action research group brings together local parents, primary teachers etc. It emerges that one group of parents who were anxious about the local secondary school had negotiated that their children remained in the same class as their friends from the primary school. It worked out well for this group, and word spread through the primary school networks. As a result the following year more children were sent to the local comprehensive school. Only this time the comprehensive decided that it wanted to 'spread the influence' of the Greendown pupils and divided them across the classes. The parents were less organised and let this go without intervening. Their children started to struggle and one by one they were pulled out of the comprehensive. This restarted the process of dispersal that was further exaggerated as parents from the next year began to hear that things were not working out at the comprehensive. The action research group unravels this process through stories and dialogue. It then invites the comprehensive school to join the action research group. Here members begin to understand how the micro-decisions that they have made (outside the neighbourhood) are impacting on individual parent decisions (within the neighbourhood), which in turn have a cumulative systemic impact on the neighbourhood as a whole – significantly affecting its demographic profile. The whole group co-constructs a solution and monitors its impact. Understanding of system dynamics within the neighbourhood is enhanced by looking at the unintended outcomes of the process, the blockages, the cumulative impacts of micro level changes and so on. This helps participants to see where the possibilities for change might lie and how an enabling environment for neighbourhood change might be facilitated. This process is then played into strategic learning groups for the city.

The process outcome assessment maps the way in which parents have successfully mobilised around the issue and the environmental factors that enabled it to happen. The quality of life outcome assessment looks for a reduction in mobility in the population of parents with secondary-age children and an increase in class sizes at Year 6. It also looks to see if there is an impact on educational attainment over time at the secondary school.

An action research strand of this type would combine with parallel action research strands (with a completely different focus) to build a picture of dynamics and interrelationships within a neighbourhood.

Notes

[1] Barry Percy-Smith led the project. Dianne Walsh, Susan Weil and I provided facilitation support. The peer research process with young people was developed and supported by Barry.

[2] I am grateful to Susan Weil for the many discussions that we have had on supporting learning to travel.

[3] There has also been a strong interest in mixing methods in what Midgley describes as third-wave systemic theory (see the Introduction to this book) in order to enhance the flexibility and responsiveness of interventions (Flood and Jackson, 1991; Flood and Romm, 1996).

SEVEN

Issues for action research facilitators

Action research is a multi-skilled job. It is also one in which action research facilitators may be very exposed. This chapter looks at the complexities of action research from the perspective of action research facilitators and those managing action research projects. It explores the following key issues:

- the relationship of systemic action research facilitators to the research
- key roles for systemic action research facilitators
- recording inquiry group sessions
- support for action research facilitators.

Although many of the issues that I discuss I would see as relevant to all action research facilitators, my comments are focused on the facilitation of systemic action research.

Relationship of systemic action research facilitators to the research

Before exploring the role of action research facilitators we need to understand more about the place that they occupy within the learning system. This includes their outlook and approach as well as their relationship to the research process.

One distinction that is often made is whether the researchers are 'outsiders' or 'insiders' (Cochlan and Brannick, 2001). Are they part of the 'organisation' that they are researching, or are they coming in from outside to support or engage with those who are inside? This distinction can be problematic in a systemic action research context. Because the terrain extends beyond a single group or organisation, *most* participants will be stakeholders in the process. Stakeholders are both inside and outside because they are inside their bit of the system and outside other bits of the system. An external action research facilitator is likely to be a stakeholder only in the loosest sense – in that he or she has an 'interest' in the process working; is personality sympathetic; and may share the overarching values that successful action or intervention promotes. But they are outsiders in the sense that they do not have embedded cultural knowing of any part of the system from living or working within it (although this can change with extended engagement) and they are outsiders in the sense that the actions resulting from the process do not have the same impact on them.

What all of these people have in common is that they are part of an evolving system. They will all have an impact, and in this sense they are all participants. So the facilitator is both an outsider and a participant.

> ... if it is described as "action research", they may envisage the task as being more like that of a scientist noting the growth of plants treated in different ways and intervening with suggestions to the gardeners of more sunlight or ways of keeping off the slugs. In practice I have found using this audit as an action researcher is more like (iii) being a chemical catalyst, trying to note the change going on all around in the test-tube while you are in it and causing some reactions yourself. The difference is that a catalyst is supposed to be itself unchanged while the action researcher will learn and change too. (Heywood, quoted in Burns et al, 2004b, p 31)

It is important that action research facilitators are aware of this. It is easy to drift into extremes, believing on the one hand that you can keep an objective relationship to the research and on the other that you have a greater stake in the research than you actually do (because you are immersed in the research process and the relationships within it). Perhaps the best we can do is to try to build personal relationships of equals while recognising that there is necessarily an unevenness of power and ownership within the research process.

I deliberately use the phrase 'building personal relationships' because I have found it surprisingly common for action research facilitators to construct harsh boundaries around what part of them is in the research and what part is not. They recognise that as action research facilitators they are part of the research, but they keep their personal lives on the outside. This may be to protect themselves, or because they believe that to blur the boundary between researcher and participant is to be unprofessional, or because they think that they have nothing to offer the process, or because they recognise their power and want to minimise their impact. The same issue applies to other professionals who are participants in action research processes. Often they also bring only their role to the group. For good inquiry it is important to break through this barrier. We all have other lives. We have beliefs, experiences and lenses through which we view issues. Participants in an inquiry on smoking cessation are smokers, non-smokers and ex–smokers. Professional social care workers may themselves have been (or may be) victims of domestic violence in their own homes. A health visitor is not only a health visitor. She may also be a mother, daughter, friend, patient, artist or badminton player. She may have been bullied at school or pregnant at 16. She may be lesbian, married, a single parent or.... We cannot discard those experiences and put them in a holding bay. Not least because it is this very wealth of experience that enables sense making to emerge within an inquiry process. This 'knowing' should not be left at the door when the inquiry begins. Let me be explicit. Not only am

I saying that the facilitator must understand their role as participant, I am also saying that the process may be enhanced if they actively bring themselves into their work, Wadsworth and Epstein observed that:

> ... professional has referred to the way in which their role changes in the group. "When I come into this group I don't feel like I am a professional. I come as me". (Wadsworth and Epstein, 1998)

Returning for a moment to the reflections of Matthieu on the facilitation process, this raises an interesting question about how facilitators engage.

> MD: We had quite an interesting discussion within the facilitation development day that we did the other day, about what X called "equalisation", and that was a really interesting discussion where we were talking about do we enter the room in role, as someone from the university who is facilitating a group of people in Hartcliffe or in what way do we, in a sense, bring ourselves to the same level as the group if that's possible, level is not the right word, and equalising isn't quite the right word but it's finding a common ground, but a common ground as me as a person, and you as a person in the group; and we had an interesting discussion in that session about honesty and transparency, or about not hiding who you are, but also about creating a space in which you can be equal in this moment. (Burns and Daum, 2004)

Trust is a crucial part of an inquiry process. In a professional model participants trust the expertise, or the process, or the conduct (ethical and otherwise) of the professional. In a participative action inquiry they trust the person. If we do not come as who we are then the power differentials within a group inquiry may go unspoken but they do not go away. This does not mean that action research facilitators should feel obliged to disclose all of the details of their personal lives (none of the participants should), but they should go through the same process of judging what to disclose as any other participant. I do not believe in holding strict boundaries between facilitators and participants in adult learning situations. These reinforce the perception of the facilitator as expert and can prevent participants from taking responsibility for their own learning and the action that needs to flow from it.

None of this means that facilitators come to the process without skills. The facilitator brings process expertise including action research design, facilitation and systemic thinking. They may also have interpretative and analytical skills that can be brought to bear on the issues being considered, but they should not assume that they are the only ones with those skills or that their interpretation or approach to interpretation is better than that of other participants. They have to have authority in order to ensure confidence in the process, but this should not be confused with seniority.

Like everyone else facilitators interpret what they encounter through a particular world view. SOLAR has at various times employed action research facilitators with entirely different outlooks on knowledge and knowing. Matthieu Daum, for example, came to SOLAR with a background in group relations and psychosocial studies. The extensive quotation below illustrates the sort of interpretation that he was processing.

> MD: The insight that came through my work on the review was how smoking links to dependency, obviously you are dependent on smoking but also how perhaps smoking brings us back whether we are smokers or not, to a very primitive dependence that we have towards our mother and how this experience of dependency gets replicated, gets re-enacted in our relationship to institutions to people in authority within these institutions so, for example, as a member of staff within Sure Start I may see that I may project into the project manager, who is a woman, dependency stuff that I have towards my mother, but also how the community who's been under-privileged, under-nurtured for many years, might in a collective way, in a systemic way, regard an institution like Sure Start coming in as some kind of, how that might re-enact all this experience that we have about dependency, if you smoke as a way of dealing with your dependency, with what you didn't have, with what you've missed, and this is what we've been hearing from people who are saying, smoking is the only good thing that happens in my life, or one of the few good things, it's for me, it's my own time, it's my holiday, I can't buy myself a Porsche, but I can buy myself a packet of fags, I can buy myself time, just for myself, all this positive nurturing. If you then have an institution that comes in and says: "the way you're dealing with this dependency isn't right, you need to change", then what impact is this going to have at a very deep level? This is the insight that came up for me. (Burns and Daum, 2004)

Although this reflection was lodged at end of the project, it was not entirely untypical of the reflections that Matthieu and I worked through in supervision. Matthieu had a critical awareness of the implications of his own outlook:

> MD: But that raises the question of what is the role of the facilitator because if you are using those models in order to guide your interventions and you're not disclosing those models to the participants because, for whatever reasons, they wouldn't perhaps engage with it in the same way that you would, then in a sense, aren't you then setting

yourself up as the disengaged professional who is making judgements about people or, I don't mean disengaging in a sense that you're not present, I mean, in a sense of somebody who is apart rather than a part of. (Burns and Daum, 2004)

The issues that Matthieu raises are complex because when he did disclose his analysis he sometimes got a strong negative reaction. On the other hand, that negative reaction sometimes triggered a conversation that led to important breakthroughs. The danger lies in the positional power of the facilitator whose reflections can assume an authority that the reflections of others do not have. Because facilitators commonly do the 'writing up' they have the opportunity to reflect in depth, which most others did not have. The other issue here is that the facilitator's perspective is only one perspective. I know from the supervisions with Matthieu that our perspectives on unfolding issues were quite different. Yet despite (or because) of this we generated a deep collective understanding of what was going on through dialogue and challenge. At its best this is what happens when the multiple lenses of the different stakeholders are brought to bear on an issue. When the facilitator holds their world view lightly and recognises it as a starting point that has particular resonance with their life there is the possibility for real creative emergence.

It is not wrong for the facilitator to come in with a perspective. Wadsworth points out the dangers of any attempts at neutrality:

> The "neutral" facilitator may be doomed to fail to enter and grasp any of the relevant discourses, and instead, be only mildly trusted or mildly distrusted from all side. The outcome may be only shallow depth of understanding and weak change. (Wadsworth and Epstein, 1998, p 378)

But it can be disastrous if it is (or is perceived to be) imposed on the inquiry. In my view this outlook fundamentally distinguishes participative action research from models of action research that are rooted in either 'professional' or 'therapeutic' expertise.

Key roles for systemic action research facilitators

In this section I identify five key roles for action research facilitators:

- facilitating and supporting group inquiry
- bridging across systems
- supporting distributed leadership
- supporting peer research
- recording inquiry group sessions.

These are clearly not the only roles that facilitators will hold but they are among the most important.

Facilitating and supporting group inquiry

Self-evidently one of the core roles of a systemic action research facilitator will be to directly facilitate inquiry and or to support others to do so. The natural tendency of a group is often to identify problems and to move immediately towards solutions. If this approach is adopted then we are actually creating task groups not inquiry groups.

Matthieu Daum distinguishes between a task group and an inquiry group as follows:

> ... an action research group opens up, makes connections, makes associations between seemingly unrelated bits of experience, bits of life, bits of behaviour, whereas, a task group focuses on a particular point and acts on it. (Burns and Daum, 2004)

A key role for an action research facilitator is to ensure that the group remains open to inquiry. Perhaps the most important aspect of that process is to enable emergence in the conversation. In practice this is not always encouraged by action research facilitators. When we were recruiting for the BCI project we realised that because facilitation means very different things to different people, very good and very experienced group facilitators do not necessarily make good action research facilitators. Often facilitators are working toward a set of predetermined outcomes. They may feel that they need to have 'achieved' something at the end of each session, and as a result they can be over directive in their approach. In eliciting what they perceive to be the groups views, they strongly guide the direction of the discussion.

Other common approaches to group facilitation work badly in group inquiry situations. For example, facilitators tend to use flip charts as a way of capturing what people have said. But in my experience this disrupts the conversational flow of the meeting and separates the facilitator from the other group participants. Some inquiry group participants have commented that it has felt like going back to school.

When I have observed action research facilitation I sometimes see what appear to participants as counter-intuitive results. On one occasion I asked participants to comment on a discussion that had been facilitated at a high tempo. The facilitator was bubbly and enthusiastic and actively guided the process. Participants felt that they had been engaged and felt happy about the conversation. Another facilitator took a low key role. She intervened to guide the conversation, but did not 'run it'. After the sessions participants felt less energised and were less satisfied with it. I was observing both sessions, and in fact it was only in the second that people laughed. The conversation was deeper, the exploration went further and the conversation produced tangible outcomes. So we have to be careful that we are not drawn to over-structured inquiry styles because that is what participants are used to and expect.

Overall I have found that a good action research facilitator needs to feel comfortable with the unknown, allowing the content of the discussion to emerge. But they need to quite assertively:

- ask questions that enable participants to ask the right questions
- ask questions that enable participants to challenge their assumptions
- focus participants on the nature of relationships rather than on individuals or organisations
- challenge dominant discourses on research, inquiry and participation
- ensure that participants follow through their own emergent ideas
- explore the implications of the connections that have been surfaced
- ensure that the 'essence' of conversations is recorded.

In this way the facilitator is able to take an authoritative role in 'holding the process' while avoiding steering the content. I once described the way in which I worked with groups to a potential client. His response was 'it sounds like you are a counsellor – but to an organisation or a system rather than a person'. There is some truth in this. As an action research facilitator your role is to encourage participants to explore issues through different lenses, to pose challenges to them and to support them to take action and learn from it. This often requires you to play back to them what they have said and ask them to reflect on it. That said, the roles of facilitator and counsellor are quite different, and it is important not to confuse them. For the one-to-one counsellor a professional relationship puts a tight boundary between him or her and the 'client'. Information gleaned from the therapeutic setting should not be taken outside. In contrast, a key role of an action researcher working across a system (bearing in mind issues of disclosure and confidentiality) is to make links between all of the different people that the participants are working with. Also, inquiry is not therapy. While it is a way of breaking entrenched patterns, freeing up log jams and so on it is not an individualised process.

As well as facilitation, action research facilitators have to pay attention to the environment within which the facilitation takes place. This means ensuring that it is supported by efficient organisation and providing an environment conducive to good inquiry. To do this facilitators need to pay attention to simple things such as who is organising the next sessions and who is making the tea. In one of our groups we had an interesting confrontation about why the facilitator did not make the tea. Getting this wrong can undermine trust from an early stage in the inquiry process. When designing a project it is important to remember that building a trusting relationship with a group is crucial, and it often takes much longer than we anticipate.

It is also important to think through the practical structuring of the day-to-day work. Every action inquiry process will be different. Some people need to meet in the day, some in the evenings and so on but I have found that a regular half-day session every six to eight weeks works well, particularly if it is possible to write up the session in the other half day. It is important for inquiry sessions to be written up almost immediately – particularly where there are multiple inquiry streams. Otherwise it is easy to build up a backlog, and then it becomes difficult to remember the true meanings of what was said in the group. In organising the schedule of meetings a balance needs to be struck between momentum on the one hand and, on the other, (a) a need for participants to feel that it is part of their work, not an additional burden, and (b) enough time between sessions for action to take place and be assessed.

One of the fundamental differences between a large system action research process and a cooperative inquiry is that it is often necessary to deal with resistances within groups. A cooperative inquiry is a 'protected space' where willing co-inquirers can engage in sense making together. In a large system inquiry, stakeholders with very different perspectives are brought together. A doctor, for example, may be crucial to the inquiry but because she is imbued in a positivist tradition of research, she may spend a great deal of the session challenging the idea of action research. Those with a vested interest in the status quo often mount an attack on the 'methodology' because they do not like the 'challenging' work that the group is doing. It is often easier to attack the method than to attack the sense making that the inquiry is doing.

As well as resistances to the process, we have also encountered strong gate keeping. People in positions of power can use that power to stop people who should be involved in the inquiry becoming involved. In the Bristol project, while the ethos of the Sure Start projects was profoundly participative, there were still examples of individual professionals limiting the capacity of the community to self-organise. In one local Sure Start area, where there was a local resident who was willing to take a leadership role, this was blocked:

> '… we tried to involve the parents to go round the area to look at shops and stuff like that, she said "no! parents have got enough to do".… X is a local woman, full of enthusiasm and she makes things happen.… She volunteered to do that, I mean, I didn't ask her to do it.'

In another area, one senior manager stopped one of her staff from taking on the leadership role in an action inquiry group. She was only able to pick it up again when her manager left. In Easton (the neighbourhood that left the consortium) there was an even stronger cultural clash. Here we were instructed not to talk to parents (let alone involve them!) until they had been properly trained.

DB: 'I got into some quite heated discussion actually with X, and a couple of other people there about engaging with parents, "no you can't work with parents, they are not ready. We are going to train them. We are going to support them." I said "this process can't work if you are not engaged with parents." She said you can work with the community groups, you can't work with parents", and by the end of it they were completely irritated, so what ended up happening was that Dianne went to work with the community groups and the community groups said "don't talk to us, you should be talking to our parents".'

MD: So, that's interesting, it's almost as if you know, we can't talk to parents (…) through the chatabout group, but we can talk to them and engage them through the parents manager who's got a designated role. But there is some interesting things about dependency in that and there is clearly a pattern of other people saying that people who are enthusiastic aren't in the position to take something on. (Burns and Daum, 2004, p 18)

Even when the espoused values of the organisation are highly participative a paternalistic view of 'participation' can still be enacted by key gatekeepers. In the third example, residents could only participate once they had been prepared by the professionals. In the first two examples the problem lay with the attitude of individuals in positions of power. The surfacing of these examples could provide the basis for a fruitful local inquiry that would start with assessing whether or not there was an underlying systemic pattern. Rather than starting in Hartcliffe, Highridge and Withywood with a an inquiry group on participation, which made little progress because the discussion was too abstract, we might have done better to wait for tangible examples like these to work on. So in facilitating inquiry we often have to actively intervene to ensure that people are able to participate, and actively challenge those who try to undermine the process.

Bridging across systems

A central role for a facilitator in a large system is to make connections between different parts of the system. There are many different bridging scenarios that they may find themselves involved with. They may need to place strategic intelligence into the right arenas without identifying those who might be made vulnerable by the disclosure. Equally, they can link people who are grappling with similar problems or who are developing similar approaches to solving problems. Much is disclosed to a facilitator in different parts of the system that reveals major failures of understanding and communication:

> I became a messenger, a communicator. I saw the terrible misunderstandings, the gaps, the failings. (Heywood, quoted in Burns et al, 2004b, p 30)

In some circumstances facilitators will need to act as intermediaries, and very occasionally (although this is difficult territory) as advocates. Facilitators will also need to facilitate groups that cannot come together initially. This may be because they are in conflict, or do not think other groups are relevant to them, or because there are huge power differentials that need to be worked through before they come together, or because groups need time to make sense of their own situation before they can engage with others. Their role is to nurture the parallel development and perhaps later find ways of bringing them into relation with each other.

> If groups of people are co-constructing realities, the nominal researcher (or research convenor) cannot be "outside" this joint discourse (or indeed the separate ones which are "coming to the table"). Indeed, in order to understand, the researcher or facilitator enters each of the different discourses to grasp their structure, content and consequences. Even "going back and forth" between them may be a witnessing of the engagement in a speaking back and forth from them – or an enabling of "nature language speakers" to speak directly to one another. (Wadsworth and Epstein, 1998, p 378)

None of this is straightforward. In this extract from her work on acute psychiatric services, Wadsworth highlights the difficulties inherent in the 'bridging' roles of systemic action research facilitators:

> The "shape" of what we did seemed to involve our attempt to act as a go-between to bridge a gap between staff and from clients to staff. But our own efforts could not bridge that gap – or the moments of successfully so doing seemed so limited as to confirm that we would need to design a far less flimsy bridge. That less flimsy bridge is the model – and particularly on-site, of patients, who are employed as staff to permanently assist communication between other staff and in-patients. But for the duration of the project it felt very much like it comprised a staff salt shaker, and a consumer pepper shaker more than a handspring apart on the table-top without us realising that – if we had come from staff and our thumb was connecting with them, consumers would not have deeply trusted the effort and our little finger would not have reached them, but – coming from consumers, our thumb fell short at the other end with staff being the ones not to feel easy enough to break their silences. To have been a "neutral"

facilitator might have been to miss deeply connecting with either. Sometimes the contradictions, paradoxes and conflicts of perception and efforts to come up with ways to resolve them nearly defeated me. (Wadsworth, quoted in Wadsworth and Epstein, 1996)

In building the trust of the people that disclose issues through their own inquiries, action research facilitators can develop split loyalties that may be difficult to manage. Very often people in different locations grow to see the facilitator as 'their person'. It is very important that this impression is managed early on in the process:

> The model must perpetually work with the systems' tendency to safeguard fears and anxieties by keeping control and distance. It must instead persistently and with great care, continuously find ways to re-connect broken feedback loops, re-open lines of communication, and at the same time support and strengthen people's capacities to stay connected. As the disconnections resulting from individuals' anxiety and control responses become concretised in systems, so a model to ensure and support re-connections must also be systemic. (Wadsworth and Epstein, 1996, p 178)

This description evokes 'the image of a person with a set of knitting needles wandering across an unravelling garment and knitting in the loose threads, helping the garment to evolve, as knitters with different colour wool try to fashion the piece of clothing that is suitable for the conditions that are emerging' (Wadsworth, 2007[2]). A key part of this role is actively negotiating 'spaces for dialogue' and where necessary to use positional power to confront gatekeepers. Sometimes a facilitator will literally need to walk into the room of a senior decision maker and say 'you need to listen to this'.

The management of the emergent design of the action research is a key part of the bridging role. When an action research facilitator says 'we need some cluster groups to test the resonance of what is happening on the ground and to link it to decision making at the centre', they are bridging. Similarly if they bring different stakeholders together in a new inquiry stream then they are making necessary connections that had not been made before. The design of the research can either support or diminish the possibilities for bridging.

Supporting distributed leadership

Another crucial role for an action research facilitator is to identify and nurture distributed leadership within the system (see Chapter Five). This supports the work of the action research facilitator, diversifies the impetus for new inquiry and action and lays the foundations for a sustainable process – which will continue and grow after external action research facilitators have left.

Distributed leaders are people who can make things happen. Earlier I described an action inquiry on domestic violence that was significantly inspired by two women, who picked up the action inquiry process and ran with it. One of the women was a family link work coordinator. The other was a manager in a local family centre. Neither had direct responsibility for any domestic violence services. By taking responsibility these women:

- ensured that other professionals felt that this was a place for them
- coordinated action that had been agreed at the action inquiry group
- organised regular meetings
- ensured that group notes and any other papers were sent out
- invited new members into the group
- liaised with the formal structures of their organisations
- instilled belief that change could come about through the work of the group.

They acted as 'link people' who took joint responsibility with the action research facilitator for organising the group. Identifying 'link people' enables us to build a day-to-day relationship with the action research facilitator and can ensure swift communication between the action research facilitator and group participants, giving the process dual authority.

Between them they can organise both the practical things (for example, the when and where of meetings) and those things that derive from the actions agreed at meetings. This model also worked well in the Children's Fund work where the participation team became a key 'link' in our work with young people on inclusion and exclusion.

Figure 18: A structured relationship between facilitators and local distributed leadership

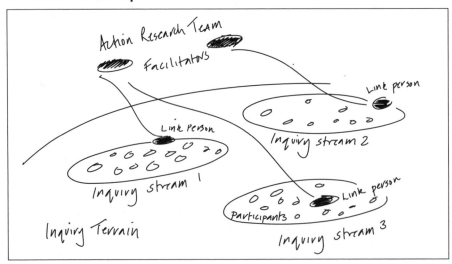

Sometimes it can be best to wait until the group is a few sessions in, so that it is clear who the group leaders are, before formalising this. I cannot emphasise too highly how important the nurturing and support of distributed leadership by an action research facilitator is.

Supporting peer research

Another important dimension of participatory action research is peer research. This is because there are limits to the depth of inquiry that can take place within an inquiry group itself. Peer research is research carried out directly by people who are affected by the issues that are at the centre of an inquiry. They carry out the research among others that share their community, life experience, neighbourhood and so on. Peer research is an incredibly important part of action research because it gives access to experiences, insights and possible actions that would almost certainly not be available to an external action research facilitator, and probably not available to many of the group. It also places ownership of the research process with the participants. Peer research can be considered as a form of distributed leadership.

Peer research does not have to be direct. We found, for example, that supporting older children to generate inquiries with younger children was an extremely effective way of engaging younger children. Because they were older they understood the process, but because they were still close in age to the younger ones, they remembered their own experience of being that age. That enabled them to ask much more relevant questions. Another example, in our Children's Fund 'large event', was to work with siblings of autistic children in order to get closer to the voice and expressed needs of those children. In Wadsworth's reporting of the psychiatric services research ex-consumers of mental health services were shown to be central to the research process:

> The involvement of former inpatients emerged as the single most important "mechanism" that the U and I project identified and trialled as a means to building in consumer evaluation of acute psychiatric hospital practice. It is a twofold mechanism: firstly, ex consumers have views they can offer in their own right and in a variety of ways about the workings of acute psychiatric hospital practice; and secondly, they can work to assist other consumers, notably inpatients, to give their views, and then facilitate those views going directly to, and being discussed by staff. (Wadsworth and Epstein, 1996, pp 63-4)

We have designed peer research processes into a number of our projects. In our project on health for young people in Hounslow my colleague Barry Percy-Smith worked for six months with a group of 10 young people (Percy-Smith et al, 2003; Percy-Smith, 2007). They developed their own insight into health through posters, stories and in one case a video. This shaped a large event attended by young people, health practitioners and policy makers. In our work with the Bristol Children's Fund on inclusion and exclusion, five Children's Fund projects carried out their own research. They interviewed each other, built a house into which they placed their aspirations and created a presentation on the experience of being autistic. What was crucial in this work was that the researchers were not just told to go away and come back with something. They were given direct support to carry out the work as they were carrying it out. This is another very important role of a systemic action research facilitator.

Recording inquiry group sessions

One of the main differences between action learning and action research lies in the recording and playback process. Action learning classically does not record the content of discussions in detail. It has a transitory quality for the participants. Individuals may capture the insights that they find valuable but the group records only the actions. Within an action research tradition recording has to encompass the process, the emergent content and researcher/facilitator reflections. The 'laying down' of this learning can take many forms: a record of a conversation, collation of 'data', visual representations of 'what is happening round here' and stories of people's experiences. Different 'methods' may be appropriate for different things. A picture or a poem may get to the heart of how people feel about things. A collage or a mind map may tell you something about how people interconnect issues. A picture may give some insight into the underlying systemic metaphors that people are working with, or remind people of something important that was surfaced.

The process that I usually use with an inquiry group is very simple. I open up a dialogue. As the dialogue unfolds I capture it in a notebook or a group scrapbook. A key question for an action inquiry facilitator is what to write down and what to write up. When I started this work I used to take notes and the write up would be a narrative summary of the notes. Over time this has changed. Now almost everything I record is direct quotes from dialogues and the stories that people tell. The quotes help people to remember the conversation and also help to capture feelings that cannot easily be conveyed in an account. These must always be recorded in the exact words that people use. Summarising a discussion is usually far less powerful, useful, actionable ... than reading a quote. I encourage others to capture phrases that resonate with their own experience. These can then be challenged and built on by the group at the beginning of the next session. Sometimes I will use a flip chart to capture visual connections and occasionally I will write a powerful quote on a flip chart, but for the most part I always sit within the group.

When I write up these notes, I do not write them up chronologically. I group quotes under key headings. Under each of these sections I add reminders of connections that were made in the group and some after-the-event reflections from me that form the basis for discussion in the first part of the next inquiry group. At the end of the record will be a list of the actions that were agreed at the meeting, and if it is not present in another part of the record, a note of actions that have been taken and any implications of those actions. These notes are sent out to a link person (if there is one) who reminds participants of the next meeting and of the actions that they have agreed to take.

One of the difficulties faced by action research facilitators is recording at the same time as facilitating. A common solution is to use the flip chart to capture 'data' as you go. I have found that, aside from separating the researcher from the participants, this tends to result in a series of superficial 'key words' that almost always fail to represent the richness and complexity of the dialogue from which it came. In 2003 I carried out a process of observations of action research facilitators. We were given clear feedback that those facilitators that had used flip charts had, by standing at the flip charts, taken themselves out of the group. This not only put them in a perceived position of power, but meant that they were unable to attend to the subtle guiding of the emergent conversation that is so crucial to the facilitation of action inquiry. So now I mostly use flipcharts for mapping relationships.

I can usually manage to record selected direct quotes while I am facilitating, especially as my style is to make strategic interventions into the conversation rather than to lead a structured discussion. Sometimes I intervene in the group by going back to a quote I have just taken down. I read back the actual words and make the connection with what they have just said. I might give some tentative suggestion of the implications. This is a way of using recording live that has the added benefit of giving confidence to the participants that they are being listened to and that their thinking is being used.

Another more interactive approach that I have used is to work with a large-scale A3 book to record themes, quotes, maps of relationships, stories and reflections with the group as they are going along. This also serves as a learning history that the group can constantly refer back to as it develops. It allows groups to keep fresh the work that they have done in previous sessions as they continue to work.

More recently I have used a tablet PC connected to a projector to record (like a flip chart) and to project onto the screen or a wall as I record it. This also has the advantage of being a live record, but like an interactive white board, it allows us to change things as we are going along, or to save one version and then develop the map in a different way on another version. It also supports trust in the group as they know what is being recorded.

Sessions may also be taped, but this is entirely in the hands of the groups. Some feel comfortable and some do not. However, it is far more important that we do not exclude people. The purpose of the tapes is not only to make available detailed transcriptions (although we may occasionally want to do so), but to ensure that key phrases and stories can be recorded in detail (not summarised or paraphrased). As I have already said, it is the words that people actually speak that often hold the nuggets of insight that help the group to move forward. Susan Weil and many action researchers in the CARPP community (Centre for Action Research in Professional Practice, University of Bath) are strong advocates of taping.

> **'I tape, because** when people are immersed in an inquiry, and insights emerge at the edge of that inquiry which cannot appreciated now, they can be re-visited later. Embodied knowing in practice is often operating in advance of the capacity to vocalise or theorise this.' (Susan Weil)

My feeling is that tapes are useful as a verbal transcript to go back to where necessary. There will be times when it is important to have the detail of what was said. But equally, in a large system inquiry with multiple inquiry streams it may be too much to routinely transcribe and analyse all of the tapes, and it is important not to set expectations that are too high.

Recording large events raises a different set of issues. Here we usually have lots of parallel dialogues that cannot all be recorded by a single facilitator. As I mentioned earlier, I have seen too many of these events waste the insight that is generated on the day because they have not paid sufficient attention to recording. I have usually found it to be a good idea to ensure that at least one person on each table takes responsibility for writing up. But even this can be unreliable. So now I ask for these people to stay at the end of the event for 30-45 minutes to sit down and record there and then. This does work well. It is far better to lose an hour's discussion in the day but have the work that has been done properly captured than to have an extra hour that everyone has forgotten within a week. One method of recording that I first encountered in a 'world cafe' event run by Juanita Brown and Susan Weil[2] is to record on paper tablecloths. In a world cafe event participants are arranged at tables 'cabaret style'. Multiple time-limited conversations are opened up and after a set period of time people are asked to stop talking. Each of the tables has a white paper tablecloth on which participants are encouraged to write or draw anything that conveyed an important part of their conversation. They are then asked to change tables, with one person remaining as the 'host' who can link the conversational threads. The host uses the tablecloth to link the discussions. The new group are encouraged to develop the conversation and continue to write or draw on the tablecloth. This can work extremely well as a 'process' tool (see also p 114), but as a 'record' it risks only catching the headlines of the emergent conversation. So, just as with open space events, without adequate recording the process will frequently triumph over content. Having said that, if time is given to collecting and analysing the tablecloths by someone who was there, the material generated can be incredibly rich. In one of our recent events with the British Red Cross, where facilitators took responsibility for writing up, they were able to take the tablecloths and write them up. This worked extremely well. Bits of the tablecloth can be digitally photographed to support bits of the write up. These trigger memories for participants who were there.

There is an important methodological question to explore here, and that is the question of context. In much qualitative research and particularly in participative work it is regarded as crucial that 'data' is not separated out from its context. Action research theory underlines this because all knowledge is regarded as contextually specific. Yet sometimes the whole story can get in the way. It may be that the whole story needs to be written up 'behind the collage' but the collage is what enables us to identify connections through resonance. A line of a poem or even a few words juxtaposed in a poem can convey meaning that would get completely lost in full narratives. Furthermore, in complex inquiry there is a real problem of data overload. A poem or a collage (to use the cliché) allows us to get to the heart of the matter.

Support for action research facilitators

> But let me emphasize that this kind of research makes demands on the research worker that are far more severe than those made by the specialised and isolated kind. It requires of him a more advanced and many sided training, and in addition a personality which can sustain, in suspension, complex wholes and which can entertain – yes, and be drawn and impelled by – human values and policy purposes while yet holding them disinterestedly far away. (Neilson, 2006, p 393)

Not only do action research facilitators have an incredibly difficult and complex task to do, they are immersed within a web of complex relationships that they have to manage. They can quickly become exposed to too many stressful relationships. Somebody who is facilitating multiple inquiry streams is constantly engaging with people and each one of those relationships has the potential to go wrong. The tension to be absorbed by facilitators is very high. This can put them under great strain and is quite different from a 'non-participant' researcher role where there is a degree of protection from the process. In traditional research the researcher can 'hide' behind the method. If people are angry their anger is recorded but the researcher does not have to build bridges across the discord. The systemic action research facilitator has responsibility for making connections across the system. This means that they continuously have to 'hold the whole'. Again this is different to traditional qualitative work that can be relatively easily compartmentalised and sequential.

Action research facilitators also have to put a lot of emotional energy into holding the anxiety of the group within an emergent process. People get anxious when they have talked around an issue but have not yet come to a solution. Much of that anxiety gets directed towards the facilitator.

Furthermore, if as Lundy and McGovern (2006) argue:

> Action research methodologies are framed by a commitment to social justice, giving voice to those who are usually "silenced", challenging structures of oppression and acting *with* ordinary people to bring about social change. (Lundy and McGovern, 2006, p 49)

then there will often be an element of risk in the process. Mostly this will involve engaging with people's anger, resentment, blame, challenges to authority and so on, but occasionally there may be risks of violence. This makes good supervision essential. A good supervisor can provide another lens through which to look at issues, aiding the sense-making process. They may also be able to spot opportunities for action that the group and the facilitator are missing. They can provide pastoral support to the researcher as well as methodological support. It is also worth mentioning that in a large system project, a team can become too stretched and task-focused. This may limit the potential to make the connections that need to be made, so it is also very important to build regular team reflection days into the process.

Conclusions

Action research facilitators should recognise themselves as active participants in the process. They should explicitly take a position as co-learners in the process and they need to be present both in role and as a person.

Good facilitation of action research depends on mobilising passion and building trust. It encourages emergence rather than pushes for solutions, and it sometimes requires the action research facilitator to go out on a limb and make strategic challenges.

Systemic action research is a highly skilled complex job that needs good support from supervisors and teams. It is crucial that this is built in.

Notes

[1] Yoland offered this metaphor in her reflections on the draft test of this book.

[2] 'Learning on the Run' (1999-2001), a project directed by Susan Weil for senior health service managers funded by the UK NHS Executive.

EIGHT

Quality and ethics in systemic action research

Quality in systemic action research

Much of the debate on action research quality has emerged in response to a perception that action research is vulnerable to arguments that it is not 'scientifically' robust. Various responses to this have been advanced. Checkland and Holwell's (1998) view is that because action research is not repeatable, the only way that it can claim validity is for it to clearly articulate its methodology in advance:

> Our argument here is that the aim in AR [action research] should be to enact a process based on a declared-in–advance methodology (encompassing a particular framework of ideas) in such a way that the process is recoverable by anyone interested in subjecting the research to critical scrutiny. (Checkland and Holwell, 1998)

But this does not take into account the sorts of emergent processes that we have discussed in this book. Peter Reason and colleagues have argued (Bradbury and Reason, 2001; Reason, 2006) that within a participatory research paradigm a notion of quality is more important than notions of validity, attribution, reliability, repeatability and transferability. Validity is not relevant because it presumes one truth. Complexity theory renders the notion of linear causal attribution unrealistic. Reliability suggests that 'experiments' must be able to be repeated and produce the same result. But as we have seen, all social processes are contextually situated and subject to multiple influences. Not only is it impossible ever to repeat the same process, but even if you could, you would never get the same result. And as Greenwood and Levin point out, while generaliseability is still important, action research facilitators would not describe it in the same way as would positivist science:

> AR [action research] does not generalize through abstraction and the loss of history and context. Meanings created in one context are examined for their credibility in another situation through a conscious reflection on similarities and differences between contextual features and historical factors. (Greenwood and Levin, 1998, p 84)

Reason articulates a more emergent view of quality:

> My argument then is that quality in inquiry comes from awareness of and transparency about the choices open to you and that you make at each stage of the inquiry; and as Lyotard might suggest, creatively making and articulating quality rules as you go along. Quality comes from asking, with others, what is important in this situation? How well are we doing? How can we show others how well we have done? I would also suggest that it is not necessarily a question of whether you have done well, but of how well you have done, and whether you have done well enough for the claims you may wish to make. It is through understanding the choices that have been made that judgements can be made about the nature of the knowledge and practice that has been generated. (Reason, 2006)

For Reason, like Checkland and Holwell, quality is guaranteed through an explanation of why we have made the choices that we have made, but here it is embedded in an iterative process that develops through the cycles of action research. While I would broadly agree with this approach it is not without difficulties. One problem with the emergent process described is that although cyclical, it still assumes a linear relationship between deliberation and action. Richard Bawden expressed this beautifully in his address to the 2003 ALARPM world congress (Action Learning, Action Research and Process Management international association), when he described action research cycles as 'a series of bent straight lines'. From the perspective of an individual agent it could be argued that there is always a process of deliberation and planning preceding action even if it is highly accelerated and almost instantaneous. But when we are looking at multiple interdependent actions where every action changes everything else around it, I am not convinced that the process can ever be as sequential as this. Linear cycles can be attractive if we want to demonstrate the sequential logic behind the decisions that we make and the interpretations that we draw. But as we have identified earlier, actions cannot always be attributed to simple causal roots.

> **'The people to** whom I describe the "mental architecture'" of action research get excited when they think about there being logic in their own daily "research" or "evaluation" practice, and that mastering a simple model of this helps them to better tackle their next inquiry. This suggests to me that tracing complex chains of this-leads-to-that causality can supply helpful evidence within a bigger picture or overarching inquiry process. It can of course never adequately describe the whole of life itself.' (Yoland Wadsworth)

In an improvised process, action can lead to action without deliberation; combinations of factors change the environment shifting the flow of action along a different course; change may result from multiple actions taken in different places for different reasons and so on. Just as in the real world, decisions about what intervention to make, how to guide and shape the action research and so on, may be complex processes of 'real time' judgement. Trying to rationalise these might be as realistic as trying to rationalise each decision in an improvised theatrical performance. As I have already illustrated, even some of the more structured action research projects carried out by SOLAR staff and students have much more the flavour of a collage than a systematically designed research project.

In their introduction to my paper on large system processes in evaluation (Burns, 2006a) Bob Williams and Iraj Imam (2006) wrote the following:

> In previous chapters you have been exposed to the smooth machine of method. Each method has been burnished over the years to give off a shiny aura of confidence and predictability. In contrast Danny's paper shows you what a systemic inquiry often feels like; a messy and sometimes confusing brew of method, inspiration, success, failure, negotiation and above all learning. Pulling people away from the traditions of linear cause and effect often creates confusion and uncertainty. Which is why, at least in Europe and Australasia, there has been a very close relationship between action research and systemic inquiry. (Burns, 2006a, p 181)

I wrote myself in that article:

> In this approach there is no formal system modelling or process-modelling characteristic of much systems work. This is an important point because although large system inquiry facilitators will want to take into account many of the key factors identified in for example Soft Systems Methodology or Total Systems Intervention, their *systematic* approach runs counter to the ethos of our work. We have found that many of the people we have worked with have been happy to discuss issues, tell their stories, and even try to understand the systemic dynamics of which they are a part, but begin to withdraw as soon as the process becomes too "modelled". I suspect this is partly because the model can never do justice to the complexity of their reality. It is also because working through the detailed steps of a complex model will often fail to sustain the interest of non-researchers. Maintaining engagement is crucial, because it is participation that provides the underlying legitimacy and validity for the analysis. (Burns, 2006a, p 192)

While there can be an 'emergent order' that enables meaning to be assembled systematically, it is not systematic in the sense of following a set of predetermined steps that define a methodological process or model. This makes justifications of action research based on method problematic. Quality is not denoted by following a set of criteria, or systematically working through a process. It is denoted by the researchers' skills in responding flexibly to the emerging demands of the research. Quality may depend on, for example, our capacity to identify and act on resonances, and our skill in interweaving a collage of insights (each of which may have emerged in completely different ways for completely different reasons). So if the logic of method is not intrinsically an indicator of the quality of action research, what might it be?

As Greenwood and Levin point out, action research must be credible, and

> ... only knowledge generated and tested in practice is credible. (Greenwood and Levin, 1998, p 81)

In terms of the content of the research we need to assess whether it has produced a depth of insight. This will depend on the extent to which it has been able to build a systemic understanding of the dynamics of change. This in turn will require multiple inquiries to ensure that a diversity of perspectives are articulated, providing a strong foundation for 'triangulation' and 'resonance testing'. A high quality action research project must also be able to show how and why it has made judgements about boundaries. Ultimately, good quality action research will produce actionable knowledge (even if clear outcomes cannot be demonstrated). So to assess quality we need to keep track of what action results and what is the result of action.

There are still challenging questions to be asked within the action research community. Quality criteria for action research cannot exist in abstract. They are fundamentally connected to what we are trying to do. A good hammer may enable high quality nail banging, but is unlikely to enable high quality sawing. So if the purpose of action research is social and organisational change then it has to be able to demonstrate its applicability to the wider world, and I am not convinced that all action research can do this. I have, for example, seen PhDs that are based on first-person action research that appear to me to be entirely introspective and at times self-indulgent. This does not mean that they do not have quality; only for the purposes of social change they do not have quality. Let me take this argument a few steps further. If we accept the central premise of this book, then good quality action research has to be systemic in its outlook. Without this it is unable to work effectively with the complexity of the real world. We have seen that in order to build a systemic picture an inquiry has to be rooted in multiple perspectives. This means that even at a local level quality has to involve more than an individual. What flows from our discussion of systemic thinking is that to be of high quality the research must:

- involve action to see how things work out
- ensure exposure to ever-increasing circles of peer review
- explain the interconnections between diverse sources of data
- employ multiple methods in multiple arenas to check that our conclusions are relevant to more than just one bit of the picture.

So what does systemic action research add to the robustness of the research process?

First, it enables us to understand the dynamics of change. If we are able to witness what happens between *a* and *b* rather than logically deducing it through predictive chains of causality, then our analysis is likely to be more accurate. Systemic action research takes that process a stage further. Because multiple inquiry strands are connected into wider social networks there is a real possibility of understanding the unintended consequences of actions as they cross systemic boundaries.

Second, by creating multiple inquiry streams, systemic action research, almost by definition, triangulates data. Patterns are identified through multiple starting points. They are then tested through processes of resonance. Resonance testing is more socially robust than representative analysis because it tells us about the importance of issues, not only their incidence.

> Rigorous evidence based on action inquiry requires a dense network of inquiry groups through which insight can be generated and corroborated. The quality of the meaning making process (analysis) lies in the exposure of information, reflections and interpretations to ever increasing circles of peer review at multiple levels within the system. What should be clear by now is that the methodology *is* the gradual creation of a dense action inquiry system. In contrast to the traditional process of collecting and analysing data and then disseminating it, the inquiry and resultant action *is* part of the data, and its journey through the networks of individuals and groups *is* the dissemination. (Burns, 2006a)

Third, like other forms of action research social robustness is assessed partly in the capacity of the process to generate actionable knowledge.

Fourth, flowing from the above, systemic action research can be judged on the actions that it generates and the impact of those actions. This does not mean that if it does not deliver tangible outcomes it is of poor quality, but if there is evidence of it generating significant action that leads to significant outcomes this would suggest quality.

Fifth, the systemic action research process not only involves extensive documentation but it interrelates different data strands as the process evolves. Records of each inquiry group meeting are produced; the evidence processed in those meetings is compiled; live analysis is constructed that can be compared with later interpretations and so on. The process continually produces dynamic data that in time becomes a longitudinal record.

Sixth, because the process works through networks and in the informal spaces it picks up crucial information and insight that does not appear in many alternative forms of research. The richness of the data is infinitely greater than simple question and answer data.

Seventh, one of the great strengths is its participatory ethos that means that quality criteria can also be generated by the participants. These criteria came from one of our projects:

- Has it generated innovative action?
- Has it led to greater understanding?
- Has it generated insight into disabling patterns within the system?
- Has it developed strong distributed leadership?
- Has it led to the integration of evaluation, policy and practice development?
- Has it built effective cross-boundary working and relationships?

Of course, just like any research, not all action research will be good research. It is also worth bearing in mind that the quality of action research generated across a large social and organisational system is inevitably going to be variable. This is particularly true of systemic action research that has multiple strands. One strand of inquiry may be completely transformative; another may go round and round in circles never quite getting to the bottom of the problem. So parts of the research process may demonstrate quality while others do not.

Good quality research is also ethical research, which takes us to the next section.

Ethics in large system action research

There are ethical issues raised by action research, and there are particular ethical issues raised by large system action research. In this chapter I explore both.

In traditional research there is an assumption that the researcher knows best and that only the researcher can make sense of data that arises from the research. In action research the assumption is that 'stakeholders' are likely to be better placed to make sense of the complex systemic dynamics of which they are a part, and make judgements about how such knowledge might be applied. In large system action research the terrain may be very large, so a wide range of stakeholders may be involved, all of whom have different views and interests. As a result a significant part of the action research process involves negotiating those interrelationships across different inquiry streams. This constantly raises ethical dilemmas about who to bring into relationship with who, what information to share and how.

Action research involves human interaction, dialogue, differences of opinion, strong emotions and so on. In this sense it is inherently more risky than many other research approaches. In human interaction things can go wrong as well as right. People can get upset or angry with each other. They can misunderstand each other and talk past each other. It is not possible to hide behind the research method when things get difficult. This means that an ethical way of being, which relates to human interrelationships, is likely to be more important than procedural ethical codes.

In the sections that follow I explore some of these issues under the following headings:

- informed consent, ethical regulation and other formal processes
- individual protection versus the resolution of community problems
- ethical implications of narrowing boundaries
- researching from a stance
- researcher power in large system processes
- resonance, peer review and democratic processes

Informed consent, ethical regulation and other formal processes

Increasingly social research is subject to the scrutiny of ethics committees before it is carried out. In health service research in the UK it is difficult even to interview a senior manager without ethical approval. Within this process, one of the emerging norms is that participants should give informed consent to participation in research. A recent publication of the Social Policy Association (Becker et al, 2006) ranked 'informed consent' as the 6th of 35 factors identified as a quality criteria for social policy research. A total of 66% of the sample of 251 specifically identified it as a quality criteria. At face value this seems to be a laudable way of protecting the individual against abuse, but if our purpose is to create social change, then it is deeply flawed. 'Informed consent' as currently articulated creates a number of serious problems for systemic action research facilitators.

First, the way in which relationships are conceived in participatory action research is quite different to that of traditional social research. Social research guidelines talk of 'human subject' research, but if the researchers are not subjects but co-researchers or co-inquirers then the research is not being done to them. There are still issues of power that need to be addressed here (particularly when working with children), but these are unlikely to be answered by a consent form.

Second, because action research is an emergent process, much of it cannot be specified in advance. As we have articulated in Chapter Four, it is possible to articulate a holding structure for the emergence, and to outline the path that the research is likely to follow, but even that is likely to change to some degree. The content of the inquiries is even more difficult to predict. While we may be clear about the question, issue, problem or topic that we are exploring, we do not know what will emerge through the conversations. If we do not yet know that a major issue is going to emerge, we do not know that we need to set up a new inquiry stream, and we do not know who will be involved in it, or what it will lead to and so on. In large system action research it is not even clear that the consequences of our work will all be visible let alone attributable to the research. One of the implications of this that we explored in Chapter Two is that we are necessarily working with partial knowledge. This means that while it is always possible to 'consent' in advance to an emergent process it is impossible to specify what that will involve. Susan Boser (2006) articulates this position very clearly:

> Informed consent and confidentiality cannot be assured in an action research process in the same way they are handled in conventional research. For instance, informed consent presents a problem as it is currently construed. Participants cannot give informed consent to research activities in advance because the full scope of the process of the research is not determined in advance by one individual (Williamson, 2002). Rather research activities are typically negotiated by participants at each stage of the action research cycle. Thus participants will have a voice in determining what these research processes, will be. However they can only begin with the knowledge that this will be a negotiated process and elect to participate or not as the process unfolds. (Boser, 2006, p 12)

In large system action research this process is amplified, because the design of the whole process is constantly negotiated.

Even in a highly specified local group context the assumption that those giving formal written or verbal consent fully understand the implications of what they are doing cannot be taken for granted. How can you know what a process of dialogue will trigger? The vignette that follows illustrates many of the complexities that can arise when engaging interactively with social issues.

One of the most powerful group processes I have facilitated was a session of a Children's Participation Learning Network. The network initially involved adults who were working with children's projects and children's services across the city. The meeting was held in a relatively small room. People were standing around the edges. It was hot. One of the participants (let us call her Maria) had offered to show a film that had been made with young people about their experiences of coming into this country and going to school for the first time. I remember a little boy talking about the moment that he first felt able to put up his hand to ask a question – the moment that he first felt included. The film finished and a dialogue ensued. The discussion was very emotional. We went around the room and each of 25 people spoke of how they experienced the film. Three broke down in tears as they recounted their own stories of coming into this country for the first time perhaps 30 or 40 years ago. Layered on this was a heated discussion about the ethics of the film itself. Most of the reflections were constructive. The interviews had been carried out by young people, but it had been edited by adults. Would it have looked different if the children had edited it? The participation team and the project worker agreed to try a different edit. Then perhaps we would look at the two films together and learn something. But other comments were harsher. One woman said that the focus was on the 'wrong' children and gave a distorted view of the school that the film was made in. Maria (who incidentally was heavily pregnant – potentially raising other ethical issues) got upset and left the room in tears.

This example raises an important question about who decides what is acceptable and what is not. Some participants in the aftermath of this meeting were unhappy that a meeting that made some people so upset was allowed to proceed. Many more felt that it was precisely because it touched people that the learning was so powerful. Three years on when I talk to participants about the network, this is the meeting they all remembered. Its power lay in the raw exposed emotion, in the close physical proximity of the participants, in the images on the screen. When working with emotions there is always risk involved. When working with the most important issues there is always emotion involved. So an ethic of risk minimisation means that we will often fail to engage with the most important issues.

'**Participative action research** is closely associated with the idea of empowerment. Underlying this is the idea that we are adult, human beings, who think and feel a range of different things, and are responsible for managing how we behave in relation to what we think and feel. Empowerment is about enabling more favourable conditions, not about protecting people. The tendency to move to considering adults as vulnerable is actually a very disempowering process.' (Matthieu Daum)

'**There are two** particular issues that I think should concern us in the increasingly bureaucratic field of research ethics. Firstly, submission forms now routinely include questions that focus on the possibility of distress to research participants. This often leads researchers to respond by indicating that they will arrange for counselling or therapy for the "distressed". In this, we are seeing a shift towards constructing the researched as potential victims. Secondly, processes of significant learning challenge taken for granted assumptions. This can be simultaneously enabling and disabling to participants. There are periods when we yearn to go back to the comfort zone of our previous assumptions and ways of working, while at the same time, we need to overcome our anxiety about alternatives. What concerns me is that many taken for granted assumptions about ethics favours research that does little to challenge or disrupts the status quo.' (Susan Weil)

Another issue that arises in relation to consent is that of formality. There is a close relationship between formality and exclusion. Formal consent formalises the research. Often those who are most vulnerable in our society are least likely to engage in a formal process. If we confront people with forms we often generate suspicion that was not there before. Because they are used to seeing consent forms in the context of high-end medical interventions where the consequences of something going wrong is very high, they are immediately thinking about what might go wrong.[1] For other people forms have the hallmark of bureaucracy and the state. Many researchers will have encountered difficulty in gaining consent from, for example, sex workers, those engaged in criminal activities or young people who are not at school. Often it is far more effective to just 'hang out' and build a relationship. Sometimes we learn as much by doing things with people as by asking them about things. In this way we build a rapport, and might later have a greater chance of finding out why they are doing what they are doing. If I set up a formal interview it is doubtful that young people truanting from school will even turn up. Why would they? They do not go to school!

It is often necessary for 'the research' to travel to where the people are, rather than the people coming to the research – for example, by going to events that are already happening such as a fun day you might gain access to parts of a community that are not normally accessible at other times of the year. Alternatively action research facilitators might attend a Sure Start drop-in. In action research processes the informal often provides the most crucial data yet in much research only formal material is considered legitimate. Crucial insight might lie in:

- the emotional responses of participants
- the things that are said informally outside of interviews
- the relationship between things that happened before the research commenced and that which is happening during it
- the material that is edited out of the story.

The formal interview is considered to be legitimate. The informal comment made in the corridor as the researcher is being shown out of the room is discarded even if it brings into question everything that was said in the interview:

> ... **"formal" qualitative** interviews can be critiqued because the interviewee is much more likely to construct their story in a way, consciously or unconsciously, which is more acceptable to themselves and to their idea of what the researcher will find acceptable. Picking the bits where the interviewee is "off guard" will indeed be much more revelatory; and much more an evidence of what may be going on than a formatted, self-edited story. In that context, it is the very notion of a consent form that should be questioned; for rather than demonstrating the interviewee's consent to be interviewed, it might actually serve the much deeper function of manifesting

> the INTERVIEWER'S consent to be told an embellished, formatted, self-edited, and somewhat-far-from-reality story by the interviewee. (Matthieu Daum)

One group participant put this very nicely in a piece of work that Susan and I did with a health network in London. She said that the most important material often lies 'on the cutting room floor'. By this she meant that in answering a question, or in creating a narrative that appears coherent to an audience, we often leave out crucial parts of our story. What is interesting about the cutting room floor metaphor is that once it has been cut the material is not retrievable. It is swept away, and the only version of reality that is left is that represented on the film. This can amount to writing people's perceptions out of history, which is in itself coercive and exploitative.

Many research ethics committees assert that material generated prior to the formal start date of the research cannot be used. This is because the data emanating from that research is not subject to the appropriate consents. Yet if the researcher is part of the research then it is impossible for them not to bring in their past, because their whole history is part of the research. If they have explored something crucial to their research prior to getting research ethics committee approval, is it ethical that they leave it out? This is another example of the effects of boundary placement on research that I discuss later in this chapter. Where you place the boundary materially affects the insight that it is possible to generate.

Individual protection versus the resolution of community problems

Sometimes in the interest of protecting the individual, we can jeopardise our understanding of a systemic problem that affects a whole community. In my view if we are to understand the dynamics of negative social norms, it is important to create spaces where people can talk openly about things that they would not otherwise disclose to the authorities. Action inquiry groups can be a space in which the unspoken is spoken. If we want to understand why domestic violence is a social norm within the community, we need to hear the stories that are not being told. These may include not only those of people who are in fear of their partner, but the stories of those who fear the consequences of revealing their circumstances to the state.

There are places where people can talk confidentially about issues that concern them. They might, for example, go to a doctor, a counsellor or a trusted figure in their local place of worship to talk without fear of disclosure. However, while this serves certain purposes (people can talk to someone about their problems and perhaps get support without fear of intervention), it does not necessarily enable something to be done about the underlying social problem. This in my view is an important role for an action inquiry group. In other words, if things that would not otherwise be disclosed emerge within an inquiry process, and these help us to understand the problem at a systemic level, then we should be ethically obliged to protect this space.

Clearly we need to be mindful that individuals also need to be protected, and if we believe someone to be at risk (particularly a child) then we have a responsibility to do something about it. But I would argue that it is more ethical to work with these issues than leave them because we fear the consequences of individual disclosure. One informal solution to this problem has been to encourage people to tell their stories in the third person, so that it is not explicit who they are talking about. This may work in traditional research where these accounts are the primary data source but it is more problematic when it is the dialogue that is central. If a mother is able to say 'when I was hit by my partner my little girl used to stop eating', and another person says 'I hadn't thought of that, my Billy started to get thin about that time, I wonder if that was connected', and then they start to explore what was going on, the possibilities for understanding and for generating action are opened up. If they fear to disclose this information because they fear that their children might be taken away then we have a problem. This issue is crucial for systemic action research because its primary concern is to generate action and understanding through an understanding of system dynamics. If an issue affects 30% of the population then we are dealing with the tip of the iceberg if we treat the problem at the individual level rather than at the community level.

In the BCI project we took a position that was entirely pragmatic. If concerns were raised that related to child abuse then we were obliged to disclose it. If issues were raised that concerned adults (such as domestic violence) then it would not be disclosed. We also ensured that the action research facilitator had a social work supervisor who he could talk to about any issues of concern. Nevertheless, an interesting observation was made in the domestic abuse action research strand of the BCI project:

> How can Sure Start work productively with organisations that don't share its statutory duties, without reducing it to its statutory obligations? In other worlds it is likely that WISH (Women Involved in Self-Help) will achieve some very good work precisely because it doesn't have statutory requirements linked to child protection and can therefore work with women with zero threat of CP procedure. (review of action research group on domestic abuse)

Ethical implications of narrowing boundaries

A decision that is ethical in one sphere may have unintended unethical consequences in another sphere. Frequently narrow boundaries are drawn to avoid confronting the ethical implications of impacts that lie outside of that boundary. In Chapter Two, drawing on the work of Gerald Midgley and others, I illustrated the way in which the drawing of different boundaries around an issue can lead us to completely different conclusions, In that case the issue was the routine catheterisation of older people:

> If we assess the micro ward practices solely in the context of a budgetary constrained clinical environment, we may conclude that the ward is efficiently managed. If we draw into our analysis the consequences of dependence for the patient we might conclude that the cost of that efficiency is too high. If the boundary is taken wider to include the social care system, then not only does it become apparent that there is a negative impact on the social care system, but this is leading to a much higher cost for the hospital. (Burns, 2006a)

I also explored issues that were raised in relation to NGO intervention against FGM in Kenya. Here, if the boundary is drawn around the specific issue of FGM, then it could be argued that it is ethical to remove young girls from that threat, but if we are aware that the longer-term implications of this for the girls are that a significant proportion will end up as sex workers, then it could be considered as entirely unethical. In Chapter Five we explored some of the issues relating to AIDS interventions in Kenya. Here, if the boundary is placed around the individual we might draw different ethical conclusions to if it is drawn around the community. It is not my place to judge; the important thing here is to understand that the way in which we draw boundaries around our inquiries has profound ethical implications.

Returning for a moment to quality criteria, one strong indicator of quality is that systemic action research has a process of boundary critique built into it. A considerable amount of traditional research produces highly spurious results because it draws conclusions about causal relationships within highly prescribed narrow boundaries, seeing as irrelevant the effects of those relationships across boundaries.

Researching from a stance

One of the key definitions of good action research is that the research has to stay inquiring. The researcher has to be able to challenge his or her own assumptions throughout the research process. Nevertheless all social research starts with a set of values and in my view research *can* be built on a clear political and ethical stance. To reject this position would be equivalent to suggesting that no theological research could take place without first proving the existence of god.

One of my students has been carrying out PhD research into how collective will can be awakened against climate change. After two years she had to take a progression examination.[2] Her papers were considered by a university committee. While they were broadly happy with the thrust of the research they asked her to note that 'climate change' was a contested concept and recommended that the words 'climate change' be taken out of the title. She was working with some of the top scientists in the world and to her the idea that climate change could be contested was about as credible as the idea that 'smoking does not cause cancer'. She was explicit that her research was built on an assumption that might be challenged along the way, but that for the time being was a bedrock on which the research would be built.

Everything we do exists within the belief system that we hold now. We cannot operate with a blank mind, with no history and no beliefs. The assumptions underpinning our work do not have to be regarded as truth by the establishment. They only have to be good enough for us to take the next step.

Researcher power in large system processes

Packham and Sriskandarajah (2005) articulate the ideal role for facilitators in emancipatory research:

> ... the facilitator/researcher plays a key role as they often have a greater theoretical background and more time for contemplation than other members of the group. The facilitator also has the task of ensuring unimpeded group communication which allows understanding to emerge which forms the basis from which enlightenment will flow. In this the facilitator must guard against manipulating the group process, particularly by ensuring that truth and power do not reside in the facilitator alone through them adopting an expert role: the reflective discussions of the group should involve interaction between a variety of ideas from group members in relation to a particular event or situation ... the responsibility for action rests solely with the actors, and the action may be both practical and political. (Packham and Sriskandarajah, 2005)

There is a risk that this participative ideal will be more easily compromised in large system contexts. This is because as scale is increased a point can quickly be reached when it is impractical for everyone to maintain an interrelationship with each other. The learning system thus becomes 'held' by facilitators, giving them considerable power in steering, prioritising and even interpreting. While they may not be interpreting meanings of specific inquiries, they are making judgements about what is important. So there is a sense in which the facilitator has both to work with and on behalf of participants.

There are also important questions of accountability in large system action research that do not arise in the same way in other approaches such as cooperative inquiry. In a cooperative inquiry process accountability is to the group. In a systemic inquiry process, where there is an outside facilitator who may be engaged with different stakeholders in complex power relationships to each other, then accountability could lie in a variety of different places. Is the facilitator accountable to the group that they are working with at any particular moment? To their commissioning body? To groups that are on the ground (as opposed to management)? The way we have got around this is to see ourselves as accountable 'to the relationship between the whole system and a set of objectives'. This is not straightforward (a) because the system is constructed and reconstructed over time, and (b) because the set of objectives may also change as the action research process progresses. In the Communities First programme we felt accountable to support capacity building in the service of long-term community regeneration. In the Red Cross project our accountability was to all of those who had a stake in the British Red Cross being able to mobilise more effectively around vulnerability to crisis. In both of these examples, although we had a contractual accountability to two clients (WAG and the British Red Cross) we had an operational accountability to the multiple stakeholders involved including residents, volunteers, communities, staff, senior managers and so on.

There is always a potential tension between different parts of the system. In the Communities First programme we were working with local coordinators and with the central policy and implementation teams. Both had views about each other. Effective systemic learning required real honesty to emerge from a local context. The paradox is of course that this might not emerge if it is perceived at local level that disclosures might travel via action research facilitators to the centre. Wadsworth (2001) highlights the same issue: 'an example of direct damage might be the revealing of a consumer's negative views about particular staff person in such a way as to be identifiable and risk retribution. These are fine matters of judgement and any ethical statement that seems clear, simple and certain may be glossing over these important matters' (Wadsworth, 2001, p 9). So judgement and a high level of ethical self-awareness by facilitators is crucial. There are important training and development issues that flow from this, but as Saville Kushner says about evaluators:

> In the end, recourse can only be made to personal values and beliefs and the rest of the world makes its own decision about the evaluator it has been landed with. (Kushner, 2000, p156)

Resonance, peer review and democratic processes

Ultimately ethical social research is participative research. Where important decisions and actions result from research it has to have a process to ensure that assumptions, meanings and impacts can be tested. I described earlier the way in which large system action research supports exposure to 'ever-increasing circles of peer review' (see also Burns, 2006a). Through it, action researchers support meaning making across the system, reflecting the multiple views of stakeholders. This is an inherently democratic process. Having said this it is crucial to acknowledge that however democratic our process, power is still working through it:

> ... common to participatory research is to assume that the democratic ethos and practice of such research assures ethicality (Rowan 2000, Stringer 1999). Yet this position assumes equal voice among all participants, neglecting the potential for a power imbalance among research participants. (Boser, 2006)

I would take this argument a step further and assert that there is always a power imbalance and that this has traditionally been one of the great weaknesses of action research. Because action research has largely constructed around dialogic processes, it has not always taken into account the importance of conflict, confrontation and diversity. While we can build a response to this critique into our process, we are still limited by the partiality of its reach. In any large system process there will always be choices about where to focus the limited resources available to the inquiry. These involve privileging some lines of inquiry at the expense of others. Looking back you always see gaps and areas in which you might have worked productively and effectively. In the end, perhaps the best we can do is to be aware of power and hold on to a set of core intentions. As Boser says:

> ... action research projects are often conducted with an explicit social change agenda, and work from the belief that the very process of participating in constructing knowledge about one's own context has the potential to redress power imbalance. (Boser, 2006, p 11)

To some extent we have to have faith that this will happen, while being mindful that we always have the potential to create new power imbalances.

Conclusions

The whole point of systemic action research, from my point of view, is to get to grips with the messy, complex, difficult issues – issues that have often defied resolution in arenas of conflict and deprivation and poverty. To work in these arenas necessarily involves risk. Not to work in these arenas is unethical. Procedural quality control and ethical regulation in practice often become a way of gate keeping and preventing real change. Under the rhetoric of protecting the individual we can fail to get to grips with issues that are facing whole communities (and frequently we do not protect the individual anyway). In my view both quality and ethical practice come down to the relationship that external facilitators have with individuals and communities. This cannot be codified into standard procedures.

Notes

[1] This is another example of an unintended consequence of actions taken across a different organisational boundary.

[2] PhDs have a point of transition about 18 months to two years into the process. This is variously articulated as an upgrade, transfer from MPhil to PhD, and progression. It usually involves the production of a number of papers and a viva, during which the student outlines the progress that they have made.

NINE

Systemic action research in policy and politics

Given that this book was not intended to be primarily methodological, it is important to place the issues that it raises in the context of policy and politics. With this in mind I want to conclude succinctly with some implications for organisations and for public participation. In this chapter I highlight the importance of the following:

- building emergence into organisational decision-making processes
- generating a different sort of evidence
- rethinking dissemination and roll-out
- re-assessing investment risk (commissioning uncertainty)
- replacing the principle of consistency with the idea of appropriate action
- enabling sustainable interventions
- re-conceptualising participation.

Building emergence into organisational decision-making processes

One of the biggest challenges facing organisations is the failure of centralised planning. Among the reasons for planning failure are that plans are often out of date by the time they are finished; they limit options (because we frequently do not know what new possibilities are available until we have taken some steps down the road); they result in unintended consequences and so on (see the Introduction to this book and Chapter Two). Despite this, organisations continue to rely on planning because there appears to be no alternative, and because it provides a form of accountability against which activities can be assessed.

Embedding action research into the decision-making process offers an alternative but it requires us to focus on the direction of travel and core values rather than trying to anticipate all of the details of implementation. This can be seen as a process of strategic improvisation that enables strategic intervention in ways that can respond flexibly to real world change. It also means that the action research has to be viewed as much more than a method of generating ideas that are then placed into traditional decision-making arenas for agreement. Systemic action research has to be constructed as part of the management and leadership process. This means that we have to let go of the traditional distinctions between different organisational tasks and roles such as leadership, management, research, organisational development and evaluation. These categories need to be collapsed.

Systemic action research is essentially about learning in its many forms, and learning does not respect role and task boundaries. So a critical question for organisations now is how to locate inquiry-based learning and action at the heart of *the* decision-making process for the organisation. We also need to ask how we manage, organise and commission integrated learning processes rather than separate ones.

There is a parallel here in the education system where teaching, research and knowledge transfer are all seen as separate and different things. If they are all regarded as parts of the learning process the distinction evaporates. Like the silos of service delivery, which dominate most governmental and public service organisations, these functional distinctions create disjunctures in organisations that make it very difficult to create holistic solutions to problems. Seeing leadership as a systemic learning process enables us to meaningfully design for emergence.

Generating a different sort of evidence

There is nothing wrong with the notion of evidence-based practice. The issue at stake here is what counts as evidence. Stories and pictures, maps of interrelationships, insight into the emotional dynamics of interventions and so on will often provide much richer evidence than the aggregated quantitative data that so frequently informs policy. This will not provide proof, but it will help us to understand the changes that have resulted from action, and how and why these have come about. Some years ago I was asked to look at the annual reviews of 40 Children's Fund projects. What convinced me of the success or otherwise of these projects was not the statistics on attendance, for example, but the stories of change. I concluded that if each project was able to tell the story of 10 children and how they had changed then the programme would have an evidence base of 400 stories that would be a far richer source for informing future change across the system than monitoring data. Evidence has to include the many forms of knowing that have been discussed in this book. It has to be based on real situations. It has to build dynamic pictures of how different actions interact with each other. Evidence that is based solely on modelling causal relationships between individual variables will fail to build the depth of understanding we need to fashion effective policy and practice.

Rethinking dissemination and roll-out

The way in which we record, document and disseminate information is not congruent with the ways in which ideas travel through organisations. Long written reports that land on people's desks are often not read or engaged with. Systemic action research is more than a forum for evidence gathering, insight generation and experimental action. It is also a form of dissemination in itself. Because we are interacting with the insight that is generated (rather than being informed of it) it sticks in our minds. To move to more dialogic or visual forms of dissemination can seem risky because they appear to lack the substance of a formal report. Managers, consultants, policy makers and evaluators no longer have a 'proper' product with which to justify their endeavours. However, if dialogue, as I have asserted, is actually the way in which knowledge and understanding already travels through social and organisational systems, then it is crucial that we purposefully construct dialogic spaces in which conversations are generated, and from which they will travel through organisations, and that we support this process with forms of representation that people can meaningfully engage with. This does not mean that reports are unnecessary, but that these may need to be more visual in form if they are to stay in people's minds, and that they should be seen as supporting dissemination rather than being the dissemination itself.

Re-assessing investment risk (commissioning uncertainty)

The approach to risk that we need to develop is counter-cultural to a public sector which is increasingly dominated by processes of formal accountability. If you were a private sector company and you invested in 10 experimental projects and one took off, you would be delighted by your investment, whereas if you are in a public sector environment and you invest in 10 strands of work you expect nine-and-a-half of them to deliver excellent outcomes. If this does not happen then a failure of performance is interpreted as a failure of accountability. In the more experimental world of unravelling and finding solutions to difficult issues, the private sector analogy will often be closer to what we are trying to do. The approach to governance that we adopt must be linked to what we are trying to do. If you are developing a new product then you need flexibility to enable creativity and to develop an understanding of how the product might answer real world questions. Once developed you might need a different process to ensure that it is delivered to high standards of quality and reliability. It is crucial for action researchers to be able to articulate this distinction clearly to clients.

While the notion of managing uncertainty is increasingly accepted, the idea that we might commission uncertainty is most definitely not. If action research is to be built in to social and organisational systems this will be necessary. To advocate an emergent approach to policy and practice development – whether as an internal 'champion' or an external action researcher – requires the ability to reassure the 'clients' of the benefits of uncertainty. We have found that the best way to do this work is to 'grow' conversations in which people see for themselves the need for something different, rather than to try to 'sell' the approach.

Replacing the principle of consistency with the idea of appropriate action

Most public service organisations highlight the importance of consistency in relation to different clients. This is the basis on which justice systems are constructed. But it does not always produce the best social outcomes. Gilligan (1992), in outlining the distinction between an ethic of justice and an ethic of care, lucidly articulated an alternative built on the idea of relational practice. Let me give an example of relational and outcomes-based approaches to policy making.

Local housing managers may 'turn a blind-eye' to squatting in properties that need substantial work on them. They accept the need to allocate according to needs-based criteria but are prepared to be pragmatic and hold the contradiction. They know that they are not going be occupied in the near future because there is no money for renovation. They are also aware that houses that are not occupied disintegrate extremely fast and that it may be in the best interest of the landlord to have someone living there even if they are not official tenants. The housing managers use their judgement to assess real relationships and judge outcomes. Thus they may initiate eviction procedures for squatters that they felt were not looking after the properties.

This scenario highlights the importance of values for providing guidance and setting boundaries in the absence of rules. For housing managers in this instance the central value is the most effective alleviation of homelessness. They sought a solution that provided a short-term solution to those in immediate need and protected the fabric of the properties for those 'priority' homeless who would eventually live in them. Here housing managers recognise the principle behind the waiting list, but break with it where appropriate, in order to ensure the best systemic outcome. This sort of process has underpinned the breakthroughs in Northern Ireland and other complex situations. In my view it needs to be much more firmly embedded within contemporary organisational culture.

Enabling sustainable interventions

We live in a world of short-term policy intervention where the rhetoric of government is sustainability, but the reality is more often 'quick wins' in the context of impending elections. However, for policy to (a) be implementable and (b) sustainable, it is crucial to develop a systemic perspective. Throughout this book I have told stories that illustrate this, for example: social care (page 23); FGM (page 25); water resource management (page 26); HIV/AIDS (page 89); school catchment issues (page 134); and squatting and housing management. The following example further illustrates this relationship between sustainability and systemic thinking.

In the UK there has been a sustained debate about the combined mumps, measles and rubella (MMR) vaccination. The vaccination is widely perceived by the public to be linked to autism, and consequently many parents have been afraid to give it to their children. As a result vaccinations levels are lower than they ought to be to be to ensure population-level immunity. The government has been convinced that the research indicating a link to autism has been comprehensively disproved and has responded with an extensive and sustained health promotion message, reinforced by financial incentives to doctors who meet target levels. This has had limited impact because many people do not believe the government. Public perception on the reliability of government health advice has been influenced by a variety of factors including images of ministers feeding beef to their children before the CJD (Creutzfeldt-Jakob disease) epidemic exploded. It is probably affected by the perceived influence of the drug companies, and even by perceptions of government honesty over the invasion of Iraq. In other words, the possibilities of implementing a policy have been profoundly affected by events elsewhere. It actually does not matter what the 'facts' about the safety of the vaccination are. What is crucial is what people 'think' the facts are. This means that solutions have to be found that take these systemic effects into account. In this case the more expensive 'single jab' was rejected, but the costs of not supporting its introduction may prove to be higher in the long run. Interventions that do not take into account impacts outside tightly defined operational boundaries are far less likely to be sustainable. A systemic approach to change is crucial to sustainability.

Re-conceptualising participation

Solutions to problems are also far more likely to be sustained if those affected by them have been involved in their creation. This strongly binds together the agendas of sustainability and participation.

In recent years the word 'participation' has proliferated but increasingly it actually refers to consultation, not participation. Where it does refer to participation, it almost exclusively relates to participation in formal decision making. While this has undoubtedly had some benefits, in that more people are involved in the governance of more organisations and institutions, it also raises a number of concerns. I want to highlight three in particular here.

First, contemporary norms of participation are locked into a 'planning' model. Needs are articulated, they are assessed against available resources and then they are formulated into action plans, which may or may not get enacted. The underlying assumption is that action should follow decision making, and public participation is in the decision-making process. In fact, as we have discussed, decisions frequently emerge from action, and in action. The most effective participation strategies will often be those that engage people in action, not in decision making.

Second, in virtually every inquiry process that I have facilitated it has quickly become clear to participants that we rarely know the right questions let alone the solutions. It takes time for clarity to emerge. Without being embedded in some sort of inquiry process it is difficult to see how local participation can be meaningful.

Third, contemporary forms of stakeholder participation are built almost exclusively on the notion of representation, where the participatory process is all about representing the views of a community to the decision-making body. As communities become more diverse and personal identities become more complex the idea of representativeness becomes more and more problematic. Increasingly I believe that participation initiatives need to focus on direct stakeholder engagement in policy and practice construction, coupled with a process of resonance testing.

The example from the Hounslow project (page 118), where SOLAR was working with teenagers on health issues (Percy-Smith et al, 2003), seeded a new way of thinking about participation in my mind. In this account the possibility emerged for the key stakeholders (young people, headteachers, director of education and so on) to actively construct the sex education policy together. The young people were not 'representative' but they 'represented' a wide range of real local life histories. In the BCI project, although it was genuinely hard to maintain the involvement of parents (often because of the complexities of their lives), those that were involved were absolutely not the 'usual suspects'. Starting an action research process with these people offers a stronger participative foundation than pulling in notional representatives to decision-making forums. The solutions that they construct with other stakeholders can then be tested for their resonance in a wider arena, and developed iteratively through testing and further dialogue. The experience of systemic action research heralds a new and more powerful model of public engagement, one that starts with direct participation in public life, and is linked through inquiry-based processes to more formal spaces for engagement.

Conclusions

It is quite extraordinary that we continue to produce plans when we know that they will be out of date by the time they are published; we continue to validate linear cause-and-effect explanations of highly complex social phenomena even though we know that they cannot be so simply explained; we spend vast amounts of time in 'decision-making meetings' to formalise decisions that have been made elsewhere; we disseminate our organisational knowledge through long reports that we know do not get read; and we base our democratic practices on a mythical notion of representativeness. It is not that these practices are absurd in theory, only that as soon as they hit reality they implode. Systemic action research is based on different assumptions and offers a robust alternative.

A final reflection

The thinking that I have laid out in this book lays down a challenge to traditional researchers, policy makers and organisational leaders. it also poses a challenge to the action research community. This is because it suggests a significant shift in emphasis:

- from consensus to parallel development
- from a focus on individual events to working with systemic interrelationships and patterns
- from linear causal attribution to understanding the dynamics of complexity
- from representativeness to resonance
- from action research as a method, to action research as a hub or container for a variety of methods
- from a focus on the formal to the informal spaces in between
- from planning to strategic improvisation.

This does not mean that consensus, individual agency, linearity, representativeness and so on are no longer relevant or important, only that they should be seen as one part of a greater whole. We need to build on them, and move beyond them in order to make sense of the complex world that we live in, and fashion flexible ways to act within it.

References

Argyris, C. (1993) *Knowledge for action*, San Francisco, CA: Jossey Bass.

Argyris, C., Putnam, R. and Smith, D. (1985) *Action science: Concepts, methods and skills for research and intervention*, San Francisco, CA: Jossey Bass.

Atwood. M., Pedler, M., Pritchard, S. and Wilkinson, D. (2003) *Leading change: A guide to whole systems working*, Bristol: The Policy Press.

Barcal, D. (2006) 'Personal and intellectual influences leading to Lewin's paradigm of action research: towards the 60th anniversary of Lewin's "action research and minority problems (1946)"', *Action Research*, vol 4, issue 4.

Bateson, M.C. (1990) *Composing a life*, New York, NY: Penguin.

Bawden, R.J. and Packham, R.G. (1991) 'Improving agriculture through systemic action research', in V. Squires and P. Tow (eds) *Dryland farming systems: A systems approach*, Sydney: Sydney University Press, Chapter 20, pp 262-71.

Becker, S., Bryman, A. and Sempik, J. (2006) *Defining 'quality' in social policy research: Views, perceptions and a framework for discussion*, Lavenham, Suffolk: Social Policy Association and Joint University Council.

Bennet, N., Wise, C., Harvey, J. and Woods, P. (2003) *Distributed leadership*, Nottingham: National College for School Leadership.

Boal, A. (1979) *Theatre of the oppressed*, London: Pluto.

Boal, A. (1992) *Games for actors and non-actors*, London: Routledge.

Boser, S. (2006) 'Ethics and power in community–campus partnerships for research', *Action Research*, vol 4, no 1, pp 9-21.

Boushel, M., Burton, E., Bums, D., Daum, M. and Walsh, D. (2003) *Three years of Sure Start: Hartcliffe, Highridge and Withywood in Bristol*, Bristol: Barnardos.

Bradbury, H. and Reason, P. (2001) 'Broadening the bandwidth of validity: issues and choice points for improving the quality of action research', in P. Reason and H. Bradbury, *Handbook of action research: Participative inquiry and practice*, London: Sage Publications.

Brocklesbury, J. and Cummings, S. (1995)' Combining hard, soft and critical methodologies in systems research: the cultural constraints', in *Systems Research*, no 12, pp 239-44.

Brown, J. (2001) 'The world café: living knowledge through conversations that matter', Doctoral dissertation, Pegasus Communications.

Burns, D. (1992) *Poll Tax rebellion*, Edinburgh/London: AK Press/Attack International.

Burns, D. (2000) *Auditing community participation: An assessment handbook*, Bristol/York: The Policy Press/Joseph Rowntree Foundation.

Burns, D. (2003) 'Whole system action research in complex governance settings', Key note presentation to the ALARPM world congress.

Burns, D. (2006a) 'Evaluation in complex governance arenas: the potential of large system action research', in B. Williams and I. Imam, *Using systems concepts in evaluation*, Fairhaven, MA: American Evaluation Association.

Burns, D. (2006b) 'Interim evaluation of the Welsh Assembly Communities First Programme', Action Research Report 1: Systemic Action Research in the Communities First Evaluation, Unpublished

Burns, D. and Daum, M. (2004) Unpublished transcript of a dialogue on 'Facilitating action research groups', Bristol: SOLAR.

Burns, D. and Taylor, M. (1997) *Mutual aid and self help*, Bristol: The Policy Press.

Burns, D. and Weil. S. (2006) 'Co-generating knowledge with communities: learning in dynamic systems', Inaugural professorial lecture, University of the West of England.

Burns, D., Heywood, F., Wilson, M. and Wilde, P. (2004b) *What works in assessing community participation?*, Bristol: The Policy Press.

Burns, D., Heywood, F., Wilson, M., Wilde, P. and Taylor, M. (2004a) *Making community participation meaningful*, Bristol: The Policy Press.

Burns, D., Daum, M., Walsh, D., Bowers, L., Mountain, D. and Coates, M. (2003) 'The first three years of Knowle West Sure Start', unpublished report.

Buzan, T. (1991) *The mind map book*, New York, NY: Penguin.

Byrne, D. (1998) *Complexity theory and the social sciences: An introduction*, Abingdon: Routledge.

Carr, W. (2006) 'Philosophy, methodology and action research', *Journal of Philosophy of Education*, vol 40, no 4, pp 421-35.

Checkland, P. (1981) *Systems thinking, systems practice*, Chichester: Wiley.

Checkland, P. and Holwell, S. (1998) 'Action research: its nature and validity', *Systemic Practice and Action Research*, vol 11, no 1, pp 9-21.

Checkland, P. and Scholes, J. (2004) *Soft systems methodology in action*, Chichester: Wiley.

Churchman, C. W. (1970) 'Operations research as a profession', *Management Science*, vol 17, pp 17-33.

Clegg, S. (1989) *Frameworks of power*, London: Sage Publications.

Cochlan, D. (2002) 'Interlevel dynamics in systemic action research', *Systemic Practice and Action Research*, vol 15, no 4, pp 273-83.

Cochlan, D. and Brannick, T. (2001) *Doing action research in your own organisation*, London: Sage Publications.

Daum, M. (2003a) 'Domestic abuse action research notes', HHW, 17/01/03, unpublished.

Daum, M. (2003b) 'Review of the action research group on domestic abuse, HHW Sure Start', unpublished review paper.

Daum, M. and Burns, D. (2003) 'Does the Bristol Children's Fund function effectively as a whole system?', unpublished report, Bristol: SOLAR.

Davilla, J. (1993) 'Foucualt's interpretive analytics of power', *Systems Practice*, no6, pp 383-405.

Denicolo, P. and Pope, M. (1990) 'Adults learning - teachers thinking', in C. Day, M. Pope and P. Denicolo (eds) *Insight into teachers thinking and practice*, Basingstoke: The Falmer Press, pp 155-69.

Flood, R.L.(1990) *Liberating systems theory*, New York, NY: Plenum Press

Flood, R L. (1996) 'Total systems intervention: local systemic intervention', in N. Romm and R. Flood (1996) *Critical systems thinking: Current research and practise*, New York, NY: Plenum

Flood, R.L. (1999) *Rethinking the fifth discipline: Learning within the unknowable*, London: Sage Publications.

Flood, R.L. (2001) 'The relationship of "systems thinking" to action research', in P. Reason and H. Bradbury, *Handbook of action research: Participative inquiry and practice*, London: Sage Publications.

Flood, R.L. and Jackson, M.C. (1991) *Critical systems thinking: Directed readings*, Chichester: Wiley.

Flood, R.L. and Romm, R.A. (1996) *Critical systems thinking: Current research and practice*, New York, NY/London: Plenum.

Foth, G. (2006) 'Network action research', *Action Research*, vol 4, no 2, pp 205-26.

Foucault, M. (1984) *The history of sexuality: An introduction*, Harmondsworth: Peregrine.

Francis, T. (2006) 'Introducing constellations at work', unpublished reflection piece.

Gave, M.E. and Walsh, D. J. (1998) *Studying children in Context: Theories, methods and ethics*, London: Sage.

Gilchrist, A. (2001) 'Strength through diversity: networking for community development', Unpublished PhD thesis, University of Bristol.

Gilligan, C. (1992, [first published 1973]) *In a different voice*, Cambridge, MA: Harvard University Press.

Greenwood, D. and Levin, M. (1998) *An Introduction to action research: Social research for social change*, Thousand Oaks, CA: Sage Publications.

Gregory, W.J. and Romm, N. (2001) 'Developing critical facilitation: learning through intervening in group processes, *Management Learning*.

Gregory, W.J. and Romm, N. (2004) 'Facilitation as fair intervention', in G. Midgley and A. Ochoa-Arias (eds) (2004) *Community operational research: OR and systems thinking for community development*, New York, NY: Kluwer academic, Plenum publishers, pp 157-74.

Gustavsen, B. (2003) 'Action research and the problem of the single case', *Concepts and transformation*, vol 8, no 1, pp 93-9.

Gutmann, D. with Millat, J.-F., van der Rest, F.-M., Ternier-David, J. and Verrier, C. (2005) *Disillusionment, dialogue of lacks*, London: Karnac ed.

Gutmann, D. with Millat, J.-F., van der Rest, F.-M., Ternier-David, J. and Verrier, C. (2006) 'Ethics for the leader and consciousness for the entrepreneur', Conference contribution, Palermo, Italy May 2006.

Hechter, M. and Opp, K.D. (eds) (2001) *Social norms*, New York, NY: Russell Sage Foundation.

Heron, J. (1981) 'The philosophical basis for a new paradigm', in P. Reason and J. Rowan (eds) *Human inquiry: A sourcebook of new paradigm research*, Chichester: Wiley, pp 19–35.

Heron, J. (1996) *Co-operative inquiry: Research into the human condition*, London: Sage Publications.

Heron, J. and Reason, P. (1997) 'A participatory inquiry paradigm', *Qualitative Inquiry*, vol 3, no 3, pp 274–94.

Heron, J. and Reason, P. (2001) 'The practice of co-operative inquiry: research "with" rather than "on" people', in P. Reason and H. Bradbury (eds) *Handbook of action research: Participative inquiry and practice*, London: Sage Publications.

Ison, R. (2000) 'Exploring some distinctions for the design of learning systems', *Cybernetics and Human Knowing*, vol 7, no 4, pp 43–56.

Ison, R. and Russell, D. (2000) *Agricultural extension and rural development: Breaking out of traditions*, Cambridge: Cambridge University Press

Ison, R. and Armson, R. (2006) Leadership from a second order cybernetic perspective, Learning Organisation, September.

Johnstone, K. (1981) *Impro: Improvisation and the theatre*, London: Methuen.

Kemmis, S. (1993) 'Action research and policy research: a challenge for social movement', *Education Policy Analysis*, vol 1, no 1.

Kemmis, S. (2001) 'Exploring the relevance of critical theory for AR', in P. Reason and H. Bradbury, *Handbook of action research: Participative inquiry and practice*, London: Sage Publications.

Kolb, D.A. (1984) *Experimental learning: Experience as a source of learning and development*, New Jersey: Prentice Hall.

Kushner, S. (2000) *Personalizing evaluation*, London: Sage Publications.

Lawrence, D.H. (1920) *Women in love*, New York, NY: Thomas Seltzer.

Lewin, K. (1952) *Field theory in social science*, New York, NY: Harper and Brothers.

Lincoln, Y. (1995) 'Emerging criteria for quality in qualitative and interpretive research', *Qualitative Inquiry*, vol 1, no 3, pp 275–89.

Lincoln, Y. and Guba, E. (1989) *Fourth generation evaluation*, Newbury Park, CA: Sage.

Ludema, J.D., Cooperrider, D.L. and Barret, F.J. (2000) 'Appreciative inquiry: the power of the unconditional positive question', in P. Reason and H. Bradbury, *Handbook of action research: Participative inquiry and practice*, London: Sage Publications.

Lundy, P. and McGovern, M. (2006) *The ethics of silence: Action research, community 'truth-telling' and post-conflict transition in the North of Ireland*, London: Sage Publications.

Mahr, A. (1999) *Das wissende feld: Familienaufstellung als geistig energetisches heilen (The knowing field: Family constellations as mental and energetic healing), Geistiges heilen für eine neue zeit*, Heidelberg: Kösel Verlag.

Marshall, J. (1999) 'Living life as injury', *Systemic Practice and Action Research*, vol 12, no 2, pp 155-71.

Marshall, J. (2004) 'Living systemic thinking: exploring quality in first-person action research', *Action Research*, vol 2, no 3, pp 305-25.

McGuiness and Wadsworth (1991) 'Understanding anytime': A consumer evaluation of an acute psychiatric hospital, Melbourne, Victorian Mental Illness Awareness Council.

Midgley, G. (2000) *Systemic intervention: Philosophy, methodology and practice*, New York, NY: Kluwer Academic.

Midgley, G. (1997) 'Mixing methods: developing systemic intervention' in J. Mingers and A. Gill (eds) *Multi methodology: The theory and practice of combining management science methodologies*, Chichester: Wiley.

Midgley, G. (2006) 'Systems thinking for evaluation', in B. Williams and I. Imam, *Using systems concepts in evaluation*, Fairhaven, MA: American Evaluation Association.

Midgley, G. and Ochoa-Arias, A. (eds) (2004) *Community operational research: OR and systems thinking for community development*. New York, NY: Kluwer academic, Plenum publishers.

Mintzberg, H. (1989) *Mintzberg on management*, New York, NY/London: Free Press.

Mittleton-Kelly, E. (1998) 'Organisations as complex evolving systems', Paper to OACES conference, Warwick, 4-5 December.

Mittleton-Kelly, E. (2003) 'Ten principles of complexity and enabling infrastructures' in E. Mittleton-Kelly (ed) *Complex systems and evolutionary persectives on organisations: The application of complexity theory to organisations*, Oxford: Elsevier, Pergamon.

Narayan, D. with Patel, R., Schafft, K., Rademacher, A. and Koch-Schulte, S. (1999) *Can anyone hear us? Voices from 47 countries*, Poverty Group, PREM, World Bank, December.

Neilson, E. (2006) 'But let us not forget John Collier', *Action Research*, vol 4, issue 4, pp 389-99.

Owen, H. (1992, 2nd edn 1997) *Open space technology: A users guide*, San Francisco, CA: Berrett-Koehler.

Packham, R.G. and Sriskandarajah, N. (2005) 'Systemic action research for post graduate education', *Agriculture and Rural Development in Systems Research and Behavioural Science*, vol 22, pp 119-30.

Percy-Smith, B. (2004) *Learning from the Children's Fund – Developing services for children and families*, Local evaluation report based on action inquiry, Northampton: Children's Fund Northamptonshire/SOLAR, University of the West of England.

Percy-Smith, B. (2007 forthcoming) *'You think you know? ... you have no idea':Youth participation in health policy development'*, Health Education Research.

Percy-Smith, B. and Weil, S. (2003) 'Practice-based research as development: innovation and empowerment in youth intervention initiatives using collaborative action inquiry', in A. Bennett (ed) *Researching youth*, Basingstoke: Palgrave Publishing.

Percy-Smith, B., Burns, D., Walsh, D. and Weil, S. (2003) *Mind the gap: Healthy futures for young people in Hounslow*, Bristol: University of the West of England and Hounslow Community Health Council.

Percy-Smith, B. and Walsh, D. (2006) *Improving services for children and families: Listening and learning*, Report from a systemic action inquiry evaluation process, Northampton: Children's Fund Northamptonshire/SOLAR.

Pratt, J., Gordon, P. and Plamping, D. (1999) *Working whole systems: Putting theory into practice in organisations*, London: King's Fund

Prieto-Carron, M. (2006) 'An inquiry into women workers in Central America and multinational corporate codes of conduct', Unpublished Ph.D. thesis, University of Bristol.

Prosser, J. (1988) *Image-based Research: A sourcebook for qualitative researchers*, London: Falmer.

Reason, P. (1994) 'Cooperative inquiry, participatory action research and action inquiry: three approaches to participative inquiry', in N.K. Denzin and Y.S. Lincoln (eds) *Handbook of qualitative research*, Newbury Park, CA: Sage Publications, pp 324-39.

Reason, P. (ed) (2002) 'Introduction', in Special Issue:'The practice of co-operative inquiry', *Systemic Practice and Action Research*, vol 15, no 3, pp 169-78.

Reason, P. (2003) 'Pragmatist philosophy and action research: reading and conversation with Richard Rorty', *Action Research*, vol 1, no 1, pp 103-23.

Reason, P. (2006) 'Choice and quality in action research practice', *Journal of Management Inquiry*, vol 15, pp 187-206.

Reason, P. and Bradbury, H. (eds) (2001) *Handbook of action research: Participatory inquiry and practice*, London: Sage Publications.

Reason, P. and Rowan, J. (eds) (1981) *Human inquiry: A sourcebook of new paradigm research*, Chichester: Wiley.

Savory-Gordon, L. (2003) 'Spillover effects of increased workplace democracy at Algoma Steel on personal, family, and community life', Unpublished PhD thesis, University of Bristol.

Senge, P. (1990) *The fifth discipline: The art and practice of the learning organisation*, London: Century.

Shaw, P. (2002) *Changing conversations in organisations*, London: Routledge.

Stacey, R. (2001) *Complex responsive processes in organisations: Learning and knowledge creation*, London: Routledge.

Stacey, R. (2003) 'Organizations as complex responsive processes of relating', *Journal of Innovative Management*, vol 8, no 2, pp 27-39.

Tarling, R., Burns, D. and Hirst, A. (2007) *Interim evaluation of Communities First*, Cardiff: Welsh Assembly Government.

Torbert, W. (2001) 'The practice of action inquiry', in P. Reason and H. Bradbury (eds) *Handbook of action research: Participation inquiry and practice*, London: Sage Publications, pp 250-60.

Ulrich, W. (1983) *Critical heuristics of social planning: A new approach to practical philosophy*, Berne Haupt and Swiss National Science Foundation.

Ulrich, W. (1990) 'Critical systems thinking and ethics: the role of contemporary practical philosophy for developing an "ethics of whole systems"', in *Towards a just society for future generations, Vol I; System Design*, Proceedings of the 34th Annual meeting of the ISSS, Portland: Oregon, USA, 8-13 July 1990.

Valero-Silva, N. (1996) Towards a critique of critical systems thinking within a Foucauldian framework: a "demystification process" or an "instrumental use" of critical theory,' *Systems Practice*, no 9, pp 539-46.

Vega, R. (1999) 'Health care and social justice evaluation: a critical and pluralist approach', PhD thesis, University of Hull.

Wadsworth, Y. (2001) *The essential U and I: A one volume presentation of the findings*, Melbourne: Victorian Health Promotion Foundation.

Wadsworth, Y. (2005) 'is it safe to talk about systems again yet? – self-organising processess for complex living systems and the dynamics of human inquiry', Bob White Memorial Lecture, Monograph No 3, Hobart: University of Tasmania.

Wadsworth, Y. and Epstein, M. (1996) *Understanding and involvement consumer evaluation of acute psychiatric hospital practice, 'A project concludes'*, Melbourne: Victorian Mental Illness Awareness Council.

Wadsworth, Y. and Epstein, M. (1998) 'Building in dialogue between customers and staff in acute mental health services', *Systemic Practice and Action Research*, vol 11, no 4, pp 353-79.

Weick, K.E. (1998) 'Improvisation as a mindset for organisational analysis', *Organization Science*, no 9, pp 543-55.

Weil, S. (1994) 'Bringing about cultural change in universities and colleges: the power and potential of story', in S. Weil (ed) *Introducing 'change from the top' in universities and colleges*, pp 149-168, London: Kogan Page.

Weil, S. (1997) 'Social and organisational learning in a different key: an introduction to the principles of critical learning theatre and dialectical inquiry', in F. Stowell, R. Ison and R. Armsonet (eds) *Systems for sustainability: People, organisations and environments*, New York, NY: Plenum.

Weil, S. (1998) 'Rhetorics and realities in public service organisations: systemic practice and organisational learning as Critically Reflexive Action Research (CRAR)', *Systemic Practice and Action Research*, vol 11, pp 37-45.

Weil, S., Wildermeersch, D. and Jansen, T. (2005) *Unemployed youth and social exclusion in Europe: Learning for inclusion*, Aldershot: Ashgate.

Williams, B. 'Systemic Inquiry', *Encyclopedia of qualitiative research methods*, London: Sage Publicartions.

Young, P.H. (1998) 'Social norms and economic welfare', *European Economic Review*, vol 42, pp 821-30.

Index

A

accountability 53, 168-9, 175
action inquiry 7, 8, 11-12
  dialogic processes 103-17
  embodied 130-3
  exploratory phase 88-9
  recording group sessions 150-3
  scales of 15-16
  starting points 88-92
  time frame 86-7
action inquiry streams 8, 103-4
  cross-cutting links' identification 96-8
  domestic abuse stream 104-10
  library use stream 110-13
  multiple streams 89-94
action learning 12, 150
action research 7-8, 87, 133-5, 160
  characteristics of 12-13
  definition 11-14
  as hub for mixed methods 133-5
  purpose of 14-19
  quality in 155-9
action research cycles 49, 156
action research facilitators 83, 113, 137, 142
  key roles 93, 141-50
    bridging across systems 145-7
    distributed leadership support 147-9
    group inquiry facilitation and support
    142-5
    peer research support 149-50
  recording group sessions 150-3
  relationship to research 137-41
  support for 153-4
actionable knowledge 125, 133, 158, 159
acute psychiatric services see Melbourne
    Understanding and Involvement project
after event reflections 113
appreciative inquiry 66
AIDS 25, 26, 89-91
ALARPM World Congress (2003) 156
anti-Poll Tax campaign 51, 52, 96
Archer, A. 82, 119
Argyris, C. 125
Armson, R. 17

B

Ballard, S. 82
Bateson, M.C. 23
Bawden, R.J. 156
BCI see Bristol Children's Initiatives project
bed-blocking crisis 23-4
Bennet, N. 100
Boal, A. 43, 77, 131
Boser, S. 22, 162, 170
boundaries 23-5, 26, 33, 98-9, 100, 176
  of facilitators 138, 139

narrowing, ethical implications 166-7
  placement of 165
  socially constructed 33
  widening of 27-8
Bradbury, H. 14, 15-16
bridging across systems 145-7
Bristol Children's Fund 62, 65, 67, 148, 149,
  150
Bristol Children's Initiatives project 60-9, 87,
    88, 94, 97-8, 178
  achievements 65-6
  Easton Sure Start 62, 68, 144-5
  emergent design 60
  evolving design 61-3
  HHW Sure Start 61, 62, 63-4, 67, 68, 97-8
    domestic violence 62, 65, 66, 97-8, 104-10,
    148, 166
    library use 62, 63-4, 65, 97, 110-13
    participation 65, 66
    smoking cessation 62, 65-6, 68
  inquiry process examples 63-5
  Knowle West Sure Start 62, 67
  learning from project 66-9
British Red Cross vulnerability project 76-80,
    87, 88, 119, 169
  emergent design 76
  learning from project 80
Brown, J. 114
buddying 68
bureaucratic boundaries 24
Burns, D. 24, 43, 51, 68, 75, 116, 139, 140, 141,
  142, 145, 157, 159, 167
Byrne, D. 2, 21, 28

C

capacity building 37, 69, 71, 74
CARPP (Centre for Action Research in
    Professional Practice) 152
catheterisation on hospital ward 23-4, 29, 167
Central America, female workers, PhD 81-2
centralised planning 173
CFSN see Communities First Support
    Network (CFSN)
change 1, 31-5
chaos theory 31
Checkland, P. 7, 155
childcare, multiple inquiry streams 92-3, 96-7
Children's Fund 84, 174
  see also Bristol Children's Fund
children's gangs and physicality 131
Children's Participation Learning Network
  162-3
citizens' juries 87
Clegg, S. 37
climate change, PhD research 167-8
cluster groups 72

collage 118-19, 150
collective impacts 30
Collier, J. 13, 14
commissioning uncertainty 175
Communities First programme (WAG) 37,
    69-75, 87, 94, 95, 169
    key learning 75
Communities First Support Network (CFSN)
    72, 74
community development and networks, PhD
    81
community participation 50, 73
complex responsive processes of relating 32,
    36
complexity theory 22, 31-3
concertive action 100
confidentiality 162
conflict
    and football 46-8
    Kikuyu and Pokot 44-6
consensus 50-1, 52, 179
consent forms 164
consequences
    unethical 166-7
    unintended 28, 29, 159, 166-7, 173
constellations work 132-3
conversation 8, 114
cooperative inquiry 98-9, 144, 168
counsellors 143
critically reflexive action research (CRAR)
    22-3
cross-cutting links across inquiry streams 96-8
crossroads events 78
cumulative impacts 28, 30
cutting room floor metaphor 165

D

Daum, M. 68, 86, 113, 125, 139, 140-1, 142,
    145, 163, 165
decision making 34, 173-4, 177, 178
democratic centralism 52
design principles, systemic action research 85,
    101
    cross-cutting links across inquiry streams
        96-8
    distributed leadership 99-101
    emergent research design 85-8
    exploratory inquiry phase 88-9
    multiple inquiry streams 89-94
    open boundaries 98-9
    organic inquiry and formal decision making
        connection 94-6
dialogic inquiry processes 103-17
    domestic abuse inquiry stream 104-10
    facilitated action inquiry streams 103-13
    large-scale events 113-17
    library use action inquiry stream 110-13
dialogic spaces 175
dissemination of information 174-5

distilled learning 129-30
distributed leadership 149
    active development of 99-101
    support of action research facilitator 147-9
domestic violence 38, 96, 165
    inquiry process 91-3
    see also domestic violence group (HHW)
domestic violence group (HHW) 62, 65, 66,
    97-8, 104-10, 148, 166
drawings, use of 120-8
Dundee Red Cross pilot 78-9
    see also British Red Cross vulnerability
        project

E

Easington Red Cross pilot 78-9
    see also British Red Cross vulnerability
        project
Easton
    anti-Poll Tax campaign 96
    Sure Start programme 62, 68, 144-5
embodied inquiry 130-3
emergence 31, 33, 83, 85-7, 173-4
emergent inquiry processes 92
emergent research design 85-8
emotion 104, 117, 129-30, 162-3
empowerment 163
entry points 48
Epstein, M. 57, 59-60, 139, 141, 146-7, 149
equalisation 139
ethics committees 161, 165
ethics in large system action research 160-1
    ethical regulation 161-4
    formal processes 161-5
    individual protection and community
        problems 165-6
    informed consent 161-3, 164
    narrowing boundaries, implications 166-7
    researcher power 168-9
    and researcher's stance 167-8
evidence, a different sort 128, 174
exploratory inquiry phase 88-9
external action research facilitators 137
    see also action research facilitators

F

facilitated action inquiry streams 103-4
    domestic abuse 104-10
    library use 110-13
facilitators see action research facilitators
female genital mutilation (FGM) 25-6, 167
female workers in Central America, PhD 81-2
field theory 43, 132
first-person action research 16
flip charts 142, 150, 151
Flood, R.L. 1, 7, 21, 22, 27, 28, 31, 38
focus groups 87
force fields 43
formality 164

formal interviews 164–5
formal qualitative interviews 164–5
formal reports 174, 175
forum theatre 132
Foth, G. 17
Foucault, M. 36–7
Francis, T. 132

G

Games for actors and non actors (Boal) 131
gate keeping 144–5
Gilchrist, A. 5, 81
Gilligan, C. 176
government health advice, public perception
    of 177
Greendown primary school 134–5
Greenwood, D. 12, 14, 15, 51, 155, 158
group facilitators 142
    see also action research facilitators
Guardian, The 24
Gustavsen, B. 17
Gutmann, D. 120

H

hard systems 7
Hartcliffe, Highridge and Withywood Sure
    Start programme *see* HHW Sure Start
    programme
health issues for young people inquiry 115–16,
    149–50
Hechter, M. 35
Heron, J. 3, 5
Heywood, F. 138, 146
HHW Sure Start programme 61, 62, 63–4, 67,
    68, 97–8
    domestic violence 62, 65, 66, 97–8, 104–10,
        148, 166
    library use 62, 63–4, 65, 97, 110–13
    participation 65, 66
    smoking cessation 62, 65–6, 68
Hirst, A. 75
HIV/AIDS 25, 26, 89–91
Holwell, S. 155
homelessness, alleviation of 176
hospital bed-blocking crisis 23–4
Hounslow Children's Health inquiry 88, 115,
    118, 178
housing management 176
housing support, voluntary organisation 42–3
human interaction 160–1

I

image theatre 132
images
    to convey meaning 117–19
    as distilled learning 129–30
    evidence of change 128
    mapping connections 129
    to surface systemic assumptions 120–8

Iman, I. 157
improvisation 41–50, 132
    accepting offers 42–3
    conflict and football 46–8
    conflict, Kikuyu and Pokot 44–6
    re-incorporation 48–50
    small interventions in opportunity spaces
        43–8
individual protection in systemic action
    research 165–6
informed consent 161–5
inquiry 7, 8, 11–12
    dialogic processes 103–17
    embodied 130–3
    exploratory phase 88–9
    recording group sessions 150–3
    scales of 15–16
    time frame 86–7
inquiry collage 118–19, 150
inquiry streams 8, 103–4
    cross-cutting links' identification 96–8
    domestic abuse stream 104–10
    library use stream 110–13
    multiple streams 89–94
insider facilitators 137
    see also action research facilitators
insight generation 8, 11, 19, 34, 55, 63, 130
    physical playback as process of 131–3
integration of methodologies 133–5
interdependencies 26, 27, 33
interrelationships 7, 8, 21, 22, 27, 41, 83, 93
intervention 9, 13, 29
    multiple interventions 52–3
    seeding into opportunity spaces 43–8
    sustainable 176–7
investment risk 175
invisible theatre 132
Ison, R. 17

J

Johnstone, K. 48

K

Kemmis, S. 14, 15, 16, 22
Kenya 126–8
    conflict and football 46–8
    conflict, Kikuyu and Pokot 44–6
    female genital mutilation 25–6, 167
    Moiben Dam 26–7
    SNV, HIV/AIDS inquiry 89–91
knowing 3, 138
Knowle West Sure Start programme 62, 67
knowledge 3
Kolb cycle 12
Kolb, D. 12
Korrir, Selline 44, 46, 48
Kushner, S. 169

L

large events 87, 113–17, 152
large system action research 7–8, 18, 19, 93, 133, 144, 160
  accountability in 168–9
  ethical issues 160–8
  ethical regulation 161–4
  formal processes 161–5
  individual protection and community problems 165–6
  informed consent 161–3, 164
  narrowing boundaries, implications 166–7
  researcher power 168–9
  and researcher's stance 167–8
large system action research projects 55–6, 81
  Bristol Children's Initiatives project 60–9
    achievements 65–6
    evolving design 61–3
    inquiry process examples 63–5
    learning from project 66–9
  British Red Cross project 76–80, 87, 88, 119, 169
    emergent design 76
    learning from project 80
  Melbourne Understanding and Involvement project 24, 55, 56–60, 87, 89, 149
    bridging across systems 146–7
    dialogues' structure 56
  Welsh Assembly Government, Communities First programme 69–75
    emergent design 70
    key learning 75
Lawrence, D.H. 3
leadership 98, 99–101, 147–9
legislative theatre 132
Levin, M. 12, 15, 51, 155, 158
Lewin, K. 11, 13, 14, 43, 130
library use group (HHW) 62, 63–4, 65, 97, 110–13
linear causality 1–2, 28–9, 31, 157, 178
link people 148, 151
'living life as inquiry' 131
local social norms 35, 37, 38
log jam metaphor 44
Ludema, J.D. 66
Lundy, P. 154

M

Mahr, A. 132
mainstream programme bending 71, 84
Making community participation meaningful 73
mapping 89, 90, 115, 129
Marshall, J. 15, 131
McGovern, M. 154
McGuiness, M. 24
Melbourne Understanding and Involvement project 24, 55, 56–60, 87, 89, 149
  bridging across systems 146–7
  dialogues' structure 56

Merthyr Communities First evaluation 71, 73
methodologies, integration of 133–5
Midgley, G. 7, 23, 34–5
Milton Keynes Red Cross pilot 78–9
  see also British Red Cross vulnerability project
mind-mapping software 129
mind maps 89, 90, 129, 150
Mintzberg, H. 34
Mittleton-Kelly, E. 32, 33, 36
mixed methods 133–5
MMR vaccination 38, 176–7
Moiben Dam 26–7
Moreno, J. 14
movement 130
multi-stranded inquiry processes 18, 81, 89–94, 159
  cross-cutting links 96–8
  see also Bristol Children's Initiatives project
multiple interventions 52–3

N

Narayan, D. 38
National College for School Leadership (NCSL) 99–100
Neilson, E. 13, 14, 153
network action research 17
networked systemic inquiry 8, 18–19, 76, 81–3
  see also British Red Cross vulnerability project
neutral facilitator 141
  see also action research facilitators
non-governmental organisations (NGOs) 25, 26, 50, 167
non-linear causality 28, 29, 31–3, 52–3
Northamptonshire Children's Fund project 87

O

observing 12
older people
  care of 23–4
  housing support organisation 42–3
open boundaries 98–9
  see also boundaries
open space events 87, 114, 116
Opp, K.D. 35
opportunity spaces 37
  and small interventions 43–8
organisations
  culture 35
  decision making 34
  dissemination of information 174–5
  emergence and decision-making 173–4
  evidence-based practice 174
  planning failure 173
outsider facilitators 137–8, 168–9
  see also action research facilitators
Owen, H. 114

P

Packham, R.G. 21, 168
paper tablecloths *see* world cafe
paradoxical effects 30-1
parallel development 50-3, 146
participation 13, 50, 67, 144-5, 163, 178
participation group (HHW) 65, 66
participatory action research 149, 160, 161,
    168, 170
partnership 29, 64, 70, 71, 72
peer research 116, 149-50
peer review 169-70
Pembrokeshire Communities First programme
    71, 73
Percy-Smith, B. 88, 115, 178, Centreplate
    pictures 1-3
performance targets 29, 50
PhDs, networked systemic inquiry 81-2
photographs 119
physicality 130-1
pictures 117, 120-8
    difficulty with 125
    evidence of change 128
planning 12
    failure of centralised 4, 28, 31, 38, 173
poems 150, 153
police, approach to inquiry 133
Poll Tax 51, 52, 96
power 36-7, 170
Prieto-Carron, M. 5, 81
psychiatric services *see* Melbourne
    Understanding and Involvement project
public service organisations
    appropriate action 176
    investment risk 175
    participation 177-8
    partnership 29
    performance targets 29
    sustainable interventions 176-7

Q

quality in systemic action research 155-60,
    161, 167

R

RDA (Regional Development Agency) 128
re-incorporation 48-50
Reason, P. 3, 4, 5, 11, 14, 15-16, 99, 156
recording group sessions 150-3
Red Cross *see* Rethinking Vulnerability, Red
    Cross project
reductionism 28-9
reflecting 12
Regional Development Agency (RDA) 128
reports, formal 174, 175
representativeness 53
research ethics, bureaucracy 163
resistances within groups 144
resonance 53-4
resonance testing 158, 159

Rethinking Vulnerability, Red Cross project
    76-80, 87, 88, 119, 169
    emergent design 76
    learning from project 80
reviews of events 113
Rhonda Cynon Taff 73, 74
risk 175

S

Savoury-Gordon, L. 5, 81
Scholes, J. 7
second-person action research 16
second-wave systems theory 7
seeding small interventions into opportunity
    spaces 43-8
Senge, P. 48
sense making 2-4, 117, 129-30, 138
sensory data 117-30
    to convey meaning 117-19
    distilled learning 129-30
    evidence of change 128
    mapping connections 129
    to surface systemic assumptions 120-8
sex education policy 115-16, 178
Shaw, P. 8, 31, 33, 116
SIM (System in the Mind) 120
small interventions 43-4, 48
    conflict and football 46-8
    conflict, Kikuyu and Pokot 44-6
smoking cessation group (HHW) 62, 65-6, 68
Snow White and the seven dwarfs 49
SNV 25, 44
    HIV/AIDS inquiry 88-91
    metaphorical pictures 126-8
social change and action research 15
social intervention theory 52-3
social norms 35-6, 37-8, 165
Social Policy Association 161
soft systems 7, 32
Soft Systems Methodology 129
SOLAR (Social and Organisational Learning
    as Action Research) 5-6
    projects 18, 55, 60-80, 84, 87, 88, 114-12,
        115, 118, 119, 120-28, 178
    PhD 5, 81-2, 119, 167
spaces of opportunity 37, 48
squatting and housing management 176
Sriskandarajah, N. 21, 168
Stacey, R. 31, 32, 33, 35, 36
stakeholder participation 178
stakeholders 137
steel plant, worker buy-out, PhD 81
stories 104
storyboards 77, 80
Sure Start programme 84
    see also Easton Sure Start programme; HHW
        Sure Start programme; Knowle West Sure
        Start programme
sustainable interventions 176-7
Swansea Red Cross pilot 78-9

see also British Red Cross vulnerability
    project
System in the Mind (SITM) 120
systemic action research 1, 4, 7–8, 10, 159
    in organisations 173–4
systemic action research cycles 49
systemic action research design principles 85,
    101
    cross-cutting links across inquiry streams
        96–8
    distributed leadership 99–101
    emergent research design 85–8
    exploratory inquiry phase 88–9
    multiple inquiry streams 89–94
    open boundaries 98–9
    organic inquiry and formal decision making
        connection 94–6
systemic action research facilitators 83, 113,
    137, 142
    informed consent problems 161–2
    key roles 93, 141–50
        bridging across systems 145–7
        distributed leadership support 147–9
        group inquiry facilitation and support
            142–5
        peer research support 149–50
    recording group sessions 150–3
    relationship to research 137–41
    support for 153–4
systemic action research projects *see* large
    system action research; networked systemic
    inquiry
systemic change 31–5
systemic effects 28
    collective impacts 30
    consequential outcomes 29
    cumulative impacts 30
    paradoxical effects 30–1
    unpredictable outcomes 28–9
systemic patterns 30, 35–6, 37, 72, 96, 120, 126
systemic thinking 7, 21–3, 33
systems 7
systems theory 7, 22

T
tapes, use in sessions 151–2
Tarling, R. 75
Taylor, A. 82
Taylor, M. 43, 73
theatre improvisation 41–2
    accepting offers 42
    re-incorporation 48–50
    small interventions in opportunity spaces
        43–4
Theatre of the oppressed (Boal) 43, 131
third-person action research 16
third-wave systems theory 7
timeline of inquiry-based processes 86–7
top-down policies 29, 38
Torbert, W. 16

Toroitich, C. 25
traditional research 13, 133, 160, 167
transformative theatre work 131–2, 133
triangulation 158, 159
trust 139, 147, 151

U
U&I *see* Melbourne Understanding and
    Involvement project
Ulrich, W. 7, 23
uncertainty, commissioning 175
unethical consequences 166–7
unintended consequences 28, 29, 159, 166–7,
    173
unpredictable outcomes 28–9, 31, 43

V
vaccination *see* MMR vaccination
video, use of 119
violence *see* domestic violence; domestic
    violence group (HHW)
visual and other sensory data 117–30
    to convey meaning 117–19
    distilled learning 129–30
    evidence of change 128
    mapping connections 129
    to surface systemic assumptions 120–8
voluntary organisation for housing support
    42–3
vulnerability project *see* Rethinking
    Vulnerability, Red Cross project

W
Wadsworth, Y. 17, 18, 24, 34, 57, 59–60, 85–6,
    117, 139, 141, 146–7, 149, 169
WAG Communities First programme
    see Welsh Assembly Government,
    Communities First programme
Walsh, D. 119, 129
water resource management 26–7
Weick, K.E. 41
Weil, S. 1, 3, 5–6, 13, 17, 18, 22–3, 35, 44, 52–3,
    77, 86, 115, 119, 152, 163
Welsh Assembly Government, Communities
    First programme 37, 69–75, 87, 94, 95, 169
    key learning 75
Welshpool Communities First programme
    71, 73
whole system change 1
whole systems thinking 21–2
Williams, B. 7, 157
WISH (Women Involved in Self-Help) 109,
    166
Women in love (Lawrence) 3
worker buy-out of steel plant, PhD 81
world cafe 87, 114–15, 152
write up of events 110, 144

Y
young people, health issues inquiry 115–16,
    149–50

DATE DUE
